THE UNIVERSITY

LEGAL ETHICS AND
PROFESSIONAL RESPONSIBILITY

Legal Ethics and Professional Responsibility

Edited by

ROSS CRANSTON

Cassel Professor of Commercial Law,
London School of Economics
and Political Science

CLARENDON PRESS · OXFORD

This book has been printed digitally and produced in a standard specification
in order to ensure its continuing availability

OXFORD
UNIVERSITY PRESS

Great Clarendon Street, Oxford OX2 6DP

Oxford University Press is a department of the University of Oxford.
It furthers the University's objective of excellence in research, scholarship,
and education by publishing world-wide in

Oxford New York

Auckland Bangkok Buenos Aires Cape Town Chennai
Dar es Salaam Delhi Hong Kong Istanbul Karachi Kolkata
Kuala Lumpur Madrid Melbourne Mexico City Mumbai Nairobi
São Paulo Shanghai Taipei Tokyo Toronto

Oxford is a registered trade mark of Oxford University Press
in the UK and in certain other countries

Published in the United States
by Oxford University Press Inc., New York

ISBN 0-19-825931-X

Antony Rowe Ltd., Eastbourne

Preface

ONE of the unfortunate consequences in this jurisdiction of the division between the academic and vocational stages of legal education is that subjects such as procedure, drafting, and ethics have not been subject to the same level of academic examination as in other countries, notably the United States. These subjects may be taught, and taught well, but their very location in a vocational programme means that there is little time or incentive to subject the black letter rules to a critical examination as to their rationale, context, and social implications. No more so is this than with professional responsibility and legal ethics, which until recently has been sadly neglected, even at the vocational stage. The situation is scarcely better in other European jurisdictions. Professor Henssler, of the University of Köln, has written to me:

In Germany there is practically no education of students on ethical rules. The only university in Germany having an institute for the law of the legal profession is Cologne. Additionally there is no obligation for students to enrol in my courses so they are offered to a small and interested audience. Neither in the written examination or during the four month period for trainee solicitors are students tested on ethical rules.

Professor Henssler then goes on to say that his aim in Germany is to reform the educational system in this area.

And that is the reason that in my presidential year of the Society of Public Teachers of Law (SPTL) I chose professional responsibility and legal ethics as the theme of the annual conference. The chapters in this book are based on some of the papers presented to that conference. (The exceptions are the chapters by Michael Brindle and Guy Dehn, and by Derek Morgan, which were specially written for the present book.) I am grateful to the authors for revising their contributions for publication, in most cases very extensively. I must also thank both Professor Jay Westbrook of the University of Texas, Dr Doreen McBarnet of Oxford, and Cyril Glasser who made stimulating presentations to the conference.

The conference would not have been the success it was without the flair and administrative ability of Mildred Schofield and Nicola Jones. Indeed during my presidential year Mildred was an invaluable support. In this regard I must also mention the honorary secretary of the SPTL, Professor Peter Birks. In so many ways the Society has been reinvigorated by his enthusiasm and dedication; all academics in this country are in his debt. Finally, there is Richard Hart of the publishers, who from the outset pursued the idea of a book on what he rightly regards as a most important topic.

A very brief conspectus of the book is in order. It begins with my overview chapter, which is followed by three chapters analysing the ethical rules pertaining to the judiciary, the bar, and solicitors (chapters 2–4). Chapter 5 turns to the specific issue of confidentiality, and chapters 6 and 7 to the particular ethical problems in the family and criminal law jurisdictions. Chapter 8 discusses the teaching of legal ethics. Then chapter 9 puts the subject in its wider social and professional context. The book closes by asking whether medical ethics can throw light on legal ethics.

Ross Cranston.

Contents

List of Contributors

ANDREW ASHWORTH: Edmund Davies Professor of Criminal Law and Criminal Justice, King's College, London.

SIR THOMAS BINGHAM: Master of the Rolls.

CHRISTOPHER BRAMALL: Head, Professional Ethics Division, The Law Society.

MICHAEL BRINDLE: QC, of Fountain Court Chambers, London.

ROSS CRANSTON: Cassel Professor of Commercial Law, London School of Economics.

ALISON CRAWLEY: Head of Policy, Professional Ethics Division, The Law Society.

GUY DEHN: Director, Public Concern at Work.

MARC GALANTER: Evjue-Bascom Professor of Law, University of Wisconsin-Madison.

DEREK MORGAN: Lecturer, Cardiff Law School.

ALAN PATERSON: Professor of Law, Strathclyde University.

THOMAS PALAY: Professor of Law, University of Wisconsin-Madison.

ANTHONY THORNTON: QC; Circuit Judge; Chairman, Professional Standards Committee of the General Council of the Bar (1992–1993).

SIR ALAN WARD: A Lord Justice of Appeal.

1

Legal Ethics and Professional Responsibility

ROSS CRANSTON

STAUGHTON LJ recently reminded us that some of the profession's ethical rules have had the appearance of protectionism and as being not at all concerned with the public interest or the proper administration of justice.[1] Certainly important ethical rules have not been ethical truisms: they have often been concerned with the gathering and retention of clients or been directed more at professional conformity rather than right behaviour.[2]

Yet any association with the profession dispels the suggestion that the profession's ethical codes are self-interest writ large. There is a genuine concern with high ethical standards, not least so as to maintain the profession's public standing. Nor would it be correct to suggest that professional standards are completely divorced from ordinary morality. There is authority, for example, that despite fidelity to the client being a paramount consideration, lawyers must not, in the words of Lord Esher MR, 'degrade' themselves personally for the purpose of winning their client's case.[3] But this example raises important issues to which we return. The first is the need to reconsider the boundaries between, on the one hand, a lawyer's obligation to a client and, on the other, the public interest. And the second is the danger that focusing simply on the profession's ethical rules can lead to moral blindness: legal ethics and professional responsibility are more than a set of rules, they are also a commitment to honesty, integrity and service in the practice of law.

This chapter offers an overview of legal ethics and professional responsibility. I divide it into four main parts. The first addresses briefly the contours of the regulatory regime for legal ethics; the second is a broad brush outline of the key ethical rules; the third raises some of the difficult issues with which students of legal ethics must grapple; and the fourth refers to the broader implications of professional responsibility.

---

[1] *R. v. Visitors to the Inns of Court, ex p. Calder* [1994] QB 1, 63. See M. Zander, *Lawyers and the Public Interest*, 1968.
[2] eg, B. Abel-Smith & R. Stevens, *Lawyers and the Courts*, 1967, pp.138–9, 160–1, 196.
[3] *In re G. Mayor Cooke* (1889) 5 TLR 407, 408.

THE REGULATORY REGIME

The general law has a great deal to say about professional behaviour; the law of agency, contracts, torts, fiduciary obligations, evidence, and, in its blunt way, criminal law, all have a bearing on lawyers' behaviour in their professional lives. Sometimes the general law speaks in surprising, although not completely unwelcome, ways. In one recent case a firm of solicitors was held to be potentially liable for restitutionary orders under the Financial Services Act 1986 for loss to an investor. Liability was held to be possible if the solicitors were knowingly concerned in the contravention of the Act, notwithstanding that they received nothing under the impugned transactions.[4] Nowadays solicitors are on guard against being the vehicles of fraud, given the reinvigorated application of proprietary claims for the proceeds and the more likely personal claims for having 'assisted' in the fraud.[5] Getting to grips with money laundering has meant legislative incursions on to the lawyer's duty of confidence.[6] It is not before time since there is clear evidence from other jurisdictions that legal professional privilege and the duty of confidence have been used to cloak the identities of the real beneficial owners of laundered bank accounts.[7]

In addition to the general law there are, secondly, the specific standards of good professional conduct which the courts have elaborated both through their direct control of lawyers and through their review of the decisions of professional disciplinary bodies.[8] Direct control has often been based on the commonplace observations that lawyers are officers of the court and therefore can be disciplined for misconduct.[9] Coupled with the inherent jurisdiction of the court to control lawyers are the specific statutory controls, for example the wasted costs 'jurisdiction' which enables a court to sheet home to solicitors and barristers the loss and expense to litigants caused by the unjustified conduct of litigation.[10]

[4] *Securities and Investments Board* v. *Pantell S.A. (No.2)* [1993] Ch. 256.
[5] The leading case is *Lipkin Gorman* v. *Karpnale Ltd.* [1991] 2 AC 548, although in fact it was a claim by, not against, solicitors. See P. Birks, 'Persistent problems in misdirected money: a quintet' [1993] *LMCLQ* 218.   [6] Criminal Justice Act 1993, ss.16, 18.
[7] eg *Republic of Haiti* v. *Duvalier* [1990] 1 QB 202, 207 (continental lawyers expert in concealment of funds). See R. Bosworth-Davies, 'Money laundering and lawyers' (1994) 138 *Solicitors J.* 626; W. Park, 'Anonymous bank accounts, narco-dollars, fiscal fraud, and lawyers' (1991–2) 15 *Fordham Int. L.J.* 652.
[8] On the inherent jurisdiction of the court: eg *In re the Justices of Antigua* (1830) 12 ER 321; *In re S (a barrister)* [1970] 1 QB 160; *John Fox* v. *Bannister King & Rigbeys* [1988] QB 925.
[9] On the position as officers of the court: see for barristers: *Rondel* v. *Worsley* [1969] 1 AC 191, 227 *per* Lord Reid; for solicitors: *Regulations in Bankruptcy* (1801) 31 ER 908; *Sittingbourne & Sheerness Railway Co.* v. *Lawson* (1886) 2 TLR 605; *Brendon* v. *Spiro* [1938] 1 KB 176; Solicitors Act 1974, s.50(1). Personal misconduct may constitute professional misconduct: *Ziems* v. *The Prothonotary of the Supreme Court of NSW* (1957) 97 CLR 279.
[10] Courts and Legal Services Act 1990, ss.4(1), 111, 112; RSC, 0.62, r.11. See eg *Ridehalgh* v. *Horsefield* [1994] Ch 205; *Bolton* v. *Law Society* [1994] 1 WLR 512; *In re a Barrister (Wasted Costs Order) (No.2 of 1991)* [1993] QB 293; *Gupta* v. *Comer* [1991] 1 QB 629. For an argument for greater use of wasted costs orders: *The Royal Commission on Criminal Justice*, Cm. 2263, 1993, p.108.

Examples of the behavioural standards which the courts have evolved for the profession arise throughout the chapter. Suffice it to say here the courts reiterate that in matters of professional discipline the touchstones are the standing of the profession in the eyes of the public and public protection from the unscrupulous or incompetent. Notwithstanding that its exercise may cause deprivation to the lawyer involved, the power of discipline is protective in purpose, rather than punitive. As Lord Mansfield said in 1778 the question is: 'Whether, after the conduct of this man, it is proper that he should continue a member of a profession which should stand free from all suspicion . . . It is not by way of punishment . . . '.[11] For this reason the considerations which ordinarily weight in mitigation of penalty for a particular individual have less effect in cases of professional discipline.[12] Whether disciplinary action has any general deterrent effect is a matter for enquiry; it may enter the consciousness of most lawyers too sporadically to influence behaviour.

The third set of rules governing professional behaviour are the codes of practice issued by the Bar and the Law Society.[13] Historically the codes have evolved from the practical workings of the discipline which the profession itself has exercised. The inns of court have a long history of controlling both the admission and conduct of barristers subject, however, to the jurisdiction of the visitors and now review by the courts.[14] A disciplinary committee for solicitors was established under the Solicitors Act 1888, although it was not until 1919 that legislation empowered the committee to exercise actual disciplinary powers.[15] The courts have generally deferred to a positive finding of misconduct by the profession's disciplinary bodies, and have also been reluctant to mitigate penalty, on the basis that the representatives of the profession itself are the best judges of misconduct and its seriousness.[16]

Public pressure has meant that the professional machinery of discipline has become increasingly elaborate. In 1986 the Law Society established the Solicitors Complaints Bureau as a quasi-independent body to handle, as the

[11] *Ex p. Brounsall* (1778) 98 ER 1385, 1385.
[12] *Bolton* v. *Law Society* [1994] 1 WLR 512, 519.
[13] The General Council of the Bar, *Code of Conduct of the Bar of England and Wales* (1990, loose-leaf) [hereafter BC]; The Law Society, *The Guide to the Professional Conduct of Solicitors*, 6th ed, 1993 [hereafter LSG]. On the code of conduct for lawyers in the European Union, see John Toulmin QC, 'A worldwide common code of professional ethics?' (1991–1992) 15 *Fordham Int.L.J.* 673.
[14] *Lincoln* v. *Daniels* [1962] 1 QB 237. See also *R.* v. *General Council of the Bar ex p. Percival* [1991] 1 QB 212; B. Lee, 'The constitutional power of the courts over admission to the bar' (1899) 13 *Harv.LR* 233; J. H. Baker, 'Judicial review of the judges as visitors to the Inns of Court' [1992] *Public Law* 411.
[15] See B. Abel-Smith & R. Stevens, *Lawyers and the Courts*, 1967, pp.188–90; R. Abel, *The Legal Profession in England and Wales*, 1988, pp.133–6, 248–60, 285–7.
[16] See *McCoan* v. *General Medical Council* [1964] 1 WLR 1107, 1113; *Bolton* v. *Law Society* [1994] 1 WLR 512.

name suggests, complaints about solicitors. The majority of complaints are resolved by agreement between the client and the solicitor concerned although a small number of cases undergo formal investigation, some of which are then considered by the Adjudication and Appeals Committee of the Law Society.[17] Insurance cover under the Solicitors' Indemnity Fund has since 1987 extended to any legal liability, including dishonesty. Since a solicitor cannot insure against personal dishonesty, a compensation fund was inaugurated in 1941 to cover situations where there is no one else against whom a claim can be made. The drain on the fund has led to increased scrutiny by the Law Society of solicitors' practises. Under the Courts and Legal Services Act 1990 the government has appointed a legal services ombudsman to review how both branches of the profession handle complaints.

The codes are not like some ethical codes, which are purely exhortatory in character. As indicated they can lead to legally enforceable consequences, and ultimately disbarment of a lawyer from practice. In many respects the codes are simply restating and expanding the general law; they are not exhaustive of all the ethical problems which lawyers face. While the codes surface in judicial decisions, they have a far more important, daily application in rulings by the profession's disciplinary bodies, decisions by the Bar and the Law Society about their application, and advice given to members of the profession by the professional bodies and others on the basis of the code provisions.

The codes are not law and are not applied as if they were. In their application the professional bodies adopt a creative role in interpretation. Many situations do not fall within the four corners of the codes, but it is not uncommon for the professional bodies to reason by analogy from other provisions and to invoke principle. The justification for this liberal, purposive approach is that lawyers should know that certain conduct is wrongful, even if not expressly proscribed by the codes. Any uncertainty in application, however, may expose lawyers to disciplinary action when their behaviour is only questionably unethical or represents the unconventional or politically unpopular. This last point is certainly not an argument against the codes but simply a caution about their application.

Even if the codes only repeated the standards contained in the general law they would be more accessible and provide a more practical basis for professional discipline. In fact the codes do more: they identify the main lines of the profession's thinking on professional responsibility and have both educative and moulding effects. New members of the profession can be more easily instructed into acceptable standards of behaviour, and members of the profession generally may be dissuaded from unacceptable behaviour, and may have any disposition to act correctly reinforced.

---

[17] Solicitors Complaints Bureau, Annual Reports. With very serious matters proceedings may be begun before the Solicitors Disciplinary Tribunal, a statutory body.

An important policy issue is the extent to which the codes ought to be infused by wider ethical notions. There are two aspects to this. One is encapsulated in the question: 'Can a good lawyer be a bad person?'[18] In other words, are the standards in the codes untenable when laid alongside ethical thought or common morality? The second aspect is that if there is a discrepancy between the codes and secular ethical thought, what is special about lawyers that exempts them from the precepts of the latter? To put it another way, how is it that lawyers can decide ethically on a course of action for a client which is different from that which they would adopt for themselves?

While there is a certain force in these questions, it seems to me that those who might argue for the primacy of ethical considerations do not give enough attention to their contingency in real life. One person's immorality is another's standard practice. One response to this might be to try to give ethical values a greater objectivity in the legal context. For example it might be said that in litigation the prime goal is seeking truth and that this is therefore the lodestar for lawyers engaged in it.[19] Even if this were the case—which is doubtful— that still does not give sufficient guidance to the lawyer wanting to know how to act ethically in particular situations. Ethical issues arise in specific contexts and we need detailed guidelines for resolving the practical problems which arise.

None of this is to advocate moral relativism. In many cases the rightness or wrongness of conduct can be identified and reflection on what ethical thought might demand should inform any discussion of professional responsibility. Lawyers cannot remain free from moral responsibility simply by pointing to a provision in the codes. Lawyers are not simply technicians; they must not submerge their own moral standards to the pursuit of a client's interest irrespective of what that might be. In any event, there is high authority that they must also serve other interests such as those of third parties and, more generally, justice.

There are grave problems, then, in putting ethical thought to the fore, not least lawyers' own unfamiliarity with this field. That does not mean that it has no role to play, just that it cannot be determining. There is also another possibility. In important respects the present professional codes are too vague. In some especially difficult areas lawyers are given no guidance as to how they should act, although in a few they are told that they have a discretion to withdraw from providing further services to a particular client. We return to some of these later in the chapter. While it is impossible for the codes to be more specific in many areas, there seems to be more scope in them for standards such as reasonableness—familiar to lawyers in other contexts—

[18] D. Luban, *Lawyers and Justice: An Ethical Study*, 1988; D. Luban (ed), *The Good Lawyer: Lawyers' Rôles and Lawyers' Ethics*, 1983.
[19] The seminal article is by Judge Frankel, 'The search for truth: an umpireal view' (1975) 123 *U.Penn.LR* 1031.

which would force lawyers to confront more directly the creative aspect of professional judgment and require them to justify a particular course of action.[20]

The final point to make is that many of the issues are as much political as ethical. This is apparent in matters such as *pro bono* work and the unmet need for legal services. But even with the codes themselves there is the obvious point that control over their content rests largely in the profession itself, the very group whose ethical behaviour is in issue. In this area self-regulation has many advantages, not least in identifying wrongdoing and fissures in the codes. As I have said, it is just plain wrong to characterise the codes as wholly, or mainly, self-serving. Yet there are dangers in self-regulation here as elsewhere. One is cartelisation and another is that the codes might not adopt a strict line if economic pressures push in the opposite direction. The obvious conclusion is that lawyers should not have a completely free hand in writing the codes; there must be some mechanism additional to the Lord Chancellor's Advisory Committee on Legal Education and Conduct for ensuring that what is contained in them is subject to public scrutiny and really is best for society as a whole.

SECRECY, DILIGENCE, FIDELITY

In an address to the new serjeants at law in 1648 Law Commissioner White-lock said that the duties of advocates to their clients were general and particular.

The general consist in three things, secrecy, diligence and fidelity.
1. For secrecy, advocates are a kind of confessors, and ought to be such to whom the client may with confidence lay open his evidences, and the naked truth of his case, *sub sigillo*, and he ought not to discover them to his client's prejudice, nor will the law compel him to do it.
2. For diligence, much is required in an advocate . . . in giving a constant and careful attendance and endeavour in his clients' causes.
3. For fidelity, it is accounted *vinculum societatis*, the name of unfaithfulness is hateful in all, and more in advocates than others, whom the client trusts with his livelihood, without which his life is irksome, and the unfaithfulness or fraud of the one is the ruin of the other.[21]

These three duties, identified three hundred and fifty years ago, provide the pegs for an exposition of the central rules of professional responsibility.

[20] W. Simon, 'Ethical discretion in lawyering' (1988) 101 *Harv.LR* 1083.
[21] Sir Bulstrode Whitelock, *Memorials of the English Affairs*, 1853, v.2, p.454. Whitelock was one of the commissioners of the Great Seal in the period of the Commonwealth.

Secrecy

So first, secrecy or, more familiarly, the duty of confidentiality. In general terms the law implies a term into the contract which a lawyer has with a client 'to keep [the] client's affairs secret and not to disclose them to anyone without just cause'.[22] Consent of a client to disclosure lifts the duty of confidentiality. (A client might well condone disclosure, when the lawyer thinks the circumstances demand it, even though the law does not require it.) But the purposes behind and contours of the duty of confidence are as uncertain for lawyers as they are for other professionals. Privacy, and protecting the client's expectations and other interests, are clearly important rationales of the duty, although as we will see there are larger public interests as well, such as encouraging utilisation of legal services and enhancing the system of civil justice. The duty applies to 'secrets which are confidentially reposed' in the lawyer,[23] and that goes some way to embracing other than what is directly communicated by the client (for example information generated by professional skill). The duty is not absolute in character, and there is the so-called public interest defence to an action for breach of the duty if the balance of interests favours disclosure.[24]

There are general injunctions about preserving the confidentiality of a client's affairs in the professional codes.[25] The duty for solicitors extends to making sure that their staff as well maintain confidentiality. In accordance with the general law, the duty of confidentiality stated in the codes continues after the lawyer/client relationship has ended. Apart from these general provisions there are a limited number of specific rules in the codes relating to confidentiality. For example, barristers must cease to act if having accepted a brief or instructions on behalf of more than one client there is or appears to be a risk of a breach of confidence, and the clients do not consent to the barrister continuing to act.[26] Another example is that solicitors must not disclose the content of a will they have drawn before probate, except with the consent of the executors.[27]

Under the general law disclosure in breach of confidence is permissible in some cases on grounds of public interest.[28] The Bar Code does not seem to acknowledge this public interest exception. It posits withdrawal from a case where, for example, the barrister has a duty of disclosure to the court and the client refuses to sanction it.[29] The Law Society Code is more in line with the general law. It says that a duty to keep a client's confidences can be overridden 'in certain exceptional circumstances'.[30] Apart from mentioning statutory

---

[22] *Parry-Jones* v. *Law Society* [1969] 1 Ch 1, 7 *per* Lord Denning.

[23] *In re a Firm of Solicitors* [1992] QB 959, 966, citing *Rakusen* v. *Ellis Munday and Clarke* [1912] 1 Ch 831, 834.

[24] See F. Gurry, *Breach of Confidence*, 1984, esp. p.149 ff; P. Finn, 'Professionals and confidentiality' (1992) 14 *Syd.LR* 317.   [25] BC§ 603; LSG§§12.12, 16.01–04.

[26] BC§504(b)(ii).   [27] LSG§16.01, Note 3.

[28] *Attorney-General* v. *Guardian Newspapers (No. 2)* [1990] 1 AC 109.   [29] BC§504(e).

[30] LSG§ 16.04.

provisions and rules of court which permit or oblige disclosure, the commentary to this principle in the Law Society Code gives only three general examples: firstly, disclosure of communications made by a client to a solicitor for the purpose of being guided or helped in the commission of a crime (an exception which restates the common law); secondly, where the solicitor has been used by the client to perpetrate fraud or other criminal purpose; and thirdly, where disclosure is reasonably necessary to establish a defence to a criminal charge.[31] It is important to appreciate how narrow these exceptions are. Firstly, and obviously, disclosure in such instances is not obligatory, however serious the wrongdoing. Secondly, the exceptions are limited to crime, or in the second case crime and fraud, and do not extend generally to deliberate wrongdoing or breaches of a court order.[32]

Running along parallel lines with the duty of confidence, but narrower in scope, is lawyer/client privilege.[33] Legal professional privilege is an evidential rule which precludes other parties by way of pre-trial discovery, or in the course of judicial or quasi-judicial proceedings, from obtaining access to communications between a lawyer and client.[34] The rationale of the privilege is that it encourages clients to reveal all to their lawyers, thereby facilitating effective legal advice and assistance. Lord Brougham's justification is often quoted in this regard:

The foundation of this rule is not difficult to discover. It is not (as has sometimes been said) on account of any particular importance which the law attributes to the business of legal professors, or any particular disposition to afford them protection, though certainly it may not be very easy to discover why a like privilege has been refused to others, and especially to medical advisers. But it is out of regard to the interests of justice, which cannot be upholden, and to the administration of justice, which cannot go on, without the aid of men skilled in jurisprudence, in the practice of the Courts, and in those matters affecting rights and obligations which form the subject of all judicial proceedings. If the privilege did not exist at all, every one would be thrown upon their own legal resources; deprived of all professional assistance, a man would not venture to consult any skilful person, or would only dare to tell his counsellor half his case.[35]

---

[31] LSG§16.04, Notes 1, 5, 8.

[32] In the previous version of the Law Society code disclosure was also permitted which the solicitor believed was necessary to prevent the client from committing a crime which the solicitor believed, on reasonable grounds, was likely to result in serious bodily harm. That provision was accidentally omitted from the current version of the code although it will be restored in the next. It might extend to a continuing crime, but certainly does not cover crimes which result in serious damage to property, the environment, or financial interests. It means that the solicitor who learns of a client's clear intention to murder has a right to disclose. *The Guide to the Professional Conduct of Solicitors*, 5th ed, 1990, 12.04, Note 8.

[33] On the distinction: *Webster* v. *James Chapman & Co. (a firm)* [1989] 3 All ER 939.

[34] Not all communications are covered and whether there is protection turns on whether or not litigation is contemplated (where a wider range of communications is covered). The rule covers what lawyers produce ('work product').

[35] *Greenough* v. *Gaskell* (1833) 39 ER 618, 620-1. See *English & American Insurance Co.* v. *Herbert Smith* [1988] FSR 232; *Balabel* v. *Air India* [1988] Ch 317, 329-30. The justification for protecting work product must be quite different: see *Hickman* v. *Taylor* 329 US 495 (1947).

Lawyer/client privilege is sometimes represented as an ancient right, fundamental to liberty and liberal democratic society.[36]

All this must be treated with healthy scepticism. It seems doubtful whether empirical evidence would lend any support to the rationale of encouraging client disclosure. Whether legal advice is sought depends in most cases on factors other than legal professional privilege. There is a plain necessity on the part of commercial interests to use lawyers and it would be surprising if they did not finely calculate whether and what they needed to disclose for the purposes of obtaining legal advice. It is highly likely anyway that most people are ignorant of the privilege.

Among the arguments Jeremy Bentham advanced against the privilege was that the innocent had no need of it and that it protected only the guilty. In his view the privilege should not exist and lawyers should have to warn their clients that their revelations could be disclosed.[37] Certainly on first impression the privilege would seem to be as likely to lead to more effective avoidance of the law as to more effective utilisation of legal services. A client can shop around to discover from one lawyer what will ground a claim, then tailor what is told to a second lawyer retained to bring the claim. Subject to the possible application of the fraud/crime exception, of which more below, the communication with the first lawyer would be privileged.

Although the privilege is of ancient lineage too much should not be made of this since over time its content has moved in unpredictable and surprising ways, and its present shape has been importantly determined by redundant evidentiary rules.[38] The notion that the privilege is somehow fundamental to liberty takes a battering with the reminder that lawyers' self-interest might dissolve the privilege.[39] The fact that the courts have refused to extend the privilege to other professions, especially those doing similar work, must also give pause to the notion that it is somehow a fundamental right.[40] This is not to deny the value of legal professional privilege. As with the duty of confidence, it protects interests such as privacy, important to the dignity of the individual. But as with the duty of confidence, countervailing public interest arguments must always be weighed in the balance, or otherwise the privilege will become a mask for abuse.[41]

The privilege does not countenance communications which are not relevant to the client's legal business. This is the effect of the seminal decision *Annesley* v. *Anglesea*,[42] where the court ordered disclosure by the

---

[36] *Australian Mining & Smelting Europe Ltd.* v. *EC Commission* [1982] ECR 1575, 1610–14; [1982] 2 CMLR 264, 320–1.

[37] J. Bowring (ed), *The Works of Jeremy Bentham*, 1843, v.7, pp.474–5.

[38] M. Radin, 'The privilege of confidential communication between lawyer and client' (1928) 16 *Calif.LR* 487; G. Hazard, 'An historical perspective on the attorney-client privilege' (1978) 66 *Calif.LR* 1061.   [39] eg LSG§16.04, Note 8.

[40] eg *Price Waterhouse (a firm)* v. *BCCI Holdings (Luxembourg) SA* [1992] BCLC 583.

[41] cf *Oxfordshire C.C.* v. *M.* [1994] 2 All ER 269, 280, *per* Steyn LJ.

[42] (1743) 17 State Trials 1140, 1223–6, 1241.

Earl's solicitor of the Earl's statement that 'I would give £10,000 to have him hanged', the 'he' being a rival for his estate. More importantly, for reasons of public policy, the privilege has never been held to apply to communications by a client for the purpose of being guided or helped in the commission of a crime or the perpetration of fraud (the crime/fraud exception).[43] The House of Lords has held that this exception to the general rule applies even if the client is the innocent tool of a third party who has the unlawful purpose.[44] The exception also extends to steps taken to conceal the unlawfulness or to spirit away the resulting profits.[45] The exception does not extend to lawyer/client communications about matters of which legality is only in doubt; the requisite purpose is absent and in any event according confidentiality fits with the rationale of encouraging persons to seek legal assistance regarding compliance with the law. There is a fine line, however, between the innocent desire to comply with lawful requirements and the dishonest quest for knowledge as to how to avoid the law. In a valuable decision the Court of Appeal has held that lawyers realising or suspecting that they have been unwittingly used as a conduit for fraud may apply to the court for an order that they be at liberty to disclose the fact to the victims.[46]

Diligence

Diligence is an obligation of lawyers demanded by the general law. Lawyers must both be skilful and must exercise the skill they have.[47] The law reports contain many examples of lawyers being liable to clients for lack of competence, and there are also cases where they have been held to be liable to third parties where a client's instructions have been negligently effected.[48] Indeed, lack of competence might be raised collaterally as in the very exceptional cases where a conviction will be quashed because of the failure of the lawyer adequately to advise or act.[49]

It goes without saying that lawyers must have a sound knowledge of the law. Thus they may be liable for wrongful advice, albeit that the questions are obscure and difficult. Clients must be advised of the legal consequences of any step which they propose to take, about the alternative remedies available, and that any particular step ought to be taken without delay.[50] But lawyers will not

---

[43] See A. Newbold, 'The crime/fraud exception to legal professional privilege' (1990) 53 *MLR* 472.   [44] *R.* v. *Central Criminal Court ex p. Francis & Francis* [1989] AC 346.
[45] *Derby & Co. Ltd.* v. *Weldon (No.7)* [1990] 1 WLR 1156; [1990] 3 All ER 161.
[46] *Finers (a firm)* v. *Miro* [1991] 1 WLR 35; [1991] 1 All ER 182.
[47] *Nocton* v. *Lord Ashburton* [1914] AC 932, 956.
[48] *Ross* v. *Caunters* [1980] Ch 297; *White* v. *Jones* [1995] 2 WLR 187; [1993] 1 All ER 691.
[49] eg *R.* v. *Clinton* [1993] 1 WLR 1181.
[50] *Re a Solicitor, ex p. Incorporated Law Society* (1895) 39 Sol.J. 219, 219; *Otter* v. *Church, Adams, Tatham & Co.* [1953] Ch 280; cf *Griffiths* v. *Evans* [1953] 1 WLR 1424; [1953] 2 All ER 1364.

be treated as responsible where the law is unsettled or where the matter is characterised by obscurity in language or expression.[51] Moreover, lawyers are not business advisers and although solicitors might offer business advice and try to protect clients against themselves, they are not under a legal duty to do so.[52]

As with others providing services, lawyers must act with reasonable competence and skill. Liability might arise simultaneously under contract and tort.[53] There is of course the immunity of barristers and solicitor-advocates from suits in negligence in respect of the carriage of a case in court and the pre-trial work connected with it.[54] This is sometimes justified on the grounds that advocates need to be able fearlessly to pursue a client's case and because of their wider duty to the court. Just how these values are promoted by immunity for incompetence is a puzzle. The strongest argument for the immunity is ensuring finality in litigation, although even this assumes that losing clients have the stamina for relitigation.

Diligence also arises in the general law in other ways. Lawyers must not misrepresent their competence. When handling moneys they must account and not make improper investments.[55] Lawyers must not stray beyond the task their client has authorised; if a lawyer acts without authority he or she may not only be liable to the client but to third parties for breach of warranty of authority.[56]

In the past there was a reluctance to treat a failure in care and skill as professional misconduct.[57] This was reinforced in practice because the professional bodies often gave precedence to the client's interest in obtaining compensation. The codes now clearly equate lack of care and skill with professional misconduct. Not only that, but they add some meat to the duty to act with care and skill. Thus both codes say that lawyers must not act if they lack the experience or competence, or if in the circumstances (for example, pressure of time) they cannot adequately represent a client.[58] These provisions are directed at the temptation, especially in today's competitive environment, for lawyers to take on any work which comes their way although, for example, it falls outside the area in which they practice. The Bar Code obliges barristers to take steps to ensure that their practices are run efficiently and are properly administered, and that proper records are kept.[59] Heads of chambers have specific obligations to ensure an efficient operation.[60] The Law Society

---

[51] *Richards* v. *Cox* [1943] KB 139; *Sykes* v. *Midland Bank Executor & Trustee Co. Ltd.* [1971] 1 QB 113; *County Personnel (Employment Agency) Ltd.* v. *Alan R. Pulver & Co.* [1987] 1 WLR 916; [1987] 1 All ER 289.   [52] *Haigh* v. *Wright Hassall & Co.* [1994] EGCS 54.
[53] *Midland Bank Trust Co. Ltd.* v. *Hett, Stubbs & Kemp* [1979] Ch 384.
[54] Courts and Legal Services Act 1990, s.62; *Saif Ali* v. *Sydney Mitchell & Co. (a firm)* [1980] AC 198; *Rondel* v. *Worsley* [1969] 1 AC 191. There is now the possibility of a wasted costs order.
[55] eg *Lee* v. *Sankey* (1873) LR 15 Eq 204; *Blyth* v. *Fladgate* [1891] 1 Ch 337.
[56] *Yonge* v. *Toynbee* [1910] 1 KB 215.   [57] *In re a Solicitor* (1974) 118 Sol.J. 737.
[58] BC§501(a)(b); LSG§§12.03, 12.11, 17.01, Note 2.   [59] BC§303(c).   [60] BC§304.

Code states explicitly that solicitors are under a duty to act with care and skill, proper diligence and promptness, and to keep their clients properly informed.[61] Solicitors must not act or continue to act in circumstances where the client cannot be represented with competence or diligence. This applies if they have insufficient time to devote to a matter, or insufficient experience or skill to deal with it competently.[62] There is also an express principle in the code obliging solicitors to deal promptly with correspondence.[63]

Care and skill under the Law Society Code covers behaviour which falls short of negligence. Unlike negligence, however, breach of the code does not lead to an award of damages although the Law Society can intervene and direct a solicitor to afford redress to the client. The most frequent causes of complaint to the Solicitors Complaints Bureau are delay and a failure to communicate. Delay can lead to the Law Society taking a matter from a solicitor and ultimately to serious disciplinary action.[64] Most importantly nowadays it is a breach of the care and skill obligation to provide services which are not of the quality which is reasonable to expect. So-called inadequate professional services cover a wider field than professional incompetence and include organisational incompetence.

An example of professional incompetence might be a case where a solicitor takes on work knowing that he or she is insuffiently experienced in that particular field to provide services of a satisfactory standard. An example of organisational incompetence would be where the solicitor is fully experienced to undertake the work but undertakes it in an unacceptably long period of time. While the solicitor's behaviour may fall short of negligence it may nonetheless be incompetent.[65]

Prejudice to a client does not have to be shown before a solicitor can be found to have failed to provide adequate professional service.[66]

Fidelity

Thirdly, then, to loyalty. As a matter of law the duty of loyalty has derived primarily from the position of lawyers as fiduciaries, a basis also of the duty of confidentiality. As a matter of public policy loyalty is probably grounded on the nature of the lawyer as a professional who places skills and knowledge at the disposal of the client. As with any professional, clients are entitled to place a certain trust in their lawyer that he or she will act loyally and competently. The strain comes when loyalty is, or ought to be, trumped by public interest.

---

[61] LSG§§12.11, 17.01.   [62] LSG§17.01, Note 2.   [63] LSG§17.02.
[64] LSG§17.01, Notes 8–9.
[65] LSG§17.01, Note 10. See Courts and Legal Services Act 1990, Schedule 15; A Paterson, 'Professional Competence' (1983) 28 *J.Law Soc.Scot.* 385.
[66] *R.* v. *The Law Society ex p. Singh & Choudry (a firm), The Times,* 1 April 1994.

(a) Devotion to the client's interests

Loyalty's first face is devotion to the client's interests. That demands competence, commitment and zeal. The Bar Code says that barristers must act
towards their lay clients and professional clients (ie instructing solicitors) 'at
all times in good faith'.[67] If there is a conflict, loyalty to the client comes
before loyalty to the instructing solicitor. For example, the Bar Code says that
in as much as barristers form the view that there is a conflict of interests
between the two, they must advise the lay client to employ another solicitor.[68]

The Bar has always put its claim to loyalty boldly in espousing the
fearless promotion and protection of a lay client's best interests, without
regard to the barrister's own interest or to any consequences which might
befall.[69] Lord Brougham's defence of Queen Caroline is portayed as an
exemplary example of barrister zeal. Brougham alluded in his defence of the
Queen to evidence which might harm the King, but argued that no matter what
the consequences his duty as an advocate demanded that he take every step
necessary to defend his client.

[A]n advocate, by the sacred duty of his connection with his client, knows, in the
discharge of that office, but one person in the world, that client and none other. To save
that client by all expedient means—to protect that client at all hazards and costs to all
others, and among others to himself—is the highest and most unquestioned of his
duties; and he must not regard the alarm, the suffering, the torment, the destruction,
which he may bring upon any other; nay, separating, even the duties of a patriot from
those of an advocate, he must go on reckless of the consequences, if his fate it should
unhappily be, to involve his country in confusion for his client.[70]

Advocates are constantly reminded that they must not act as judges. Rights, it
is said, are determined by the courts and not by advocates. 'It is for want of
remembering this that foolish people object to lawyers that they will advocate
a case against their own opinions.'[71] It is also said advocates often find that
arguments which they do not think to be valid are accepted by the courts.
Notwithstanding all this lay people, perhaps foolishly, do not share the same
confidence as advocates that the adversarial system always works.

The Law Society Code requires solicitors to act in the best interest of their
client.[72] More detailed consequences of loyalty include the principle that
solicitors must not take advantage of the age, inexperience, want of education, business experience, or ill health of a client.[73] Moreover, the code says

[67] BC§203(c).   [68] BC§605. See also BC§203(b).   [69] See now BC§203(a).
[70] Hansard, new ser, iii, Oct.3, 1820, 114. See W. Forsyth, *Hortensius, or the Advocate*, 3rd ed,
1879, p.389; D. Rhode, 'An adversarial exchange on adversarial tactics' (1991) 41 *J.Leg.Ed.* 29.
On Lushington's involvement in the defence: S. M. Waddams, *Law, Politics and the Church of
England*, 1992, pp.144–50.   [71] *Johnson* v. *Emerson* (1871) LR 6 Ex 329, 367.
[72] LSG§1.01.   [73] LSG§12.14.

specifically that solicitors must not take unfair advantage of a client by overcharging.[74]

What are the public interest limits on loyalty? There are few common law boundaries to advocate zeal. One is honesty; advocates must present their client's case to the best of their ability, without making themselves a judge of its correctness, but they must not be dishonest.[75] Lord Denning MR, in his own inimitable way, summed up the boundaries for advocates as follows:

[An advocate] must accept the brief and do all he honourably can on behalf of his client. I say 'all he *honourably* can' because his duty is not only to his client. He has a duty to the court which is paramount. It is a mistake to suppose that he is the mouthpiece of his client to say what he wants: or his tool to do what he directs. He is none of these things. He owes allegiance to a higher cause. It is the cause of truth and justice. He must not consciously misstate the facts. He must not knowingly conceal the truth. He must not unjustly make a charge of fraud, that is, without evidence to support it. He must produce all the relevant authorities, even those that are against him. He must see that his client discloses, if ordered, the relevant documents, even those that are fatal to his case. He must disregard the most specific instructions of his client, if they conflict with his duty to the court.[76]

In other words, advocates must not assert what they know to be a lie, nor must they connive at, much less attempt to substantiate, a fraud, but they are entitled to require the other side to prove its case. The adversary system is supposed to produce a just result based on laws fairly applied to accurate facts.

The professional codes contain injunctions similar to the common law against acting dishonestly, unlawfully, or in any way likely to diminish public confidence in the profession.[77] The codes also say that although there is a duty to advance a client's interests, this must not be so as to compromise professional standards.[78] As the Law Society Code puts it, the duty to observe principles of professional conduct 'means that there will be limitations upon the freedom of a solicitor to do what the client wants him or her to do. A solicitor must not breach the principles of professional conduct in order to benefit the client.'[79]

Specific guidance on these limits is harder to come by. There is a well

---

[74] LSG§14.10. The rule at common law: *MacColl* v. *Council of the Law Society of Scotland* [1987] SLT 524; *In re Veron* (1966) 84 W.N. Pt.1 (NSW) 136. See also *Singer* v. *Sharegin* (1984) 14 Fam.L. 58, 59.

[75] Sir William Boulton, *A Guide to Conduct and Etiquette at the Bar*, 1975, p.69. In *Abraham* v. *Jutsun* [1963] 2 All ER 402, 404, Lord Denning said: '[It is an advocate's] duty to take any point which he believed to be fairly arguable on behalf of his client. An advocate is not to usurp the province of the judge. He is not to determine what shall be the effect of legal argument. He is not guilty of misconduct simply because he takes a point which the tribunal holds to be bad. He only becomes guilty of misconduct if he is dishonest. That is, if he knowingly takes a bad point and thereby deceives the court.'

[76] *Rondel* v. *Worsley* [1966] 3 WLR 950, 962. Compare a similar statement by Crampton J in *R.* v. *O'Connell* (1844) 7 Irish LR 261, 313.   [77] BC§201; LSG§§1.01, 12.02, 18.01.

[78] BC§205; LSG§§1.01, 12.02.   [79] LSG§12.13, Note 1.

known limit, restated in both codes, that lawyers must not deceive or mislead a court.[80] *Meek* v. *Fleming*[81] is an example. A press photographer brought an action against 'Chief Inspector Fleming' for, *inter alia*, assault. Between the issue of the writ and the trial the defendant was demoted to station sergeant for being a party to an arrangement to practice deception on a court. He was asked in cross-examination: 'You are a chief inspector and you have been in the force, you told us, since 1938'. His answer was yes. During the summing up the judge referred to the defendant as 'inspector' or 'chief inspector' many times. The fact of the demotion was known to the defendant's legal advisers but they decided not to reveal it to the court. A new trial was ordered, since to allow the defendant to retain the judgment unfairly obtained would be a miscarriage of justice.

By contrast, *R.* v. *Visitors to the Inns of Court, ex parte Calder*[82] involved a barrister who had made a mock-up of a receipt purportedly signed by her client, the plaintiff. Believing it to be forged she put it to the defendant in cross-examination—'Have you ever seen anything like this before?'—in an attempt to undermine the defendant's credibility. At that stage the original of the receipt could not be found, nor a photocopy. Subsequently it was found and the mock-up played no further part in the trial. The barrister was none the less charged with misleading the court by failing to explain fully the provenance of the mock-up. The Court of Appeal quashed the conviction by the Visitors; the original had not been disclosed, the barrister was entitled to assume it might well have been destroyed, and therefore it was a legitimate tactic to cross-examine on the basis of the mock-up. The court was not misled and there was no evidence that the barrister had attempted to mislead it.

Derived from the obligation not to deceive or mislead the court are the more specific duties not to coach witnesses, not to devise facts to assist a client, and to ensure that the court is informed of all relevant decisions and legislation, however unfavourable.[83] A client's admission of perjury or of misleading a court, prior to or in the course of proceedings, obliges both a barrister and solicitor to decline to act further, unless the client agrees fully to disclose the matter.[84] Presenting perjured evidence would, of course, constitute misleading the court.

These various aspects of the duty of honesty derive from the adversary system: courts must be able to rely on the honesty of opposing parties since

---

[80] BC§202, App H, §5.2; LSG§22.01.

[81] [1961] 2 QB 366. See also *R.* v. *Bridgwood* 1987, discussed LSG, Annex 22C. Advising a client to wear conventional clothing, never otherwise worn except to marriages or funerals, has never been thought to be misleading, presumably because the judge/jury realises the truth.

[82] [1994] QB 1. Generally speaking, in presenting a document to a court an advocate is in effect warranting that it is what it purports to be and that it is accurate.

[83] BC§610; App H, §§5.8, 5.10, 6.2; LSG§22.01, Note 1, 3–4; §22.16, Notes 1, 4–5. On citing all relevant authorities: see *Glebe Sugar Refining Co.* v. *Greenock Harbour Trustees*, 1921, SC (HL) 72, 73–4 *per* Lord Birkenhead, LC.   [84] Sir William Boulton, *op.cit.*, p.77; LSG§22.08.

there is no inquisitorial system whereby they can investigate facts, and the pressure of business and absence of law clerks mean that judges are reliant on the advocates to research the law fully. While placing obligations on lawyers in this way compensates for certain features of the adversary system, it does not address other matters such as any inequality of legal representation.

(b) Conflicts of Interest

The other face of loyalty is avoiding conflicts of interest, although this principle is also underpinned by the duty of confidentiality. Echoing the general law, the professional codes contain a variety of provisions addressing conflict of duty and interest (between lawyer and client) and conflict of duties (duty to different clients or duty to a new client and a former client). Illustrative in the Bar Code are the rules relating to barristers likely to be a witness in a case, barristers having a connection with a client or court, and barristers with two or more clients whose interests conflict.[85] The general thrust of these rules is replicated for solicitors in the Law Society Code, although the scope is wider, disqualifying a solicitor's partners as well as the individual solicitor with the conflict.[86]

As with general fiduciary law, to avoid a conflict of interest lawyers might have to decline to act altogether.[87] Thus the Law Society Code provides that solicitors who have acted for both lender and borrower must not subsequently act for the lender against the borrower to enforce repayment if in doing so he or she has obtained confidential relevant information, for example about the borrower's financial position.[88] Nor may a solicitor who has acted for a company in a particular matter, and has also acted separately for directors or shareholders in a personal capacity in the same matter, now act for either the company or the other parties if litigation ensues between them in respect of it.[89] Mundane examples of conflicts of duty and interest, where solicitors must decline to act, involve transactions with clients, gifts, and legacies.[90]

In general fiduciary law conflict of interest rules are as much directed against tendencies and appearances as against actual conflict. There are few instances in the codes where appearances or tendencies disqualify, possibly because it is thought that it would lead to the profession not acting where there is no real conflict of interest and where other public interests demand that the lawyer continue to represent the client.[91] In the general law fiduciaries are

---

[85] BC§501(d)–(f); 504(b)(i).

[86] LSG§§12.06–07, 15.01–03, 22.07. See, eg, *Lewis* v. *Hillman* (1852) 10 ER 239; *Brown* v. *Inland Revenue*, 1964 SC (HL) 180; *R.* v. *Ataou* [1988] QB 798; *Perry* v. *Edwin Coe (a firm)*, *Independent*, 1 April 1994.   [87] LSG§15.05.

[88] LSG§15.02, Note 4.   [89] LSG§15.02, Note 6.

[90] LSG§15.05, 15.08. See *Stewart* v. *MacLaren* 1920 SC (HL) 148; *In re a Solicitor* [1975] QB 475.

[91] BC§§501(e), 504(b); LSG§§12.06, Note 1, 15.01, Note 1. See C. Wolfram, *Modern Legal Ethics*, 1986, pp.319–21.

released from their duties if the beneficiaries give their fully informed consent to any conflict of interest. With many lay clients, consent in this context will be largely illusory; they are not in a position to appreciate the nature of any conflict and its implications, even if disclosed. None the less, in several respects the professional codes do use consent as a dissolvent for a conflict of interest.[92]

Conflicts of interest are pervasive; the problem is that they may be so common that lawyers do not recognise them as such. For this reason it is better to attack an undesirable practice directly instead of imposing on the lawyer the obligation to take action if that practice gives rise to a 'conflict'. Take the basic potential conflict between a client and a lawyer—the lawyer is being paid, which, especially if at an hourly rate, creates a potential incentive to contrive to create work. For example, litigation which is better settled might be unnecessarily prolonged. (It is fair to add that with a test case a disincentive to settle might occur for non-economic reasons.) This basic conflict is dealt with in the professional codes by general rules such as those relating to lawyers acting with reasonable skill, care, and diligence. Would it not be better to tackle the problem with specific code provisions against undertaking unnecessary work? Such a rule might also mitigate the tendency for 'legal advisors, pressed by their clients, to take every point conceivable and inconceivable without judgment or discrimination'.[93]

Another example is the solicitor acting for both lender and borrower in the case of an institutional mortgage. This is standard practice and there is nothing in the Solicitors' Practice Rules 1990 or in the Law Society Code to prevent it. Indeed the code says that normally there will be no conflict.[94] However, the code provides that where a solicitor's duty requires advice to a borrower of the dangers of a lender's scheme, there is a conflict of interest until that duty is discharged. The code adds: 'The general duty of a solicitor may require him or her to try to ensure the borrower obtains independent financial advice—sometimes a second opinion. Much will depend on the level of sophistication, the vulnerability and the general understanding of the client as well as the complexity of the scheme.'[95] The fact is, as a past president of the Law Society has written, that conflict is endemic nowadays in representing both borrower and lender, given the inequality of bargaining power and that some mortgage arrangements 'contain a number of traps for the unwary'.[96] Specific rules, rather than putting the onus on the practitioner, seem to be demanded.

---

[92] eg LSG§15.03, Note 1.
[93] *Ashmore* v. *Corporation of Lloyd's* [1992] 1 WLR 446, 453, *per* Lord Templeman.
[94] Solicitors' Practice Rules 1990, r.6; LSG§24.01; LSG, Annex 24K, III, 1–2.
[95] LSG, Annex 24K, III, 4.
[96] T. Holland, 'Representing both borrower and lender' (1994) 144 *NLJ* 822, 822. cf *Spector* v. *Ageda* [1973] 1 Ch 30; *Mortgage Express Ltd.* v. *Bowerman & Partners (a firm)*, *The Times*, August 1, 1995.

The restructuring of law firms in the 1980s has given rise to conflict problems where different parts of the amalgamated firm have represented opposing clients. The Law Society has issued detailed guidance on the matter; the amalgamated firm must cease to act for both clients, although in 'exceptional' and 'rare' circumstances the amalgamated firm may continue to act for one, or, just possibly, both clients if it is in the best interests of the clients and an effective Chinese wall is erected, provided that both clients give their consent after full and frank independent advice. The guidance adds:

However, in practice, the difficulties in maintaining the requisite separation, and the risk of embarrassment and impropriety, must be so great as to mean that the new firm can virtually never act for both and invariably not in litigation. A heavy onus would be on the amalgamated firm to displace the *prima facie* pragmatic prohibition.[97]

The guidance does not cover an increasingly regular occurrence of younger solicitors, and increasingly partners, moving firms, so that a client finds that a solicitor has moved to a firm on the other side of a matter. Here it may assist to revert to the principle that if a solicitor or his or her firm has acquired relevant knowledge concerning a former client during the course of acting for him or her, the solicitor or firm must not accept instructions to act against that client.[98] Of course this is not wide enough to cover the situation where the client was with another solicitor in the solicitor's former firm but the client fears a seepage of knowledge within that firm.

The guidance represents the ethical position, not necessarily the law. In *Rakusen* v. *Ellis, Munday and Clarke*,[99] the Court of Appeal early this century took a relaxed position and allowed one of two partners to represent a company defending a wrongful dismissal action when the plaintiff had consulted the other partner earlier in the proceedings, in the course of which he had disclosed much confidential information. There was an undertaking that the latter would not act in any way in the proceedings and would not say anything about his consultations with the plaintiff. Indeed the facts were peculiar in that the two partners effectively conducted separate practices without any knowledge of each other's clients. However, the decision dates from a different age of smaller firms and, it might be added, lower standards. When the Court of Appeal had to consider the issue in 1991 in relation to an amalgamated firm it adopted an objective test, whether a reasonable person would reasonably anticipate that there was a danger that information gained from acting for a former client would be used against that client in representing the new client. A majority held that it would only be in special cases that a Chinese wall would be considered a suitable arrangement to prevent the leakage of information since, however conscientious members of the firm, confidential information could inadvertently seep.[100] The Court of Appeal unfortunately omitted discussion of

---

[97] LSG, Annex 15A, 8.   [98] LSG§15.02.   [99] [1912] 1 Ch 831.
[100] *In re a Firm of Solicitors* [1992] QB 959. See Law Commission, *Fiduciary Duties and Regulatory Rules*, Consultation Paper No. 124, 1992, pp.144–51.

the case law of other common law jurisdictions, which have also had to consider the problem in the last decade.[101] The tests used elsewhere are tougher.

Yet in this area desirable public policy is not clear cut. The argument for a liberal standard is that there is a countervailing public interest in not unduly restricting a client's choice of solicitor, and that depriving persons of their chosen solicitor may cause inconvenience, expense, and disruption.[102] The problem is especially acute when representation is well under way so the change in lawyer will have a very considerable impact on the client who has to find a new one. In the United States disqualification suits have become a forensic tactic, generating satellite litigation and, of course, costs and delay. What seems necessary is not senseless disqualification but a close empirical inquiry as to whether there is or will be a conflict, and how that might be mitigated. Detailed billing records are now available showing whether and how much solicitors have worked on particular files.[103] These will not reveal whether confidential information has seeped, and there will still need to be a searching inquiry and an investigation into the adequacy of any Chinese wall—but at least they are a beginning.[104]

LAWYER CONTROL AND LAWYER ZEAL

A distinction—albeit glib—can be drawn between at one end of the spectrum lawyers taking advantage of clients, and at the other lawyers taking advantage on behalf of clients. The first conceives the lawyer/client relationship as one of control with lawyers imposing their agenda on clients. The second conceives of the client as autonomous, with the lawyer zealously pursuing the client's interests, as the North American literature puts it, as hired gun. In fact the reality of domination or autonomy falls along a spectrum and varies with the circumstances. Certainly the ordinary person might be relatively ignorant of and mystified by the law. However unconsciously, the lawyer might impose his or her agenda on the relationship.[105] On the other hand, the commercial client

---

[101] *McDonald Estate* v. *Martin* [1991] 1 WWR 705; *National Mutual Holdings Pty Ltd.* v. *Sentry Corp.* (1989) 87 ALR 539. The seminal US decision is *T.C. Theatre Corp.* v. *Warner Brothers Pictures*, 113 F.Supp. 265 (S.D.NY 1953). On Chinese walls see, eg, *Analytica Inc.* v. *NPD Research Inc.* 708 F. 2d 1263 (7th Cir. 1983). See F. M. B. Reynolds, 'Solicitors and conflict of duties' (1991) 107 *LQR* 536; R. Tomasic, 'Chinese walls, legal principle and commercial reality in multi-service professional firms' (1991) 14 *U.NSW L.J.* 46; Note, 'The Chinese wall defense to law-firm disqualification' (1980) 128 *U.Penn.LR* 677.

[102] See Staughton LJ's dissent in *In re a Firm of Solicitors* [1992] QB 959.

[103] cf *Silver Chrysler Plymouth Inc.* v. *Chrysler Motors Corp.* 518 F. 2d 751 (2nd Cir, 1975).

[104] The Bar needs to address the issue; chambers now are much more than a collection of individuals, not least because they permit barristers to call on each other's judgment and skill.

[105] The classic study is D. Rosenthal, *Attorney and Client: Who's in Charge?* (1974). See also M. Cain, 'The general practice lawyer and the client: towards a radical conception', in R. Dingwall & P. Lewis (eds), *The Sociology of the Professions*, 1983; A. Sarat & W. Felstiner, 'Law and strategy in the divorce lawyer's office' (1986) 20 *Law & Soc.R.* 93; G. Lerman, 'Lying to Clients' (1990) 138 *U.Penn.L.R.* 659.

might know exactly what it wants to achieve, with lawyers and others being employed as tools to facilitate this. The problem then might be not the autonomy of the client but that of the lawyer.

In one sense lawyer control is a corollary of the law's mystery: the lawyer has a superior learning and knowledge of legal processes which clients cannot hope to acquire (without a substantial investment), even if they had the inclination. Lawyer control has an additional, functional justification, in suppressing antisocial behaviour. To use a sociological term, lawyers are gate-keepers. They advise clients about how to behave lawfully, they screen out unjustified claims, they encourage the settlement of disputes, and they damp down abuses of the legal process. I suggest below that the lawyer's role as gate-keeper should be enhanced.

The profession's codes exhibit a concern with both tendencies. Concern that the lawyer might take advantage of the client is evident in the Bar's standards applicable to criminal cases. Barristers should advise defendants about their plea ('he may, if necessary, express his advice in strong terms') but must make clear that the client has complete freedom of choice.[106] They should advise clients about whether or not to give evidence in their own defence, but the decision should be taken by clients themselves.[107] Similarly, the Law Society Code says that solicitors must act in the best interests of clients.[108] There are various warnings that solicitors must keep clients properly informed.[109] The aim in relation to communications with clients is to ensure that those unfamiliar with the law receive the information needed to understand what is happening. No doubt more could be done both through the codes and in the way lawyers treat clients. Legal education has a role in lawyers learning how to be more responsive, for example to the human as well as to the legal dimensions of clients' problems.

Lawyer Zeal and its Limits

In considering lawyer zeal it is useful to begin with the rôle of a leading City of London law firm in the well publicised acquisition of House of Fraser by the Fayeds. House of Fraser was then the largest group of department stores in Europe and included the prestigious Harrods store. The firm represented the Fayeds at crucial points in the acquisition process. Inspectors were appointed to inquire into the circumstances surrounding the take-over, notably the impression conveyed to the government that the Fayeds were a family with wide-spread, international business interests who had sufficient funds to finance the take-over without assistance from any third party. In the course of their report, the inspectors (Henry Brooke QC, as he then was, and Hugh

---

[106] BC, Annex H, section 2, §2.3.   [107] *ibid.*, §2.4.   [108] LSG§1.01(c).
[109] LSG§§12.15, 13.03–4, 16.07.

Aldous, an accountant) concluded that in deciding not to refer the acquisition to the Monopolies and Mergers Commission the government had taken comfort from the assurances which were given to the Office of Fair Trading (OFT) and the Department of Trade and Industry (DTI) by the Fayeds and, more importantly, from an impression which had been created that the Fayeds' merchant bankers, the board of House of Fraser (which recommended acceptance of the bid), and the law firm had aligned their reputations with those of the Fayeds. In response to this the law firm contended that in acting, speaking, and making submissions for their clients, solicitors do not generally give an imprimatur of any sort. If regard was had to what it had said and written it would be concluded that the firm had declined to give any assurance or endorsement. The inspectors rejected this.

We have little difficulty in accepting that these submissions were correct as a matter of theory. A High Court judge or an experienced lawyer would have little difficulty in detecting when a solicitor was ceasing to act as a mere advocate and becoming more and would also probably try and stop him from changing his role because he would know the problems this causes. In their relationships with the OFT, however, solicitors are not dealing with High Court judges or experienced lawyers. They are dealing with intelligent lay people. [The OFT officer] and, at one remove, [the DTI officer] told us the impression which [the firm] created on their minds and we are not surprised that the firm created that impression. The firm has said that they should have read the words which [it] used and that they were wrong to receive that impression. We do not agree. Anyone reading [the] letter would have obtained the impression that the firm was in a certain sense vouching for the accuracy of what their clients had said.[110]

In the result the inspectors did not blame the firm for failing to take further steps to ensure that the assertions by their clients were based on fact. They thought that the problem arose from a confusion of rôles, in particular that solicitors when they act as advocates do not appreciate the dangers of identifying with their clients, ready to vouch for their cause. Barristers, of course, however passionately they might argue their client's case, do not as a practice assert a personal opinion as to the facts or the law.[111]

The House of Fraser take-over raises in stark form the dangers of lawyer zeal. Identifying (or being perceived to identify) too closely with a client's case as in that instance misled others as to the strength of the client's arguments. Of course zeal *per se* is admirable. The problem in some areas is an under-representation of interests, not excessive zealousness. The tragedy is that financial constraints mean that many ordinary people with a need for legal services are not served at all, let alone zealously. Coupled with the problem of

[110] Department of Trade and Industry, *House of Fraser Holdings plc*, 1988, p.491. On the Law Society's response to this report: HC, Trade & Industry Committee, *Company Investigations*, HC 36, 1990, pp.285–6 (with limited exceptions 'a solicitor is under no obligation to check the accuracy of any statement he makes on behalf of a client . . .'). See also R. Rice, 'Salutary lessons from the Fayed affair', *Financial Times*, 26 March 1990, p.8.   [111] BC§610(b).

unrepresentation is the unenthusiastic representation of clients. For a variety of financial and other reasons lawyers might not show the devotion, which would ordinarily be expected, in pursuing certain claims. This is one of the criticisms of plea bargaining, that it can lead defence lawyers to substitute good relations with the prosecution authorities, and other interests, for a zealous defence.[112]

Zeal, however, must have its boundaries. The client's own interests will delineate the first. Thus it may be that the client's interests are best served by compromise and accommodation with opponents, rather than the zealous insistence on pursuing legal rights to the hilt. Moreover, a lawyer might not give sufficient attention to the object of zealousness; in other words, the problem might not be excessive zealousness, but excessive zealousness on behalf of the wrong person. Instructed by a company, for example, zealousness on behalf of the company as a whole, rather than the directors with whom the lawyer actually deals, could lead to greater corporate social responsibility. A second boundary to zeal is that demanded by the interests of others directly involved in the matter. Even in the arena of criminal defence zeal needs to be mitigated in the interests of victims. An example is the shield against defence attacks which the victims in rape cases now have.[113]

The final boundary to zealousness is that imposed by the public interest. This is the hardest to define. It is clear that a Darwinian struggle between adversaries will not necessarily produce a result which is in the public interest. We now know enough about the adversary process to realise that, quite apart from anything else, the different sides might be unequally matched. Moreover, many aspects of a lawyer's work do not involve another side; for example a lawyer simply gives advice to a client as to how to structure a transaction to comply with company law and to minimize taxation.

Before proceeding further to delineate this third boundary, it is as well to recall the origins of lawyer zeal. They lie in criminal defence, and there the justification is obvious. Zealousness guarantees a thorough preparation of the case, not simply by the defence lawyers. Without it, the police and prosecution authorities would not have the same incentive thoroughly to investigate a matter, for example by investigating any corroboration for the defendant's account. Recent miscarriages of justice underlie how much worse the situation would be in the absence of a zealous defence.

Putting that to one side, however, the crucial issue is that the approach with criminal defence cannot automatically be extended to other cases, in particular the lawyer giving advice to, negotiating on behalf of, or representing a client where no litigation is in contemplation. Here we are not concerned with the state operating against the individual or with the possibility that the

[112] J. Baldwin & M. McConville, *Negotiated Justice*, 1977.
[113] Sexual Offences (Amendment) Act 1976, s.2. See A. Keane, *The Modern Law of Evidence*, 3rd ed, 1994, pp.135–9.

client might be deprived of his or her liberty. For good reasons the zeal which we expect of a lawyer in criminal defence is not necessarily appropriate in these other, more common, situations. Generally speaking, of course, the client will have no truck with illegality and will want to stay well within the four corners of the law. But sometimes clients will want to push the law to its limit and will expect their lawyer to facilitate this. They will want their bid for a target company to succeed, financing to be obtained for their enterprise, or tax to be avoided. These days in commercial law the lawyer becomes closely involved in business decision making. Competitive pressures impel lawyers to tread on very thin ice. It was probably only a matter of time before prosecuting authorities should bring proceedings against a City solicitor. Although the judge directed a not guilty verdict against the partner of a City law firm who was involved in the Blue Arrow affair, the prosecution was a salutary warning, as the *Financial Times* put it, 'of the dangers inherent in the proactive rôle commercial lawyers are required to play these days'.[114] As one expert in commercial fraud from another prominent City law firm said: 'The apparently aggressive attitude of the prosecution towards professionals is moulded by a belief that many sophisticated frauds . . . cannot be carried out without the active and knowing participation of a solicitor or other advisor.[115] It is in these areas of potential wrongdoing by clients, or suspected wrongdoing, that the problems for lawyers are most acute.

Client Wrongdoing

Over the years the Bar has been able to refine its approach to a client's confession of wrongdoing. In 1915 the English Bar Council drew a sharp distinction between confessions which were made to counsel before the proceedings commenced and those which were made subsequently. If the former it was said to be most undesirable for an advocate to whom the confession had been made to undertake the defence, since he would most certainly be seriously embarrassed in the conduct of the case. In any event no harm could be done by requesting the accused to retain another advocate. Other considerations applied in cases in which the confession was made during the proceedings, or in circumstances where the advocate could not withdraw without seriously compromising the position of the accused. In addressing this the Bar Council said it was essential to bear in mind that the issue in a criminal trial was always whether the accused was guilty of the offence charged, not whether the accused was innocent, and secondly that the burden rested on the

---

[114] R. Rice, 'Blue Arrow and the rôle of the solicitor', *Financial Times*, 20 Nov. 1989, p.15. See Department of Trade and Industry, *County NatWest Limited. County NatWest Services Limited,* 1989.

[115] D. Kirk, 'Blue Arrow: a legacy of suspicion', *Lawyer*, v.5, n.43, 5 Nov. 1991, p.4. See P. Stewart, 'Lawyers in the Firing Line', *Int'l. Financial LR*, Apr. 1991, p.12.

prosecution to prove the case. Thus the advocate's duty was to protect a client as far as possible from being convicted, except by a competent tribunal and upon legal evidence sufficient to support a conviction, although in the event of a confession there were very strict limitations on how the defence was to be conducted since no advocate should assert what he or she knew to be a lie, nor connive at, much less attempt to substantiate, a fraud.[116] This approach is, in substance, contained in the current code.[117]

Illustrative of the principle is the Australian decision, used in some of the American texts, *Tuckiar* v. *The King*.[118] The accused, a nomadic aboriginal, was charged with the murder of a police constable in the Northern Territory. During the trial counsel for the accused interviewed his client at the suggestion of the trial judge to ascertain whether he agreed with evidence given by a witness for the Crown of a confession alleged to have been made by the accused to the witness. After interviewing the accused his counsel said in open court that he was in a worse predicament than he had encountered in all his career. The implication was obvious, and the accused was found guilty of murder. In a joint judgment the High Court of Australia (Gavan Duffy CJ, Dixon J, Evatt J, McTiernan J) said of counsel:

Why he should have conceived himself to have been in so great a predicament, it is not easy for those experienced in advocacy to understand. He had a plain duty, both to his client and to the Court, to press such rational considerations as the evidence fairly gave rise to in favour of complete acquittal or conviction of manslaughter only.[119]

Outside the law this approach has never been universally accepted. Jeremy Bentham regarded the lawyer assisting a guilty client to an acquittal to be an accessory after the fact of the offence.[120] In any event, the approach addresses

---

[116] See also Sir M. Hilbery, *Duty and Art in Advocacy*, 1959, p.9.

[117] BC, Annex H, section 2, §§3.2–5 (Standards Applicable to Criminal Cases), read:

   3.2 . . . the mere fact that a person charged with a crime has confessed to his counsel that he did commit the offence charged is no bar to that barrister appearing or continuing to appear in his defence, nor indeed does such a confession release the barrister from his imperative duty to do all that he honourably can for his client.

   3.3 Such a confession, however, imposes very strict limitations on the conduct of the defence. A barrister must not assert as true that which he knows to be false. He must not connive at, much less attempt to substantiate, a fraud.

   3.4 While, therefore, it would be right to take any objections to the competency of the Court, to the form of the indictment, to the admissibility of any evidence or to the evidence admitted . . . a barrister must not . . . set up an affirmative case inconsistent with the confession made to him.

   3.5 . . . he is entitled to test the evidence given by each individual witness and to argue that the evidence taken as a whole is insufficient to amount to proof that the defendant is guilty of the offence charged. Further than this he ought not to go.

[118] (1934) 52 CLR 335.

[119] At p.346. After the defendant was convicted his counsel made a public statement in court to the effect that the accused admitted the evidence called by the Crown of a confession was correct. The High Court said that this was wholly indefensible; in the event it rendered a re-trial impossible because that would have been known through the Territory.

[120] J. Bowring, *op.cit.*, pp.474–5.

cases of unequivocal guilt, not those of doubtful guilt. In practice the former will be rare and the reality is of a 'confession' in relation to which the lawyer will rarely, if ever, be able to conclude certain guilt. No doubt there are other cases, falling outside the strict words of the code, which lawyers themselves would almost universally condemn as professional misconduct. A striking example is *R. v. Dean*.[121] Dean was tried for attempted murder of his wife and defended by Meagher. He was convicted and after the trial Dean confessed to Meagher that he was in fact guilty. (Clearly this does not fall within the words of the code since it was not a confession before or during the trial.) Knowing this, Meagher still agitated for a Royal Commission to reopen the case, and when one was ultimately appointed Dean received a pardon as a result of its recommendations. Afterwards Meagher had to concede Dean's confession and was struck off for professional misconduct.

What of those instances which do not fall squarely within the words of the code, or clear cases such as *R. v. Dean*, where a lawyer knows, or more probably suspects, that he is assisting a client in wrongful conduct, wrongful in the sense that it will be a breach of the criminal or regulatory law, fraudulent, or (possibly also) an intentional or bad faith breach of contract?[122] Consider these hypothetical examples.

- A solicitor appears on legal aid in the county court against an unrepresented landlord. The landlord puts arguments which are irrelevant to the issue. However, the solicitor knows that if the landlord were to put other arguments his client might not be able to resist the order for possession.
- An assistant solicitor in a City firm is advising a company on the application of the Environmental Protection Act to some of its intended activities. It is fairly clear to her that the activities are in clear breach of the Act, but, at the conference, her supervising partner indicates to the client that the area is doubtful legally, and that in any event it is unlikely that the enforcement authorities will discover the breach. At the end of the conference she is told by him to draft a letter of advice to the client along those lines.
- A lawyer in a law centre is advising on welfare benefit. He is unsure whether the client is telling the truth about not having worked in the relevant period, but on being assured that no work was done proceeds with the claim and as a result has been successful. A short time later he discovers that the client was not telling the truth and had full time employment for the period for which benefit was, wrongfully, obtained.[123]

---

[121] C. K. Allen, 'R. v. Dean' (1941) 57 *LQR* 85.

[122] Counselling breach of contract would not otherwise seem to be professionally objectionable, although it might be a tort.

[123] These hypotheticals are derived from P. Heymann & L. Leibman, *The Social Responsibility of Lawyers*, 1988; G. Kittleson, 'From ethics to politics: confronting ethics and scarcity in public interest practice' (1978) *Bost.U.L.Rev.* 337, 363–72.

One approach in addressing these hypotheticals is to ask to what extent non-lawyers would be in breach of the criminal or civil law—whether as aider or abettor, conspirator, constructive trustee, and so on—were they to advise or assist the client. On this approach if a non-lawyer were to be liable, exceptional reasons would have to be adduced to exculpate a lawyer. However, we saw at the outset that in the realm of legal ethics and professional responsibility we are not simply concerned with breaches of the criminal or civil law but with those broader standards which in particular will maintain the public standing of the profession. Thus this approach, while fruitful, will be too narrow in a number of cases.

Another approach is to reason from the codes and from other sources about professional misconduct. In relation to the first hypothetical, there is authority that a party asking for an injunction *ex parte* must bring all material facts to the notice of the court; this principle could extend to other cases creating or confirming rights which otherwise would not exist. With the second and third hypotheticals we can draw on various principles.[124] First, lawyers, as we know, are under no duty to assist a crime or fraud, or to become party to an abuse of process.[125] The duty of confidence is dissolved under the crime/fraud exception. Indeed there is even some older professional authority that in the case of a serious crime a solicitor has an *obligation* to convey the information to the relevant authorities—thus going beyond the crime/fraud exception—notwithstanding the duty of confidence.[126] In terms of our hypotheticals, however, these existing principles are only a baseline to providing definite guidance on what are patently troubling cases.

Whatever approach is adopted, much depends on the knowledge of the lawyer with respect to the wrong the client will effect and on what the lawyer actually does to achieve it. As to the first, culpable knowledge must extend beyond actual knowledge to encompass wilfully shutting one's eyes to the obvious, and wilfully and recklessly failing to make the enquiries an honest and reasonable person would make.[127] Perhaps *R. v. Delaval*[128] is as relevant as it was when Lord Mansfield decided it over two hundred years ago. There a young woman was removed from Bates, to whom she was apprenticed, and placed in the hands of Sir Francis Delaval, ostensibly for musical training but

[124] *Dalglish v. Jarvie* (1850) 42 ER 89. See also *Garrard v. Email Furniture Pty. Ltd.* (1993) 32 NSWLR 662, 677.

[125] *Batchelor v. Pattison*, 1876 3 R 914, 918 (lawyers cannot be asked to follow the client's instructions beyond what is lawful and proper); *Clark v. United States* 289 US 1, 15 (1933), *per* Cardozo J for the court: 'A client who consults an attorney for advice that will serve him in the commission of a fraud will have no help from the law.' Solicitors who have strong evidence of suspected fraud on the part of a client are entitled to apply to the court for directions as to how to deal with the fruits of the fraud. *Finers (a firm) v. Miro* [1991] 1 All ER 182.

[126] Sir Thomas Lund CBE, *A Guide to the Professional Conduct and Etiquette of Solicitors*, 1960, p.103. In less serious cases the lawyer might only be obliged to withdraw: *ibid.*, pp.105, 107.

[127] To use the classification of Peter Gibson J. in *Baden, Delvaux and Lecuit v. Société Général du Commerce SA* [1983] BCLC 325.   [128] (1763) 97 ER 913.

in fact for the purposes of prostitution. Not only was the information for conspiracy of Bates and Delaval upheld, but also that of the lawyer who drafted the documents of assignment. The attempt to portray the lawyer simply as an amanuensis was unsuccessful. He could not imagine that she really bound herself to Delaval to be taught music, said Lord Mansfield; he could not have been ignorant of the true purpose of the transaction.[129] In practice it should not be forgotten that lawyers by training should be able to make astute judgments as to their clients' purposes. If, as Professor Hazard notes, a lawyer can assess how the purposes of others may affect his or her client, a lawyer can have the same knowledge of how a client's purposes can affect others.[130]

Measuring the second factor, the extent of the lawyer's activity in effecting the wrongdoing, is similarly difficult. Much will turn on the circumstances. Performing an act which substantially furthers the client's wrongdoing should give rise to culpability. In *Johnson* v. *Youden*[131] a solicitor did the conveyancing of a house, knowing the price to be in breach of the price control regulations. The court held that since he did know how the price was calculated he was guilty of aiding and abetting the offence. The attempt to portray him as a mere scrivener failed. The conveyancing effected the wrongdoing. Thus, if the principles applying to accessory liability are relevant, there seems no reason why in some circumstances, if the lawyer knows what is going on, giving advice should not make the lawyer guilty of professional misconduct if it enables the client to pursue the unlawful conduct.

THE PROFESSION'S WIDER RESPONSIBILITIES

So far the focus has been on the profession's responsibilities in relation to clients. Although only partly articulated and patchy lawyers have acknowledged wider responsibilities. One aspect is the recently assumed obligation not only to end racial and sexual discrimination in the profession, but positively to advance the position of minorities and women.[132] Another aspect is the responsibility to the law itself, in ensuring its renewal and amendment in the light of changing social and economic circumstances. Then there is what could in broad terms be described as facilitating access to justice. In this regard the reduction in the number of persons qualifying for legal aid highlights the

---

[129] at p.916.
[130] G. Hazard, 'How far may a lawyer go in assisting a client in legally wrongful conduct?' (1981) 35 *U.Miami LR* 669, 672.   [131] [1950] 1 KB 544.
[132] Courts and Legal Services Act 1990, s.64; The General Council of the Bar, *Equality Code for Chambers*, 1993; LSG§7.01 Annex 7A ('Equal opportunities in solicitors' firms—practice information').

importance of new initiatives. These wider responsibilities deserve attention;
let us briefly examine a few.

The profession engages in law reform activity, primarily through official
committees of both the Bar Council and Law Society which comment on
proposed legislation and in some cases promote statutory change. But there
is nothing comparable in the English codes to the obligations stated in the
Model Rules of the American Bar Association, that lawyers 'should cultivate
knowledge of law beyond its use for clients, employ that knowledge in reform
of the law and work to strengthen legal education'.[133] The underlying rationale
of this provision, as set out in 1952 in a seminal report from the Joint
Conference of the American Bar Association and the Association of American
Law Schools, is partly to enhance the standing of the legal profession itself.
Partly also it was felt that lawyers who saw an injustice in practice, or who
brought about an injustice by their advocacy, should seek legal reform. As the
statement put it, a lawyer has both the best chance to know when the law is
working badly and the special competence to put it in order.[134] Detached from
the immediate representation of client interest, lawyers involved in law reform
activity can and should adopt a more detached view.[135]

Access to justice has a number of strands. One is ensuring that persons are
not handicapped from establishing the rightness of their position because they
are, or their cause is, unpopular. Representation of unpopular causes is an
essential component of public confidence in the legitimacy of the legal system.
The cab-rank rule for the Bar demands that barristers accept any instructions or
brief to represent any client at a proper professional fee in the fields in which
they profess to practice, irrespective of the nature of the case or any belief or
opinion which the barrister might have formed as to the character, reputation,
cause, conduct, guilt or innocence of that person.[136] Extravagant claims have
sometimes been made for the cab-rank rule,[137] and in some cases unpopular
clients have found that barristers of their first or even second choice have been
unavailable because of 'prior commitments'. On the whole, however, the rule
has worked remarkably well and unpopular clients have been better served in

---

[133] American Bar Association, *Model Rules of Professional Conduct*, 1983, Preamble, para.5,
§6.1.

[134] L. Fuller & J. Randall, 'Professional Responsibility' (1958) 44 *Amer.Bar Assoc. J.* 1159.

[135] Compare Justice Brandeis' oft quoted remarks: '[T]he leaders of the bar with a few exceptions
have not only failed to take part in constructive legislation designed to solve in the interest of our
people our great social, economic and industrial problems, they have failed likewise to oppose
legislation prompted by selfish interests. They have often gone further in disregard of the public
interest. They have, at times, advocated as lawyers, legislative measures which as citizens they
could not approve . . .'. L. Brandeis, 'The opportunity in the law' (1905) 39 *American Law Review*
555, 560–1.   [136] BC§209.

[137] Erskine's is well known in his defence of Tom Paine: 'From the moment that any advocate
can be permitted to say, that he will or will **not** stand between the Crown and the subject . . . from
that moment the liberties of England are at an end': (1792) 22 *State Trials* 358, 412.

England than in the United States, where there is no equivalent obligation.[138] Not only has the rule ensured representation for unpopular clients, but it has gone a considerable way to removing the stigma from those barristers who have stuck their neck out on a regular basis to represent unpopular causes.

Unlike the Bar solicitors are free to decline instructions, although any refusal must not be based on racial, sexual, or religious grounds.[139] Solicitors can therefore refuse assistance to those to whom they have moral or political objections. By the same token if they accept a retainer they are bound to the duties of confidence, diligence, and loyalty already examined, however morally or politically obnoxious they find their client's cause. (There is nothing equivalent for the profession here to the American ethical rule whereby a lawyer might explicitly base advice to a client on his or her personal views of morality and similar non-legal values.[140]) Representation of a client by a solicitor does not constitute endorsement of that client's morals or politics. But since solicitors are free to choose their clients on such grounds, it follows that their decisions to do so may be criticised. A solicitor's choice of client or cause is a moral decision and the solicitor must be prepared to justify it along with other decisions.[141]

Another strand of access to justice concerns the maldistribution of legal services. Corporations and the very wealthy pay for and receive excellent legal advice and assistance. Criminal legal aid ensures that most of those on serious charges are represented. This is clearly necessary when the exercise of state power might result in a custodial sentence. Otherwise there is unmet legal need, in some respects quite substantial. The profession has taken some steps in response, collectively and individually.[142] The *pro bono* working party of the Law Society has recommended a variety of initiatives to encourage voluntary legal services.[143] Others need to be considered; for example a well developed technique in Australia and some parts of the United States is to use interest on general client accounts to fund subsidised legal services and legal education. The present position in this country has direct ethical connotations because legislation, promoted by the Law Society, reverses the common law duty of solicitors not to profit from the use of their clients' moneys.[144]

Finally, those of us who are primarily law teachers need to turn the spotlight on ourselves. Partly this concerns our rôle as teachers. There are many problems which are by no means unique to law teachers. How should we

---

[138] It has been said that there ethical rules have been used **against** lawyers associated with unpopular causes: J. Auerbach, *Unequal Justice*, 1976, p.289.   [139] LSG§7.01 and Note 3.
[140] American Bar Association, *Model Rules of Professional Coduct*, §2.1, Comment.
[141] M. Freedman, 'Ethical ends and ethical means' (1991) 41 *J. Leg.Educ.* 55, 56.
[142] eg the bar supports the Free Representation Unit, a registered charity providing free advice and representation for those before tribunals.   [143] *Solicitors Serving Society*, May 1994.
[144] Solicitors Act 1974, s.33(3). See Solicitors' Accounts Rules 1991, r.20 (clients must account when sums are large or held for longer periods).

relate to our students, professionally and socially; what steps should we take to
further equal opportunities; how extensively should we engage in consultancy
or practice to the detriment of our academic duties—these are a few examples.
Partly also it concerns the responsibility to teach legal ethics. So far law
schools in this jurisdiction have washed their hands of this on the grounds
that legal ethics are for the vocational year. At the vocational level traditional
courses on legal ethics have focused on specific points of professional practice
and behaviour. Unfortunately they have also strayed heavily into areas which,
while useful to the young practitioner, have nothing to do with ethics but are
really issues of etiquette. This is changing as traditional courses are revamped
and refined.[145]

But law schools have failed to provide their students with guidance on
professional responsibility and on the ethical issues which they will face when
they enter the profession (and I do not exculpate myself from that charge). As
Professor Menkel-Meadow has rightly noted: '[Law teachers] cannot avoid
teaching ethics. By the very act of teaching, law teachers embody lawyering
and the conduct of legal professionals. We create images of law and lawyering
when we teach doctrine through cases and hypotheticals.'[146] That does not
mean that law schools need convey the technical detail of professional
responsibility, which might still be left to the vocational year. Nor should
law schools delude themselves that they can effectively socialise their students
to behave ethically when in practice groups and institutional pressures will
produce in them certain types of behaviour. Yet all law teachers have a
responsibility to give some attention to the ethical underpinnings of legal
practice. We have a responsibility to sensitize students to the ethical problems
they will face as practitioners, to provide them with some assistance in the task
of resolving these problems, and to expose them to wider issues such as the
unmet need for legal services.

CONCLUSIONS

Defalcations by solicitors, and the substantial amounts involved, have put the
spotlight on professional standards. Recent instances, in which senior City
solicitors were embroiled in financial scandals, have also focused public
attention on professional behaviour. In recognition of such developments,
lawyers and law firms are becoming more vigilant in preventing the possible
conflicts and temptations which can arise in the course of servicing clients. For
example, some City firms now operate a two partner rule on large transactions,

[145] See Inns of Court School of Law, *Professional Conduct*, 6th ed, 1994.
[146] C. Menkel-Meadow, 'Can a law teacher avoid teaching legal ethics' (1991) 41
J.Leg.Educ. 3, 3.

to ensure collective decision making on difficult advice. (The cost to the client, of course, escalates.) Similarly, a number of regulatory initiatives have been taken at the level of the profession as a whole with respect to professional standards. Just one example is the establishment of the Legal Services Ombudsman.

While the ethical rules themselves have not attracted the same public attention, there has been a quiet transformation in recent decades. From some rather general standards which it was thought all lawyers would know, there has evolved a more legalised system based on codes of conduct. One interpretation of this development is that it reflects both movements in the market for legal services and the transformation of the profession. A socially homogeneous, relatively cohesive profession, with shared understandings, has become a much larger and variegated one, with members playing a variety of new rôles. There has been a consequent need for rules and a bureaucratic machinery to assimilate and discipline the professional's disparate parts. Moreover, greater attention has had to be given within the profession to ethical standards because in many ways they are symbolic of how the profession sees itself. Disputes about the rules are surrogates for disputes about the future of the profession.[147]

An underlying theme of this chapter has been that the move to more definite rules is not only inevitable but also desirable. Intuition or appeals to secular or other morality are no substitute for a framework of rules. Not only is there no consensus over the former, but in some important respects the correct ethical position is not immediately apparent. Issues of legal ethics do not come labelled as such but arise in particular contexts of legal practice. Without definite rules it is not only difficult to see how professional behaviour will be constrained but the problems of teaching legal ethics would be considerably compounded.

By the same token—a second underlying theme of the chapter—the existing codes of professional practice cannot simply be treated as a system of specific rules. If that were to be the case they would become like any other body of rules which lawyers would manipulate, and if needs be seek to avoid. The ends lawyers are pursuing, the ethics of their clients, the standing of the profession, and the wider interests of justice—these are just some of the matters which must also be considered in channelling and justifying professional behaviour. Moreover, the present professional codes do not give specific guidance in important respects. To return to one of the hypotheticals above: if breach of a regulatory law is tolerated by officials, should lawyers counsel a client to disregard it? Arguably desuetude is distinguishable from

---

[147] Thus the debate about advertising: on the one hand advertising is correctly said to inform the public about legal services and to further competition; on the other hand there is truth in the claim that advertising will transform the profession into a body of business hucksters. See editorial, 'Trading standards' (1993) 143 *NLJ* 1249.

under-enforcement of a regulatory law because of lack of resources. Without a reasoned elaboration of the ethical position, however, lawyers will be at a loss as to which course to pursue in the absence of a definite rule.

This wider context of the rules has implications for teaching. How lawyers ought to behave in particular circumstances depends on a complex set of factors rather than the bare bones of any relevant rules. The correct ethical stance will very infrequently come ready labelled. What must be done is to sensitize students to the problems that they will face in practice and to provide them with some framework so that they can resolve difficult problems. Ideally the way to achieve this is to integrate the consideration of ethical issues into courses on substantive law. After all, it is a matter of addressing how ethical considerations will arise in daily practice. Moreover, what is said or not said in particular courses provides an agenda for students about the nature of law and legal practice. Unfortunately the integrated approach is likely to prove difficult in the short term given our lack of expertise in ethics. That points towards a separate course in law school, but it would need to ensure a deeper understanding of the ethical issues which might arise, in passing, in the study and practice of substantive law. The course would need to provide an opportunity to reflect on the nature of law and legal practice and should attempt to explain the interplay between the ethical issues which have been implicit in particular courses, and in particular cases and legislation. The course would provide an opportunity to make students more aware of the value that legal solutions carry, for a student to develop his or her own attitude to ethical questions, and for professionals to be brought in to contribute their experience.

A third underlying theme of this chapter is that in important respects the current set of ethical rules is contestable. I have focused on the duties of confidentiality and loyalty which lawyers are mandated to give to a client's interests. The linch-pin of the present rules is that lawyers need not be convinced of a client's case; that is for the courts. In single-mindedly serving a client's interest, the assumption is that a lawyer is serving justice. As a lawyer one need not be primarily concerned with any wider interest.

This argument and its conclusion is still largely valid. But there are a number of difficulties. Firstly, there is the wide-spread public perception these days that the self-interest of the lawyer is masquerading as a public service. The unequal access to legal services and the unequal matching of lawyers in particular cases undermine the validity of the model. Secondly, we have seen that however unformulated or inadequate they might be, there are limits to the lawyer acting as hired gun. For advocates, Lord Reid sums up the position this way:

Every counsel has a duty to his client fearlessly to raise every issue, advance every argument, and ask every question, however distasteful, which he thinks will help his client's case. But, as an officer of the court concerned in the administration of justice, he has an overriding duty to the court, to the standards of his profession, and to the public, which may and often does lead to a conflict with his client's wishes or with what the client thinks are his personal wishes.[148]

The corollary is that in some circumstances the law and the profession's ethical rules recognise that unquestioning zeal in a client's interest may cause social harm.

What is necessary in this area is a further refinement of the provisions in the codes. When do the interests of others and the public interest trump devotion to the client's interest? When should a lawyer question his or her client's intentions and activities and be justified by code provisions in doing so? When should a lawyer cease to act for a particular client or indeed disclose suspected wrongdoing to the relevant regulatory agency? Such questions demand careful analysis. One difficulty is that the current rules were forged in the context of the criminal law where the notion of the fearless advocate, zealously defending the client, come what may, is more understandable. But extension of the arguments in the criminal context to other areas, in particular advice to clients, does not always make sense. The enormous legal resources which powerful economic interests can marshall—whatever the cause—might well be politically contentious, socially harmful, and possibly morally objectionable. Ultimately this phenomenon might also undermine the standing of the legal profession and the legitimacy of the law.

A final underlying theme of this chapter has been that legal ethics have to be conceived of within the more general area of professional responsibility. The wider ethical issues of the operation of the legal profession as a whole are now firmly on the agenda. The obvious example is the unequal utilization of legal services and of access to them. As indicated, this wider conception links with the rules in the professional codes, since many of these are based on the notion that clients will be competently and adequately represented. Another aspect of this wider topic is inequality of access to the profession itself. The professional bodies have taken this on board in the realisation that the profession is failing to tap vital resources and denying opportunities to, for example, a significant minority of young people with ethnic backgrounds.

In conclusion let me reiterate that law schools too have failed in the areas of legal ethics and professional responsibility. We have not provided our students with more guidance on the ethical issues which they will face when they enter the profession. Successful lawyers these days reap great rewards, but in the process will face many temptations to barter their integrity. Legal educators need to provide them with some guidance as to how they might

---

[148] *Rondel* v. *Worsley* [1969] 1 AC 191, 227. See also S. Rogers, 'The Ethics of Advocacy' (1899) 15 *LQR* 259.

resolve the problems which they will face. We must remember with Holmes that: 'the business of a law school is not sufficiently described when you merely say that it is to teach law, or to make lawyers. It is to teach law in the grand manner, and to make great lawyers'.[149]

[149] This is an expanded version of my Presidential Address to the SPTL Annual Conference on 8 Sept. 1993. I am grateful to William Blair QC for his comments.

2

Judicial Ethics

SIR THOMAS BINGHAM

JUDICIAL ethics, the subject I have been asked to address in this chapter, appears to have been largely neglected in this country in recent years—by the judiciary, by the practising profession, and, less surprisingly, by academics.

No doubt this relative neglect is, up to a point, reassuring. It reflects the fact that we have in this country been spared the scandals which have given life to the subject in the United States over many years and in Australia more recently. It is indeed a striking fact that in nearly three centuries since the Act of Settlement made the superior judges irremovable save on an address by both Houses of Parliament no English High Court judge has been so removed. The practice of appointing judges from a small pool of candidates, sharing a common professional background, and known personally or by professional repute to those making and advising on appointments, has enabled much to be taken for granted. Apart from the Kilmuir Rules, which were very limited in their scope and have now been to some extent relaxed, I know of no recent attempt to state the rules which govern, or should govern, the conduct of judges, and it is of interest that, in writing the letter to the Director-General of the BBC in which the Rules were set out, Lord Kilmuir referred to 'the important qualification that, as you are already aware, the Lord Chancellor has no sort of disciplinary jurisdiction over Her Majesty's Judges'.

A moderate degree of reassurance should not, however, spill over into complacency. Though the occasions are, I feel sure, infrequent, none of us knows how often, or on what grounds, judges of the higher courts have been informally nudged or encouraged into retirement. The Lord Chancellor is of course empowered to dismiss circuit judges, district judges, magistrates, and justices, but the principles upon which he acts may not be entirely clear. The enlargement of the pool from which judges are recruited, welcome though this is, must increase the possibility of error and may mean that less can be taken for granted. Above all, whether the judges like it or not—and of course they do not—we live in a time when the judicial rôle and judicial performance are the subject of increasingly critical public scrutiny. No reader even of the quality press would be tempted to think that the judges were beyond reproach. If, as I think most of us present would hold, the administration of justice is one of the cardinal functions of civil society, and if for that purpose the judges are entrusted, as they are, with wide and sometimes unreviewable powers, it is surely a matter of some moment to consider the principles of conduct by which judges are, or consider themselves to be, bound. I am accordingly grateful to the Society for causing me to think about this subject in a more coherent way than I have had occasion to do before.[1]

Before venturing further, I should perhaps enter five caveats. First, the views I express are my own personal views, which I have not discussed with anyone. They do not carry the imprimatur of the Lord Chancellor who, as head of the judiciary, must be regarded as the ultimate, or at least the penultimate, arbiter of these matters. I do not doubt that some of my observations would provoke dissent from some of my professional colleagues. Secondly, I should make clear that my opinions have the inherent vulnerability of all opinions formed without discussion, argument, or application to specific instances. I could well imagine that situations would arise which would cause me to modify or depart from what I now think, and no doubt the passage of time and changing circumstances would anyway call at least for modification. Thirdly, it is obvious that any rules in a field of this kind must cover a wide spectrum of conduct. There are of course some acts—like acceptance of a gift from a current litigant, or conviction of conspiracy to pervert the course of justice—which would without question call for immediate removal or dismissal. There is other conduct—like using official writing paper to conduct an argument with one's insurers—which most judges would regard as 'a bit off' or 'not done' but which could not attract any sanction. Between these extremes would lie a wide range of conduct to which the appropriate response would depend on questions of degree. If it were shown, for instance, that a judge had on an isolated occasion behaved in court in an intemperate, overbearing, or unjudicial way, or fallen asleep, or neglected his duties, he might expect to be rebuked by any appellate court before which the case came or a senior judge would make an opportunity to have a quiet word. That would in all probability be that. But it might be different if a judge's unacceptable conduct in court, or somnolence, or neglect were shown to be habitual and of such an order as reasonably to undermine confidence in his ability to do justice. Fourthly, I have not attempted to cover all aspects of this subject. Despite the length of this address, there are significant areas of the subject which I shall not attempt to cover. And fifthly, I hope it will not be thought sexist if I refer to individual, hypothetical judges as 'he'. It is cumbersome to repeat 'he or she' and I am too pedantic to be happy using 'they' or 'their' after a singular noun. The alternative stratagem of saying 'she' seems inappropriate, since I know of

---

[1] I am in particular grateful for being introduced to *Judicial Ethics in Australia* by the Hon Mr Justice Thomas of the Supreme Court of Queensland, a most interesting and informative work on which I have drawn heavily.

no case where the conduct of a female judge has given serious ground for complaint.

I take as my starting point a passage in an address given by Sir Owen Dixon to law students in the University of Melbourne when professional conduct was first introduced into the curriculum of the university law school in 1953. He said:

To be a good lawyer is difficult. To master the law is impossible. But I should have thought that the first rule of conduct for counsel, the first and paramount ethical rule, was to do his best to acquire such a knowledge of the law that he really knows what he is doing when he stands between his client and the court and advises for or against entering the temple of justice.[2]

If applied to judges, the passage plainly calls for some modification, but the essential point seems to me apposite: it is a judge's professional duty to do what he reasonably can to equip himself to discharge his judicial duties with a high degree of competence. Sir Owen went on to say that acquiring such knowledge of the law meant hard work for a long time, and he added: 'It is harder work than in London because counsel here do not specialise. In England it is otherwise and a man may pass his life very comfortably as an expert in an extremely narrow field.'[3]

There is a relevance to judges in this passage also, and for them there are twin dangers. Some judges, particularly circuit judges, may pass their lives very comfortably as experts trying criminal cases. The temptation for them, after a time and in run of the mill cases, is that of over-familiarity, leading to ill-prepared, impromptu, ill-organised, diffuse, and unnecessarily lengthy jury directions. The Crown Court Study, recently made for the Runciman Royal Commission, suggests that to a remarkable and very creditable extent this temptation is resisted. Appellate judges are subject to a different temptation. Almost all of them spend much of their time dealing with areas of the law with which they have no close familiarity. The temptation then is in effect to cede decision of the appeal to the member of the court who is so familiar. This, plainly, is a dereliction of judicial duty. The litigant is entitled to the considered judgment, if not the considered judgments, of all members of the court, not just one. So Sir Owen's observations, suitably adapted, seem to me the right place to start. It is also perhaps appropriate to bear in mind Professor Dworkin's recent observations on judicial integrity and the need to give, so far as possible, adequately reasoned decisions.[4] It must be possible to improve on the performance of a High Court judge to whom I once addressed submissions which he gave no reason for rejecting beyond saying 'Well, I'm sorry, but I don't agree'.

Just as the Ten Commandments of the Old Testament were subsumed in

[2] *Jesting Pilate*, p.131.   [3] *Ibid.*   [4] *Life's Dominion*, 1993, pp.144–7.

the New by 'the first and great commandment . . . and the second . . . like unto
it, namely this', so (as it seems to me) much of what would go into a detailed
code of judicial conduct if we had one is embraced by the judicial oath to 'do
right to all manner of people after the laws and usages of this realm, without
fear or favour, affection or ill will'. This is language not only noble in its
simplicity but also rich in content, and I think some phrases may usefully be
highlighted.

The judge's obligation is to do justice 'after the laws and usages of this
realm'. In other words, he must apply the law, not his own personal predilec-
tion, reflecting the wisdom of Samuel Johnson's observation: 'To permit a law
to be modified at discretion is to leave the community without law. It is to
withdraw the direction of that public wisdom by which the deficiencies of
private understanding are to be supplied.'[5]

This obligation does not, in the field of non-statutory law, deprive the
judge of all power to innovate, and to develop the law, an almost inevitable
activity when he faces a situation to which existing authority does not apply.
But it does in my view restrict the judges' authority to engage in what might be
called wholesale judicial legislation. I will give an example. In an unreported
decision on very strong facts, the Court of Appeal recently held that there was
no enforceable right to privacy in English law.[6] In so holding the Court had
regard not only to authority, judicial and academic, but also to the public
concern directed to this subject over thirty years, reflected in reports by the
Younger Committee and JUSTICE, in a series of unsuccessful Private Members' Bills, and in the deliberations (not then concluded) of the Calcutt
Committee. The Court has been criticised for excessive timidity, in failing
to grasp a nettle which other organs of government appeared strikingly
unwilling to handle, and for failing to lay down the foundations of a law of
privacy. I do not myself accept the validity of this criticism, unsurprisingly
since I was a party to the decision. It seems to me a very good example of the
sort of task judges may not properly take it upon themselves to discharge.

When one turns to statute law and subordinate legislation, the judge's
duty to apply the law by seeking conscientiously to give fair and full effect to
the intention of the legislation is obvious. This is not simply a rule of
construction but a constitutional duty, a duty which judges assume as part of
the price of their independence. It is also in my opinion an ethical duty, in the
sense that a judge who knowingly and deliberately neglected to give effect to
the plain effect of a statute would be acting improperly. Having said that I
must, no doubt surprisingly, confess to having done so, in one context. Perhaps
I may elaborate, since I hope the example will show that ethical duties, even
constitutional duties, are not always as straightforward as might be thought.

---

[5] Boswell, *Life of Johnson*, 1976, p.496.
[6] *Kaye* v. *Robertson*, 23 Feb. 1990; see App. 1 to the Calcutt Report.

The context I have in mind is the Bail Act 1976. That Act was founded on the praiseworthy premise that prospective defendants who may be innocent and whom it is unnecessary to keep in prison should not be imprisoned during what may be a lengthy period until they are tried. Thus the general rule in section 4 of the Act is that a person shall be granted bail unless certain conditions apply, and in the case of imprisonable offences those conditions relate to the risk that the defendant will fail to surrender to custody, commit an offence while on bail, or interfere with witnesses, or that his own safety or welfare may be damaged by the grant of bail. So far so good. It is the wording of paragraph 2 of the relevant schedule[7] which causes trouble:

The defendant need not be granted bail if the court is satisfied that there are substantial grounds for believing that the defendant, if released on bail (whether subject to conditions or not) would—

fail to surrender to custody, commit an offence, and so on. The difficulty arises because the court must do more than form an opinion that one or other consequence will or may follow if bail is refused; the court must be **satisfied**, an obviously more exacting state of intellectual conviction. Moreover, the court must be satisfied on substantial grounds, so hunch or personal apprehension is not enough if (as not infrequently happens) no ground of substance is presented to the court. The court's right to refuse bail is not, however, conditional on its being satisfied that there are substantial grounds for believing that the defendant **may**, if released on bail, do one or other of the proscribed things; the court must be satisfied that there are substantial grounds for believing that if granted bail the defendant **would** do one or other of the proscribed things, a very difficult test to satisfy in relation to anything as unpredictable as the future conduct of an unknown human being over a shortish time period. The dilemma presented by this provision was not in my view cured by paragraph 9 of the schedule, which required the court in taking these decisions to have regard so far as appeared to it to be relevant to the nature and seriousness of the offence charged, the probable penalty, the defendant's character, antecedents and community ties, the defendant's previous behaviour on bail, and the strength of the evidence against him. It is not very easy to relate this paragraph to paragraph 2, which I have quoted: the rigorous conditions of paragraph 2 are either satisfied or they are not, and if they are not it will only be in a minority of cases that paragraph 9 will make good the deficiency. The fact that a defendant has a long criminal record does not of itself enable the court to be satisfied that there are substantial grounds for believing that he will commit an offence if granted bail, and the fact that a defendant has a house and assets abroad, in Northern Cyprus or elsewhere, does not of itself enable the court to be satisfied that there are substantial

---

[7] Para. 2 of Part 1 of Schedule 1 of the Act.

grounds for believing that he will fail to surrender to custody if granted bail, although in each case the court will recognise a risk. An amendment to the Act has eased but not in my view cured this problem. In cases where I could not conscientiously say (to myself) that the conditions of paragraph 2 were satisfied, but in which I have felt grave apprehension that a defendant's release involved a real danger to the public, I have on occasion refused bail. I suspect other judges have done the same. It is highly regrettable that courts should be subject to this dilemma. On the repeated occasions when judges or justices have been vilified and hounded for releasing on bail a defendant who commits other offences or absconds, I have never been aware of any acknowledgement, in parliament or the press, of the stringent duty which this Act has imposed upon the courts.

The judge's duty to administer justice 'without fear or favour, affection or ill will' plainly covers a very wide range of ethical duties. If one were to attempt a modern paraphrase, it might perhaps be that a judge must free himself of prejudice and partiality and so conduct himself, in court and out of it, as to give no ground for doubting his ability and willingness to decide cases coming before him solely on their legal and factual merits as they appear to him in the exercise of an objective, independent, and impartial judgment. This again calls for some elaboration.

Perhaps the most obvious reflection of this principle is the clear rule that a judge must have no pecuniary interest in the outcome of any litigation before him and should not be financially beholden to any litigant appearing before him. In *Dimes* v. *Grand Junction Canal Company*[8] an order of the Lord Chancellor was set aside because he had a substantial interest in the company, even though he was only affirming a decision of the Vice-Chancellor and was not in any way influenced by his interest. This was, as it seems to me, a very strong decision, but I have no doubt that it would be followed today on similar facts although I do not think a judge would stand down on account of a share-holding in a litigant company, or perhaps even disclose it,[9] unless the share-holding and the action were such that the outcome could have a more than negligible effect on his fortune. That accords with an occasion in the Court of Appeal when, at the outset of a very lengthy and obviously tedious patent appeal, one member of the court disclosed that he held shares in one of the litigant companies. 'If my Brother thinks,' said (Charles) Russell LJ,

[8] (1852) 3 HLC 758; 10 ER 301.

[9] On reading this passage a very senior retired judge observed that he would personally disclose any share-holding of which he was aware. He had found himself severely criticised in the press for hearing a case without disclosing that he held shares in a part-owner of a litigant company. The share-holding had in fact been very small, and the judge had been unaware of it since his investments were managed on a discretionary basis by brokers. He then took steps, however, to put all his shares into the name of his brokers' nominee company. This would be effective to avert unfair criticism of this kind, but would not displace the need to disclose any significant share-holding, however held, of which the judge was aware.

presiding, 'that he can escape from this case on a ground as tenuous as that, he is in error.'

The rule against acceptance of gifts from litigants or potential litigants is clear and obvious. But it is not quite absolute. Both the Lord Chief Justice and the Master of the Rolls receive annual gifts of a quarter of roebuck from the Royal Parks (on payment of a nominal delivery charge) and until recently, received a shirt-length of cloth from the Corporation of London. If not sanctioned by immemorial custom, these gifts would no doubt be questionable. It is of interest that Lord Chief Justice Hale, in the much more venal age of Charles II, 'not only refused the customary perquisites like the venison for the justices on circuit, but insisted on paying more than the regular price for his domestic supplies.'[10]

No attempt has ever been made in this country, so far as I know, to define the sources from which a judge may properly receive money in addition to his judicial salary. There can, plainly, be no objection to his receiving the proceeds of ordinary investments, or the rents of any property the judge may own, or the earnings of any estate the judge may be fortunate enough to have. It has not been thought inconsistent with judicial office to be a member of Lloyd's, although it is now (I think) some years since judges sitting in the Commercial Court thought it proper to maintain their membership, an exemption for which they are, no doubt, grateful. I do not think it would be generally regarded as improper for a judge to accept a modest honorarium for a lecture or address which he had given, although most would perhaps decline or ask that the sum be paid to charity; a gift of wine or a book a judge might, properly in my view, accept, but the identity of the donor and the value of the gift would plainly affect his decision.

In his letter to the Director-General, Lord Kilmuir (ironically perhaps, in view of the furore later caused by his acceptance of company directorships while drawing the not ungenerous pension of a former Lord Chancellor) observed that 'in no circumstances, of course, should a Judge take a fee in connection with a broadcast'. This is a rule which I think most, if not all, judges would observe in relation to any radio or television broadcast or any newspaper article. This seems to me a good rule. But there is to my knowledge no similar rule or practice in relation to the proceeds of any legal treatise, novel, play, or other literary work which a judge may publish. It is possible to see a distinction between the two situations, but it is not very obvious. Probably, however, this is an area better left to judges' recognition that they must do nothing which could or could appear to compromise their judicial integrity than to any attempt at formulation of detailed rules.

All the major common law jurisdictions would, I am sure, regard it as unacceptable for a serving judge to engage in any capacity in any commercial

---

[10] Bond, 'The Growth of Judicial Ethics', (1925) 10 *Mass. Law Quarterly* 1 at p.13.

enterprise (save for the very limited, and now unusual, exception of managing his own estate). Happily perhaps, most of us would not be tempted to emulate the Illinois judge who moonlighted as a construction worker.[11] But beyond that rule there is a surprising diversity of view. The Canons of Judicial Conduct promulgated by the American Bar Association bluntly provide that 'A judge should not act as an arbitrator or mediator.' Here, section 3 of the Administration of Justice Act 1970 expressly provides for Commercial Judges to act as arbitrators. They do not of course receive any personal benefit, since the fees payable (shortly to be increased) are prescribed and are payable to the Treasury. It may be the lack of any similar mechanism which explains the American rule. In Australia and, I think, the United States, it would be questionable whether a serving judge should serve as chairman of a sporting body. Here, judges have certainly served in such capacities, and I do not think this would be regarded as in any way objectionable unless the appointment were likely to involve the judge in controversy or the body were likely to be involved in litigation. The American Canons provide that

A judge should not solicit funds for any educational, religious, charitable, fraternal or civic organisation, or use or permit the use of the prestige of his office for that purpose, but he may be listed as an officer, director, or trustee of such an organisation.

In this country, a judge would undoubtedly be expected to exercise considerable discretion about the bodies with which he allowed himself to be associated, avoiding involvement in any campaigning organization of even a non-political kind, and would be scrupulous not to exploit his judicial office for the purpose of attracting funds. But subject to those caveats, English judges would not feel themselves precluded from soliciting funds for charitable causes, and I can think of a number who have done so. Again, the American Canons provide that

A judge should not accept appointment to a governmental committee, commission, or other position that is concerned with issues of fact or policy or matters other than the improvement of the law, the legal system, or the administration of justice.

In Australia, the desirability of such a rule has been the subject of active debate. In Victoria, there has been long standing disapproval of judges serving on royal commissions. In Queensland the judges have held that they should not do so.[12] Strong and well-argued opinions have been expressed on both sides.[13] The contrast with this country, where very many judges at all levels have served as royal commissioners or conducted inquiries and investigations, is very marked. One need only instance Lord Scarman, who perhaps holds the record, with his inquiries into disturbances in Red Lion Square, Northern

---

[11] *Re Daley* 2 Ill. Cts. Com 38 (1983).   [12] Thomas, *op.cit.*, 54–5.
[13] 'Judges as Royal Commissioners and Chairman of Non-Judicial Tribunals', Australian Institute of Judicial Administration Incorporated, 1986.

Ireland, and Brixton, and into the Grunwick labour dispute. It is scarcely an exaggeration to say that among senior judges 'my inquiry' is the equivalent, in other circles, of 'my operation'. But we do well to recognize that those in the United States and Australia who take the contrary view have a serious point. It is in my opinion consistent with judicial office for a judge to serve in these capacities if the reason for his appointment is the need to harness to the task in question the special skills which a judge should possess: characteristically, the ability to dissect and analyse evidence, appraise witnesses, exercise a fair and balanced judgment, write a clear and coherent report, and so on. If, however, that is not the reason for his appointment—if, more particularly, it were sought to lend the respectability of his office or reputation to some political end not otherwise acceptable to the public—it would in my opinion be the clear duty of the judge to decline to serve. In general, we seem in this country to have been able to operate within more liberal constraints than have been found to be appropriate elsewhere. So long as this liberality can be maintained, it is in my view desirable that it should be: justice is not a cloistered virtue, and it is in general desirable that judges should have acquaintances and experience outside the monastery.

It is now regarded in this country as a cardinal feature of judicial impartiality that the judge should be a political eunuch. If he was ever a member of any political party or organization, he must sever all ties on appointment. Thereafter he must do nothing which could give rise to any suggestion of political partisanship. A colleague once told me that he had never, since appointment, even cast his vote, although he did somewhat undermine the effect of this by adding that since he lived in Chelsea there was anyway no need.

It is perhaps worth pausing briefly to reflect how recent this tradition is. Well after the Act of Settlement, Lord Chief Justices as well as Lord Chancellors were known to sit in the cabinet.[14] Lord Stowell combined his judicial rôle in the Admiralty Court with a very active parliamentary role, concerned with the same measures on which he thereafter ruled as a judge.[15] Lord Romilly, the last member of my Inn to hold my office, held it while a member of the House of Commons. Sir James Stephen, while serving as a Queen's Bench puisne, contributed very lengthy letters to *The Times* attacking the government's policy on Ireland.[16] Lord Hewart, plainly, did not regard the office of Lord Chief Justice as any bar to participation in the political controversies of the day. Only in what, legally speaking, must be regarded as very recent times have the senior judicial offices ceased to be the preserve of the law officers of the day who wanted them. If my memory serves, Lord

[14] Eg, Lord Mansfield, who was also Chancellor of the Exchequer, and Lord Ellenborough.
[15] H. J. Bourguignon, *Sir William Scott Lord Stowell*, 1987, p.271.
[16] K. J. M. Smith, *James Fitzjames Stephen*, 1988, p.153.

Hailsham on his first appointment as Lord Chancellor in 1970 announced an intention to increase the number of appointments to the bench from the ranks of serving members of parliament, an intention he did not, happily, implement to any significant extent.

It is also perhaps worth pausing briefly to reflect how different is the position here from that in the United States, with whose legal system we tend to think our own has so much in common. A rule of total and universal political neutrality would of course be inconceivable in a country where many members of the state judiciaries are elected and accordingly campaign for election on a platform. It is furthermore accepted that appointments to the higher, especially the highest, federal judiciary are made with what are essentially political considerations in mind, even though presidential hopes are often confounded. And there is a long tradition of active political activity by members of the Supreme Court. Brandeis was a major architect of Woodrow Wilson's legislative programme. During the Second World War Frankfurter conferred almost daily with Roosevelt about strategies and policies, and assisted in drafting some of the president's speeches. Fortas advised Lyndon Johnson on topics including the Vietnam War, steel price increases, and strategy for averting transport strikes. But this gave rise to criticism, as did some of Warren Burger's activity as chief justice.[17] So it may be that even in the United States there is some movement in our direction.

Here, the rule is clear and (subject to the anomalous position of the Lord Chancellor) absolute. The Law Lords sit on the cross-benches and do not, by tradition, become involved in political controversy unrelated to the administration of justice. Perhaps the only remaining problem, and that a minor one, concerns the position of judges' spouses. When almost all judges were men and wives were expected to subordinate their personal interests to their husbands', the unwritten rule was that judges' wives should adopt the same position of strict neutrality as their husbands. But the unwillingness of wives to be treated as appendages of their husbands, recognition that there need be no identity of view between husband and wife on political any more than other issues, and—I fear it must be admitted—the increasing appointment of women to the bench, with the result that it is the husband not the wife who is expected to give up office as member of parliament or county councillor, will, I feel sure, lead to acceptance that conventional political activities of the spouse will not taint the judge provided the judge remains resolutely aloof.

The Kilmuir Rules undoubtedly had the effect of discouraging almost to the point of prohibiting contacts between judges and the media. The reason which he gave—that 'So long as a Judge keeps silent his reputation for wisdom and impartiality remains unassailable'—was not entirely flattering but con-

---

[17] Edwards, 'Judicial Misconduct and Politics in the Federal System: A Proposal for Revising the Judicial Councils Act' (1987) 75 *Calif.LR*.

tained a hard nugget of truth. As is well known, this rule (if one can call it such) has been relaxed somewhat by the present Lord Chancellor, for reasons which are in my opinion sound. If judges are fit to judge they should be able to exercise a reasonable judgment on whether to speak to the media and what to say if they do. Issues do, perhaps increasingly, arise on which it is desirable that the voice of the professional judiciary should be heard and it is unfortunate if the only audible voice is that of those retired judges most forward in offering their opinions. There is also, I suppose, a faint hope that the more grotesque caricatures of the modern judiciary will lose credibility if the public generally has a better idea of what judges are actually like. But there has now been enough experience of the new and more liberal regime to indicate the very real damage which would be done if judges did not exercise their new freedom with the greatest circumspection. It is vital that the occasions on which and the conditions under which judges contribute to public discussion are closely considered. I would whole-heartedly endorse the view more than once advanced by Mr Bernard Levin that judges should not be tempted to pontificate or offer opinions on subjects outside their professional field.[18] Nor should they, save on issues directly related to the administration of justice and then with considerable discretion, be drawn into criticising government policy. When such issues do arise—one thinks recently of cutbacks in legal aid, the Administration of Justice Act 1992, and the number of judges—it is probably desirable that public comment should be left to the Lord Chief Justice, who by tradition enjoys a seat in the House of Lords, presumably to give him an appropriate public forum in which to discuss such matters.

In his most interesting book on 'Judicial Ethics in Australia', Mr Justice Thomas of the Queensland Supreme Court addresses a topic never to my knowledge expressly addressed here, the social constraints to which a judge is subject. He suggests[19] that 'a judge should not have particularly close contact with anyone who regularly appears in his court' and also says[20] 'I should be very surprised if there is still any general expectation that judges should never go into a public bar'. On the first point, any English rule would have to take account of the Inns of Court, which inevitably bring judges and senior practitioners at the Bar into close contact. This is, no doubt, a source of strength, but there are potential dangers, to which judges should be alert. I can certainly think of one judge whose continuing contact with members of his old chambers was so close and frequent as to raise disquieting questions in the minds of those appearing against them before him. On the second point, as a very general proposition, I think most judges would be inclined to agree. But I would be very surprised if any judge were to be seen in a public house within about a mile of the Law Courts in the Strand or, perhaps, any court in which the judge was sitting. On a third point I have no doubt that there would be

---

[18] *The Times*, 28 Feb. 1986 and 17 Aug. 1993.   [19] At p.44.   [20] At p.42.

general agreement: that while a judge need not necessarily conduct his private life in accordance with the highest standards of morality he must at least do so in such a way as to avert the possibility of scandal and to demonstrate respect for the law he is appointed to serve; one could well imagine that infractions of the law which were in the past regarded as relatively venial—driving when over the prescribed limit of alcohol is the obvious example—might in future cause much more acute concern.

If, as happens from time to time, proceedings are issued against a judge as a result of something done or not done in his judicial capacity, the standard practice is to hand any papers to the Treasury Solicitor who will take the necessary steps to have the action dismissed. If it were necessary for a judge to issue proceedings to defend his judicial reputation (an almost unheard of event), I think it would again be appropriate to invoke the help and follow the advice of the Treasury Solicitor. A judge who did not follow this course would not, I think, expect to be reimbursed out of the public purse for any expenditure he incurred. Only in the most extreme or unusual circumstances does any judge go to law in relation to a private matter: this is no doubt in part because of the somewhat invidious spectacle this would present to the public, but it is also in part because judges know, better than anyone, how uncertain the outcome of litigation is liable to be.

I fear I have occupied much of your time without having, as yet, even got the judge into court. It is perhaps difficult to improve on rules for his own personal guidance which Chief Justice Hale devised for himself in the 1660s:[21]

4. That in the execution of justice, I carefully lay aside my own passions, and not give way to them however provoked.

5. That I be wholly intent upon the business I am about, remitting all other cares and thoughts as unseasonable and interruptions.

6. That I suffer not myself to be prepossessed with any judgment at all, till the whole business and both parties be heard.

7. That I never engage myself in the beginning of any cause, but reserve myself unprejudiced till the whole be heard.

This is, literally, a counsel of perfection. It is a truism that all human beings, judges included, are to some extent creatures of their upbringing, education, and experience. They inevitably hold views, entertain preferences, and are subject to prejudices. But it is plainly their duty to lay these aside and approach cases in an impartial and objective way so far as possible, and to give the appearance of doing so.

There can, I think, be no doubt that much judicial behaviour was tolerated in the past which would be regarded as simply unacceptable today. Connoisseurs will doubtless savour, as I do, the account of 'The Origin of the

[21] Thomas, *op. cit.* App B, p.203.

Commercial Court' contributed by Lord Justice MacKinnon to the *Law Quarterly Review* in 1944:[22]

Mr Justice J. C. Lawrance was a stupid man, a very ill-equipped lawyer and a bad judge. He was not the worst judge I have appeared before: that distinction I would assign to Mr Justice Ridley. Ridley had much better brains than Lawrance, but he had a perverse instinct for unfairness that Lawrance could never approach.

Examples of past judicial misbehaviour spring readily to mind. There was the occasion when Norman Birkett, appearing as a young man for a plaintiff who he thought had won, rose after his opponent's closing speech and said 'I don't know if your Lordship wishes to hear me?' 'No,' said the judge, so Birkett sat down and listened with horror while the judge delivered judgment against his client. At the end he rose and protested: 'But your Lordship said you didn't wish to hear me.' 'I didn't,' replied the judge, 'and I still don't.' One recalls the notorious partisanship of Lord Hewart.[23] One recalls the judge who, on receiving the assurance of a witness wishing to affirm that he had no religious belief, observed 'And no morals either'. One recalls the appeal which succeeded against Hallett J because the judge's interruptions had been such as to make the conduct of both parties' cases impossible.[24] One recalls, much more recently, the criminal case in which a chairman of quarter sessions (unobjectionably, as was held on appeal) on repeated occasions during a defendant's case observed in a loud voice 'Oh, God' and laid his head across his arm and made groaning and sighing noises.[25] It cannot, unfortunately, be said that such aberrations never recur, and of course they were always exceptional. But I have no doubt that the modern judiciary would, as it should, regard itself as the servant of the public, not its master; would recognize that the dignity of judicial office is enhanced and not reduced by the display of ordinary good manners; and would recognize that the appearance of justice is almost as important as its substance, if indeed the two are separable. There is much force in Sir Robert Megarry's observation that the most important person in court is not the judge or the advocate or the witness but the litigant who is going to lose.[26]

The judge's duty to be, and appear to be, completely impartial during the conduct of a case is so fundamental, so pervasive and—I must admit—so obvious that I would not be justified in wearying you with examples. But there are a number of situations which perhaps deserve mention.

Firstly, disqualification. It is the judge's duty to disqualify himself if, pecuniary interest altogether apart, he is for any reason unable to try a case on its objective merits or might reasonably appear to be so. This can give rise to

[22] 60 *LQR* 324.　　[23] C. P. Harvey, *The Advocate's Devil*, 1958, p.32.
[24] *Jones* v. *National Coal Board* [1957] 2 QB 55.
[25] *R* v. *Hircock, Farmer, Leggett* [1970] 1 QB 67.
[26] 'Judges and Judging', Child & Co Lecture, 3 Mar. 1977, p.5.

very difficult questions.[27] In the ordinary way English practice would not require a judge to stand down because he had previously decided cases against a particular party, or even because he had previously rejected the evidence of a particular material witness. But the consistency of the previous adverse decisions or the terms in which the evidence had been rejected might be such as to raise a question, however wrongly, about the judge's ability to approach a case with the necessary objectivity. In such a case the judge may prefer to stand down. The Court of Appeal has, however, emphasised very recently that a charge of bias or apparent bias is not to be lightly made.[28]

Secondly, it is quite clear that a judge should not make disparaging comments about the parties in any case he is currently trying. An extreme example of such conduct came before the Criminal Division of the Court of Appeal in the recent and notorious case of *R* v. *Batth*.[29] In that case the then Recorder of London, while presiding over a trial in which a Sikh defendant was accused of murder, was reported in a daily newspaper to have made an after-dinner speech at the Mansion House in which, referring to the case he was hearing at the time, he made mention of 'murderous Sikhs'. It was found, not surprisingly, that in the absence of any convincing contradiction of the report, it raised an appearance of bias and the court commented on 'the extreme unwisdom of any Judge making remarks outside the court in public about a case which he is currently trying'. In an even more recent civil case,[30] the Civil Division of the Court of Appeal held that 'total abstinence from comment on a current case, in public or in private, should be the rule'.

Thirdly, while it is inherent in the appellate system that judges will disagree, and it is on occasion necessary for an appellate court to express criticism, sometimes very strong criticism, of a judge's conduct, the language used on such occasions should be measured, temperate, dignified, and so far as possible polite. Such situations should never degenerate into personal vendetta. Happily, I can think of no recent parallel to the occasion on which Scrutton LJ gratuitously criticised the knowledge claimed by McCardie J, a bachelor, of women's underwear, an attack to which McCardie J responded by refusing to make his notes of judgment available to any Court of Appeal of which Scrutton LJ was a member.[31] When Lord Maugham wrote to *The Times* criticising Lord Atkin's dissenting judgment in *Liversidge* v. *Anderson*[32] Atkin rightly forbore to reply. I cannot think any judge would now feel justified in writing to a periodical to criticise a judgment of the Lord Chief Justice, as Sir James Stephen did in 1884 fiercely attacking Lord Coleridge's judgment in a blasphemy case.[33] The convention is now settled that differences of this kind are not aired in the press.

---

[27] See, eg, *Australian National Industries Ltd* v. *Spedley Securities Ltd* (1992) 26 NSW LR 411.
[28] *Arab Monetary Fund* v. *Hashim*, unreported.   [29] unreported, 9 Apr. 1990.
[30] *Arab Monetary Fund* v. *Hashim*, unreported.   [31] Thomas, *op. cit.*, pp.18–19.
[32] [1942] AC 206.   [33] K. J. M. Smith, *James Fitzjames Stephen*, p.171.

Fourthly, it is plainly improper for a judge to court publicity or seek public acclaim or newspaper headlines. There is still much force in the old aphorism that the best judge is he whose name is unknown to average readers of the *Daily Mail*. Chief Justice Hale three centuries ago was fully alive to this point. His 'Things necessary to be continually had in remembrance' included

11. That popular or court applause or distaste, have no influence into any thing I do in point of distribution of justice.
12. Not to be solicitous what men say or think, so long as I keep myself exactly according to the rule of justice.

Modern practice would, I think, endorse that approach fully, subject to two qualifications. In passing sentence in a difficult case, a criminal judge is often wise to take account, among many other considerations, of how a proposed sentence will be perceived by the public at large, or the community to which the defendant belongs, or the victim. This is not a surrender to the clamour of the mob; it is realistic recognition that a sentence widely seen as unjustifiably lenient may ultimately be damaging to the defendant himself and even, unless and until corrected, to the administration of criminal justice. In the civil field also, cases arise which are of public concern: it may then not be enough for the court to reach the right decision; it may be necessary also to give reasons for the decision in terms which the public can understand.

Fifthly, there has, particularly in the United States, been some debate about the *ex parte* communications a judge may properly have when preparing his judgment.[34] The view there seems to be that a judge may consult with other judges but not with any law teacher. It is without doubt fundamental that a judge should not decide a case on a point which has not been raised in argument without giving notice to the parties and allowing them an opportunity to make submissions. That is a rule which arbitrators are expected to observe and so are judges. But subject to that, English practice would not in my view frown on a judge who sought to clear his mind or test his views by discussing the matter with a colleague or a law teacher. Difficulties could arise if the discussion were with an appellate judge who was thereafter called upon to decide an appeal against the decision, but in a case raising some issue of judicial or sentencing policy I do not think consultation with an appellate judge would be thought improper provided the trial judge did not cede the responsibility for decision which was properly his.

Sixthly, modern practice requires expeditious delivery of reserved judgments. The press of other commitments, the incidence of vacations, and the occasional unavailability (in multi-judge courts) of all members may lead to some delay between hearing and judgment but (save at the highest level) this

---

[34] ABA Canons of Judicial Conduct, Canon 3A(4); 'Judicial Ethics: The less-often asked questions', Andrew L. Kaufman, (1989) *Washington Law Review*, vol 64, p.851.

should be measured at most in weeks and not in months. I do not think any delay beyond that is regarded as tolerable save perhaps in very special circumstances.

Seventhly, judges (being human) do not like being reversed on appeal, although some dislike it more than others. But it is the judge's clear duty to do nothing to obstruct any arguable appeal, whether by making findings of fact more conclusive than the evidence warrants in the expectation that the appellate court will be unable to interfere, by passing an unduly lenient sentence in the hope of deterring an appeal against conviction, by refusing leave or a certificate in any case where such is necessary and justified, or in any other way. Whatever the cost to his *amour propre* the judge must, so far as possible, remain detached and not seek to deprive a litigant of rights which the legal system confers.

In this context the question has arisen whether and to what extent it is permissible for a judge to edit a transcript of what he said. Authority makes plain that editing a transcript of a direction to a jury is not permitted.[35] This is in my view right, since in such cases much may turn on the precise terms in which the jury is directed; in civil cases more latitude is permitted, since that is generally not so. It is common practice to correct errors and infelicities of grammar and style in the transcript of an *extempore* judgment. But that latitude does not extend to alterations in the substance or sense of what was said, to the adding of new points or the rectifying of omissions not mentioned at the time. Still less does it sanction the wholesale rewriting of the judgment, using the transcript as little more than a draft.

Eighthly and lastly under this head, the overwhelming consensus of judicial opinion would in my view discourage or condemn attempts by judges, whether from the bench or otherwise, to answer public criticism of their decisions. Lord Cockburn burned his fingers when he entered the lists in defence of his decision in *R* v. *Bedingfield*[36] over a century ago. Other judges who have attempted to answer criticisms, particularly of criminal sentences, from the bench have tended to cut sorry and rather unconvincing figures. Judges are almost always better advised to remain silent, leaving the wisdom or unwisdom of any decision to be judged by the appellate courts, by academic commentators, and by public opinion.

On the closing stages of the judge's official journey I have only three brief points to make. First, and whatever the position before the appointment of Fisher J in 1968, it is now in my view clear that a judge may not properly retire (save of course on grounds of ill health or incapacity) before serving a minimum period of 15 years. The Lord Chancellor makes plain to prospective appointees that elevation to the bench is a one-way street and judges are morally obliged to honour that commitment. Secondly, the judge may after

---

[35] *R* v. *Klucznski* [1973] 1 WLR 1230.   [36] (1879) 14 Cox CC 341.

retirement pursue any avocation, public or private, not inappropriate for a retired judge. This may certainly include acting as an arbitrator or giving expert opinions on the law in the capacity of a retired judge. But thirdly, and here the contrast with both the United States and Australia is stark, a retired judge may not return to the practice of law. There are in my opinion a number of sound practical reasons which strongly support that rule. There is also, I think, a formal reason: that on becoming a judge a practitioner ceases to be a barrister or a solicitor (whether he remains on the roll or not) and becomes solely a judge, with the result that on retirement he lacks any qualification to practise. I would for my part be very sorry to see that rule eroded.[37]

---

[37] This is a slightly modified version of a lecture given at the SPTL Annual Conference on 8 Sept. 1993.

3

The Professional Responsibility and Ethics of the English Bar

ANTHONY THORNTON

THE ENGLISH BAR

THE professional responsibility and ethics required of barristers can only be understood by examining the structure of the Bar, the way in which its rules of conduct are promulgated, the essential requirements of practice, and the conduct a barrister must observe whilst practising. The English Bar has always been a self-regulating profession whose customs, practising arrangements and rules of conduct have evolved piecemeal over several centuries. The Bar's governing body is the General Council of the Bar, usually referred to as the Bar Council. The principal function of the Bar Council is to train and regulate a small profession that both practises as advocates in the courts of England and Wales and acts as specialist advisors in English law. The members of the profession, known as barristers, practise as self-employed referral professionals.[1] However, the term 'barrister' has two related meanings. It describes a practising member of the Bar and it is a qualification which must be acquired by all practising barristers. The qualification is, technically, a degree awarded by one of the four Inns of Court. For many years, a significant number of those who have acquired the qualification of barrister have used this qualification whilst employed to provide legal services in either the public or private sector. Thus, nowadays, practising barristers are either independent or employed practitioners, all of whom have been called to the Bar by one of the four Inns of Court.[2] In addition, there are many who no longer use their qualification but, having been called to the Bar, retain it. These people are known as non-practising barristers.

Until the Courts and Legal Services Act 1990, or CLSA, the Bar had remained largely free of statutory regulation. This is in striking contrast to solicitors, whose profession has been regulated by a series of Solicitors Acts, and to the legal professions of other common law jurisdictions. Although the

---

[1] Nowadays, the terms 'barrister' and 'counsel' are used interchangeably. Originally, 'counsel' was used of a barrister when exercising rights of audience. 'Barrister-at-law' is now obsolete as a term. It was used, until recently, when a barrister's degree of barrister was being referred to.

[2] 'Call' is the historic ceremony, still performed, in which the Inn concerned bestows the degree of barrister on a newly qualified student barrister. 'The Bar' was historically a barre or bench positioned within the hall of each Inn in which the ceremony takes place.

CLSA has made significant statutory inroads into the independence of the Bar from outside influences, the profession retains its vitality without any significant statutory foundation.

Historically, the profession has been centred on the four Inns of Court. These bodies, the Inner Temple, the Middle Temple, Gray's Inn and Lincoln's Inn, are voluntary societies and have existed since very ancient times. They had certainly become established by the fourteenth century and they evolved from the inns where apprentices in the law lodged during the sessions of the courts. Each Inn can call to the Bar those who are appropriately qualified and, until recent times, were the only place providing instruction in pleading, advocacy and the other practical essentials a barrister requires in order to practise. In 1852, the Inns established the Council of Legal Education. This body provides the compulsory training for the Bar, the Vocational Course,[3] which must be completed before any aspiring barrister can be called to the Bar and appear in court.

The Bar Council was set up in 1894 and now consists of approximately 120 members, partly elected by the practising Bar and partly nominated by the profession's constituent bodies. It is the Bar Council that promotes amendments to the Bar's Code of Conduct and which is responsible for setting practising standards and investigating disciplinary complaints. The Inns' last remaining function in disciplinary matters is to set up disciplinary tribunals to hear and determine complaints and to put into effect the most serious sanctions of being disbarred and suspended from practice.

The profession remains a small one. In 1994 there were approximately 8000 barristers in independent practice in England and Wales. Most practise in groups, known as chambers, with a clerk who manages each barrister's practice. Members of chambers are still known as tenants. This dates from the days when the accommodation was leased from the Inn by one person who then sub-let space to his tenants. Nowadays the lease is held by, or on behalf of, all members of chambers. Although sharing clerking and office facilities, each member of chambers remains independent and partnerships or other business associations are not allowed. Since 1991, barristers have been allowed to practise from home.[4]

Traditionally, barristers have practised from chambers located in, and rented from, one of the four Inns of Court. In 1994, about 4000 barristers practised from chambers located in the Inns. However, a growing number of barristers are now practising in London in chambers based outside the Inns, largely because of what are perceived to be more favourable rent terms obtainable outside. In 1994, about 1000 practised from such chambers. This

---

[3] In June 1994, the Bar Council resolved in principle that the CLE's monopoly should be broken and that the Vocational Course, validated by the Bar Council, should also be provided in other legal educational establishments. The first such courses should start in the academic year 1996–1997.

[4] In July 1995 there were about 250 barristers known to be practising as sole practitioners from home.

trend could have serious long-term consequences for the Inns, nearly all of whose income is derived from their rent rolls and for whom there is no other source of finance currently available to pay for the growing resources required for education and training, the Inns' current principal function.

In addition to the 5000 barristers with chambers in London, about 3000 practise from chambers located outside London, principally in the major provincial court centres of Birmingham, Manchester, Liverpool, Leeds and Winchester. Many London chambers also have annexes in these centres.

There are no precise figures available for the number of employed barristers. This is because many do not subscribe to the Bar Council, even though they have a professional obligation to do so. In 1994 there were about 2500 known to be in practice of whom 656 were employed as Crown Prosecutors by the Crown Prosecution Service. The majority of Crown Prosecutors are solicitors. In reality, there were probably about 5000 practising as employed barristers at that time. There are severe practising restrictions placed on employed barristers. They may only provide legal services to their employer and may only appear as advocates for their employer in the County Court, Magistrates' courts, tribunals and arbitrations. Until 1989 they had no rights of audience at all. Thus, amongst employed barristers, only CPS barristers regularly appear as advocates. However, the Government Legal Service is seeking rights of audience for all employed barristers in all courts by an application under the procedure established by the CLSA and the limited rights of audience available to employed barristers, including CPS barrister Crown Prosecutors, may be widened in the near future.

Although there are so many employed barristers, the profession is organised and regulated largely for barristers in independent practice. Only 14 places are reserved for employed barristers on the Bar Council and the Code of Conduct is principally concerned with the court conduct and practising arrangements of independent practitioners.

CONDUCT AND ETIQUETTE

Until 1980 the Bar had no code of conduct. The professional rules and obligations required of practising barristers, known colloquially as the Bar's conduct and etiquette, were passed on by word of mouth, mainly during pupillage, and were based on tradition, resolutions of the Bar Council which were endorsed by a subsequent General Meeting of the Bar, specific rulings of the Bar Council and judicial influence, usually by way of dicta in judgments raising points of court procedure.

This remarkable lack of any written code of conduct over a period of six centuries is explained by the tightly-knit nature of the profession. The judges from earliest times promulgated the requirements for an advocate's training, as to both its length and content. This training was provided in the Inns and, since the eighteenth century, by practitioners offering pupillages during which a pupil sits with a pupil master learning by example and experience for an intensive year immediately following qualification. Only since 1956 has pupillage been compulsory. Until the 1970s, it had to be paid for, nowadays chambers are encouraged to pay pupils and more than half the 600 pupils trained each year receive payments in their compulsory pupillage year. By the eighteenth century, the Inns had taken over from the judges the role of promulgating standards and, in 1852, the Inns agreed to the first set of Consolidated Regulations. These Regulations, amended annually, provide the framework for the four stages of the professional training of barristers: the academic state, the Vocational Stage, pupillage and, recently, compulsory continuing education in the early years of practice. They also provide the requirements for admission to an Inn and for call to the Bar.

Until the nineteenth century, no clear-cut series of rules of conduct, other than those associated with qualification, emerged. Barristers had acquired exclusive rights of audience in the higher courts and they worked and lived in close proximity to each other and the judges on a daily basis. Thus, conduct was, in reality, that to be expected of professional gentlemen whose working environment was the subject of intense peer-group pressure. The Inns did discipline its members from time to time but the recorded instances are largely associated with drunken or riotous behaviour, landlord disputes arising out of the occupation of rooms or chambers within the Inns and financial improvidence.

The growth of the circuit system in the nineteenth century led to change. The assize system goes back to the twelfth century. This is a system, which still operates, whereby the High Court judges visit the main centres of population on a regular basis and dispense local justice. However, the volume and extent of work on circuit only became fully developed as a consequence of the industrial revolution. As a result, barristers travelled around the circuits with the judges, often spending weeks away from home at a time. Circuit messes and circuits, which are associations of barristers practising on circuit, grew up with complex rules of membership. In part, these rules were designed to enable the Bar to retain exclusive rights of audience on circuit.

During the nineteenth century, defined rules of etiquette developed, in part due to the growing influence of the Attorney-General and, in part, due to the enormous changes in both the structure of the courts and in civil and criminal procedure. Three of the changes that led to a more pronounced use of advocacy skills and a resultant development of standard rules of etiquette for barristers were the demise of the Forms of Action, the ability of a defendant in a criminal trial to give evidence on his or her behalf and the growth in the use of documents in litigation. The Attorney-General's influence arose because he became recognised as the leader of the Bar and he would pronounce on matters of court behaviour and, where necessary, informally admonish any barrister whose errant behaviour was brought to his notice. In the mid-nineteenth century, the size of the Bar declined, largely due to the introduction of the County Courts in 1834, which were always open to solicitor advocates and which took much work from the existing courts. No-one had chambers outside the four Inns and, thus, the personal influence of the Attorney-General, coupled with peer-group pressure, enabled the profession to regulate itself even though the disciplinary influences of both the judges and the Inns were waning.

THE BAR COUNCIL

The last 50 years have seen a further erosion of the powers and influence of the Inns and also of the Circuits[5] at the expense of the Bar Council and, to a lesser extent, specialist Bar Associations concerned with the major areas of specialist practice, such as commercial law, family law, criminal law, planning law, employment law and revenue law. The Bar Council is now recognised as the authorised body for barristers by section 31 of the CLSA.[6] The Bar Council is also the relevant designated body for the purpose of giving effect to the Recognition Directive and the Implementation Regulations 1990, the vehicles for allowing appropriately qualified EC legal practitioners to obtain recognition of their qualifications by being called to the Bar. It is the Bar Council that promulgates or amends the Code of Conduct. The first edition of the Code of Conduct was approved by the Bar in General Meeting on 15th July 1980, with effect from 1st January 1981. The process of codification had started in the 1970s and was completed following a recommendation of the Royal Commission on Legal Services that had reported in 1979. There was an obvious gap created by the profession's oral tradition since no official rule book existed which could be readily consulted when a barrister's required conduct on any particular point was sought. The resolutions passed by the Bar Council and by the Bar in General Meeting and relevant rulings were printed in the Annual Statement circulated to each subscriber but these were not always readily available. An annual subscription, payable to the Bar Council was voluntary and not every practising barrister paid a subscription. In consequence, the long-serving secretary or chief executive of the Bar Council, Sir William Boulton, produced an unofficial but authoritative guide: 'Boulton's Conduct

---

[5] There are, and have been for many years, six circuits: South Eastern, Western, Wales and Chester, Midland and Oxford, Northern and North Eastern. These developed as part of the assize system with the High Court judges travelling around the assize courts on a particular circuit. Each circuit's leader had, and to some extent still has, a considerable influence on the professional behaviour of the members of that circuit.

[6] Section 27(3) of the CLSA provides, however, that no person may have a right of audience as a barrister unless he or she has been called to the Bar by one of the Inns of Court, thereby preserving the Inn's role as the provider of the essential qualification required of a barrister, namely the degree of barrister.

and Etiquette at the Bar'. This ran to six editions from 1953 until 1975 and consisted of a definitive commentary with sources and dates of relevant resolutions and rulings of the Bar or Bar Council, and was the usual point of reference for any query about conduct. Its status as an informal code was enhanced by the custom of each Inn giving a copy of the current edition to each newly called barrister.

From 1981 onwards, the profession's conduct has been regulated by an authoritative and official Code of Conduct. This Code originally provided that any amendment might be made by the Bar in General Meeting or, alternatively, by resolution of the Bar Council which would be operative forthwith but which might be revoked or amended by the Bar in General Meeting. However, a constitutional change of significance took effect on 1st January 1987. From that date, the Bar Council obtained exclusive authority to amend or replace the Code of Conduct. This change followed from the report of the Rawlinson Committee in 1986 that had made wide-ranging recommendations for the reform of the structure of the Bar. The principal consequence of these reforms was that the Bar Council became, for the first time, the Parliament of the Bar. The power of the Bar Council to promulgate rules of conduct for the profession is contained in Regulation 16 of its Constitution, which provides that the Bar Council shall have regard to, but shall not be bound to give effect to, any resolution of any meeting of the Bar and that it shall not be competent for any meeting of the Bar to exercise or to attempt to exercise any function or power which, by its Constitution, is exercisable by the Bar Council. One of these functions is to promote the standards, honour and independence of the Bar.[7]

This power is enshrined whilst the CLSA remains in force since the authorised body for barristers is defined in section 31 as the General Council of the Bar and it is that body's rules of conduct which have statutory approval and which must be observed by barristers when exercising rights of audience as barristers.

In addition to the Code of Conduct, there are the Consolidated Regulations which set out the profession's qualification and training regulations. Most of the Consolidated Regulations are promulgated by the four Inns of Court, acting through a consultative council called the Council of the Inns of Court which consists of representatives of the four Inns and observers from the Bar Council. The only exception concerns the part of the Consolidated Regulations concerned with the Bar's Vocational Course which is promulgated by the Council of Legal Education. However, the Bar Council's Constitution pro-

---

[7] Regulation 1(c) of the Constitution of the General Council of the Bar. The current edition, the fifth, is a completely re-drafted Code, replacing all earlier Codes. It was adopted by the Bar Council on 27 Jan. 1990, coming into force on 1 Apr. 1991. The re-drafting exercise had been prompted by the publication of the Courts and Legal Services Bill in Oct. 1989 and the re-drafted Code swept away many restrictive practises enshrined in earlier Codes and pre-existing etiquette.

vides, in Regulation 1(g), that the Bar Council may give or withhold consent to any amendment of the Consolidated Regulations. Moreover, it is the Bar Council that must forward any proposed amendment of the Consolidated Regulations to the CLSA approval process and no amendment may take effect until it has been approved pursuant to this process.

The Code of Conduct is an ungainly document consisting of ten parts and sixteen annexes. It is such a shapeless document because it is regulating so many different aspects of a barrister's professional life. The Code, in summary, defines how a barrister must practise and it regulates a barrister's relationship with the courts and tribunals in which barristers habitually practise, with professional and lay clients, with other barristers and with the outside world. Finally, the Code prescribes certain general behaviour regarded as unbecoming in a barrister.[8]

The principal documents are the Code of Conduct itself, two Codes of Practice called Written Standards for the Conduct of Professional Work, and a practising handbook called Chambers Administration Guidelines or 'Action Pack'. An Equality Code for chambers, being a code of practice concerned with equal opportunities, has recently been adopted as an additional annexe. Other relevant annexes deal with overseas practice and practice in England by overseas lawyers and the Code of Conduct for lawyers in the European Community, a separate code promulgated by the C.C.B.E.[9]

The Code of Conduct defines requirements that a barrister must fulfil in order to be allowed to practise. Traditionally, all barristers have always been sole practitioner advocates. Until recently, barristers have had to practise from chambers with a clerk who had to conduct all fee negotiations on a barrister's behalf but these requirements have now been removed. There are now three ways in which a barrister may practise; in independent practice, in employment and as a non-practising barrister. Moreover, anyone who has been called to the Bar retains the qualification and degree of barrister even if, thereafter, that individual ceases to have any connection with the law.

THE COURTS AND LEGAL SERVICES ACT

The CLSA has had, and will continue to have, a profound effect on the Bar and on practising barristers. Originally, the Act was conceived as the then Conservative government's means of introducing widened rights of audience in the

---

[8] Paragraph 201 of the Code of Conduct prohibits conduct whether in pursuit of a barrister's profession or otherwise which is dishonest or otherwise discreditable to a barrister, is prejudicial to the administration of justice or is likely to diminish public confidence in the legal profession or the administration of justice or otherwise bring the legal profession into disrepute.

[9] The Council of the Bars and Law Societies of the European Community.

higher courts.[10] This move followed nearly eight years of wrangling between barristers and solicitors as to whether the two branches of the legal profession could evolve a consensus as to who should have rights of audience in the higher courts. This wrangling started soon after the Royal Commission on Legal Services reported in 1979 that no change was desirable; it intensified when solicitors lost the ability to charge standard fees for conveyancing in 1982 and it continued throughout the fractured debate within the Marre Committee's deliberations between 1986 and 1989. That committee, consisting of tripartite representation of barristers, solicitors and lay people, had been appointed jointly by the Bar Council and the Law Society to seek a consensus on rights of audience, and is split roughly down the middle on the subject with a small majority of the lay representatives siding with the solicitor members. At that point, Lord Mackay, a Scot, was appointed Lord Chancellor. He had been a Law Lord and, before that, both Dean of the Faculty of Advocates (the Scottish equivalent to the Chairman of the Bar Council) and Lord Advocate (the Scottish equivalent of the Attorney-General, a non-political appointment). Lord Mackay was, therefore, able to bring to the task of reform of the English legal profession the perspective of a distinguished and informed outsider.

The complexity of the CLSA is explained by two factors, firstly, the attempt by Lord Mackay to impose a workable but complex political solution to the problem created by the outrage of both the judges and the Bar to the original proposals which would have given, at a stroke, rights of audience in all courts to most solicitors and many non-lawyers and secondly, the opportunity being taken to introduce a wide range of pending reforms affecting legal practice.

The effect of the Act on rules of conduct arises from the means whereby rights of audience and litigation are to be granted. The Act provides that these rights are to be solely determined by the Act.[11] The participants in litigation in all courts, tribunals and statutory inquiries, but not arbitrations, are divided into two overlapping categories: advocates and litigators. The power to grant rights of audience and rights to conduct litigation is given to authorised bodies. The Bar Council and the Law Society are recognised as existing authorised bodies but new authorised bodies may be created. Authorised bodies are to have appropriate rules of education, training and conduct governing the members to whom they grant these rights which must be both enforceable and enforced as appropriate. No recognition of a new authorised body and no

---

[10] The Act had been proceeded by 3 green papers and, following widespread consultation, a white paper. The Lord Chancellor, Lord Mackay, introduced the green papers soon after his appointment following the resignation of his predecessor, Lord Havers, on grounds of ill-health. The reforms were part of Mrs. Thatcher's government's political crusade against restrictive practices in all areas of economic activity.

[11] Sections 27(1) (for rights of audience) and 28 (1) (for rights to conduct litigation). The relevant provisions are set out in Part II of the Act, which came into force on 1st April 1991.

amendment of any rule of conduct, training or education of members of an authorised body may be introduced unless approved by the approval machinery of the Act. The rules of education, training and conduct of the Bar Council and the Law Society in force on the day the relevant provisions of the Act came into force received deemed approval under the Act and all barristers who were already qualified were deemed to have been granted rights of audience in all courts.[12] Whereas the Bar Council, the authorised body for barristers, has powers to grant rights of audience to its members, the Law Society was recognised as the authorised body for both advocacy and litigation purposes for solicitors since they have always had rights of audience in the lower courts.

The approval mechanism consists of a tripartite structure. Two parts of this are advisory and the third and final part, the designated judges, is the decision-making part. The principle advisory part is a committee, the Lord Chancellor's Advisory Committee. This is an unwieldy body of 17. It has a lay majority of one. The chairman is a senior judge, the current chairman Lord Steyn and his predecessor Lord Griffiths both being Law Lords. The purpose of this committee is to examine each application to create an authorised body or to amend a rule of education, training or conduct to see whether the application complies with the statutory objective and the general principle, both of which are defined by the Act and which the Act requires all approvals to be tested against.[13] The statutory objective is wide-ranging and provides that the objective of the Act is the development of legal services in England and Wales by making provision for new or better ways of providing such services and for a wider choice of persons providing them, while maintaining the proper and efficient administration of justice. It follows that any application should be allowed if it has, as its objective, the provision of new or better ways of providing legal services unless the general principle can be shown to operate. The general principle limits the application of the statutory objective where appropriate. It requires consideration of the administration of justice and the effectiveness and appropriateness of the relevant rules of education, training and conduct. Thus, these factors can over-ride the statutory objective. It follows that any amendment that has the potential for limiting rights of audience or reducing the numbers of those exercising rights of audience is likely to contravene the statutory objective and not to be one for which approval should be granted.

The Advisory Committee reports to, and advises, the designated judges whether any application should succeed. The other advisory part of the process is the Director General of Fair Trading, whose remit is to advise the designated judges whether the subject of any application has the potential for being anti-competitive. If it is, this provides a further possible reason for refusal. Finally, each of the five designated judges, the Lord Chancellor, the Lord

---

[12] Section 3 *Ibid.*   [13] Section 17(1).

Chief Justice, the Master of the Rolls, the Vice-Chancellor and the President of the Family Division, acting individually and taking into account the advice received, must decide whether to approve the application or not. If any of the five decides against the application, it fails and the proposal may not take effect.

The approval process is required to be completed as soon as possible after it has been initiated. In practice, the process has been shown to be cumbrous and very slow. In the first four years it was in operation, starting in April 1991, the only major item of work that the Advisory Committee was concerned with was the application by the Law Society for approval of rule changes which would enable solicitors in both private practice and employed by the CPS and any other employer to obtain full rights of audience. The Advisory Committee has also dealt with an associated application on behalf of employed barristers for full rights of audience. In the case of employed solicitors and barristers, the enhanced rights of audience would continue to be exercised only on behalf of their employers. Thus, for CPS Crown Prosecutors, the wider rights would be confined to prosecuting. The relevant courts concerned with these applications are the High Court, Crown Court, Court of Appeal and House of Lords.

The process has been successfully completed for solicitors in private practice and the first High Court rights of audience by a solicitor were exercised in 1994. A solicitor must show relevant experience as a lower court advocate and have completed additional training in advocacy and relevant procedural law and practice before being granted higher court advocacy rights. However, for employed lawyers, after two references to the Advisory Committee, by June 1995 the process had only reached the stage of the Advisory Committee's advice. The Committee, by a majority of one, advised against the applications. The Director General of Fair Trading advised that the applications would increase competition and should therefore succeed on competition grounds. The controversy centres around the question as to whether Crown Prosecutors, or 'state lawyers' as some pejoratively call them, should be able to appear as advocates in the Crown Court and in criminal appeals. Currently, all prosecutions in the Crown Court are conducted by barristers in independent practice. The Bar Council, which is dominated by representatives of those in independent practice, has adamantly opposed attempts to extend the rights of audience of Crown Prosecutors. Its argument is that it is against the public interest for the prosecution of trials on indictment in court to be conducted by those as intimately associated with both the decision to prosecute and the preparation of the prosecution's case as a Crown Prosecutor would be. Moreover, only those who practise on a regular daily basis as advocates have sufficient experience and expertise to prosecute in the higher courts. Criminal practitioners from the independent Bar have such experience, Crown Prosecutors, it is argued, do not. The CPS equally adamantly refutes these arguments. It points to the Code for Crown Prosecutors,[14] with its emphasis on objectivity and which contains guidelines as to whether to prosecute and as to when and how to proceed with the prosecution, as showing that the necessary detachment is already required of Crown Prosecutors. Moreover, with their regular experience prosecuting before Magistrates, in whose courts 98% of all criminal cases are conducted, Crown Prosecutors necessarily acquire the appropriate experience. These arguments should have been, but have not been, conclusively and speedily put to rest by the CLSA approval machinery.

From the standpoint of the Bar's Code of Conduct, there are three particular features of the CLSA that should be noted. Firstly, the Act creates and defines a clear demarcation between those who appear as advocates, exercising rights of audience, from those who prepare cases out of court, exercising rights to conduct litigation. Unfortunately, no clear or workable definition of these two functions is provided.[15] As the profession which has traditionally provided advocacy services, barristers were only granted rights of audience by the Act. When all court work was conducted orally, this distinction was relatively easy to apply. However, particularly in the civil field, more and more of the presentation of a case is conducted on paper. In most cases, a written summary of the case is presented by way of supplementing an opening and closing speech and the speeches themselves are often extremely brief. Evidence in chief is given in writing and time limits as to cross-examination and speeches are being introduced with growing frequency. The extent to which the preparation of documents for use at the trial constitutes the exercise of rights of audience is unclear. The significance of this uncertainty is that barristers cannot prepare these documents in so far as such preparation is to be regarded as exclusively the conduct of litigation. Equally, a litigator without relevant rights of audience can prepare them unless such preparation is regarded as exclusively falling within the field of advocacy. A similar trend, albeit not so pronounced, is occurring in criminal trials, particularly fraud trials and in the production of case statements by the prosecution. The Bar Council may well have to apply for at least limited rights to grant barristers limited rights to conduct litigation in the near future.

A second feature of the Act is the prominence given to rules of conduct and qualification regulations, the latter being the shorthand for regulations concerned with education and training.[16] Thus, the Code of Conduct and the

---

[14] The third edition was published in June 1994 pursuant to section 10 of the Prosecution of Offences Act 1985.

[15] Section 27(9) provides that qualification regulations are regulations, however they may be described, as to the education and training which members of an authorised body must receive in order to be entitled to any right of audience and that rules of conduct are rules as to the conduct required of members in exercising any rights of audience granted.

[16] See Section 27(9) summarised above.

Consolidated Regulations, at least in theory, contain three types of rule: rules that are rules of conduct or qualification regulations and the balance that fall into neither category and are, therefore, not subject to the Act at all. The definition of the first two categories is wide, the consequence of which is that most, if not all, of the Code of Conduct and the Consolidated Regulations are subject to the Act and any amendment is subject to the approval machinery. Since the Code of Conduct is subject to so many constant pressures for amendment, this creates a serious impediment to change. The Advisory Committee has attempted to improve the process by introducing a fast track system for considering minor amendments and by encouraging the introduction of general powers to be exercised by the Bar Council in its discretion and the publication of guidelines as to how that discretion will be exercised. This reduces the need to amend the Code of Conduct and the Consolidated Regulations.

A final significant feature of the Act is provided by Schedule 2. This provides a detailed list of matters that the Advisory Committee is to keep under review. The Advisory Committee can recommend to the Bar Council amendments to its rules of conduct or qualification regulations which the Bar Council is not required to comply with but, clearly, any such recommendation would have persuasive effect. The Advisory Committee, pursuant to its Schedule 2 role, initiated a three-year review of legal education in 1993 and has also embarked on a consideration of conduct associated with 'cracked trials', being trials where a change of plea from not guilty to guilty occurs on the first day of the trial. This second initiative followed publication and research into the problems associated with cracked trials revealing what was alleged to be undue pressure being placed upon defendants by their legal representatives to change their plea.

BARRISTERS IN INDEPENDENT PRACTICE

1. Sole Practice

A barrister in independent practice must fulfil three essential requirements: to be a sole practitioner, to work on referral and to observe the 'cab-rank' rule. The first requirement of independent practice is enshrined in the rule which prohibits a barrister from practising in partnership with anyone.[17] Most barristers practise from chambers, a group of up to 50 practising barristers. Each member of chambers is a sole practitioner who shares office accommodation and core services, particularly clerking and secretarial facilities. Although no longer a professional requirement, virtually all chambers have

[17] Paragraph 207(a) of the Code of Conduct.

a senior clerk and a number of assistant clerks who are responsible for booking in work, negotiating and collecting fees, avoiding fixture clashes and running the administration of chambers. The clerks to chambers are also responsible for attracting new work and helping to develop the practices of newly-joined members of chambers[18]

Barristers who practise on their own from home are subject to an essential rule of conduct which limits the numbers of those practising in this way. This is, that before practising on his or her own, a barrister must have practised in chambers for at least three years following pupillage.[19] This rule is similar to a rule of practice for solicitors, which precludes a solicitor from practising as a sole practitioner until that solicitor has been admitted for at least three years.[20]

The purpose of the rule is to ensure that a practitioner obtains sufficient experience of practice by example since so much of a practising lawyer's craft can only be learnt by experience and by following others. The rule is, however, a severe restriction on the ability of a qualified barrister to practise since only about half of the approximately 600 pupils a year are offered a place in chambers. The remaining pupils have to find a place as an employed or non-practising barrister or to take employment away from the law altogether. This limitation will undoubtedly be critically examined in the near future by the Director General of Fair Trading as the numbers wishing to practise continue to grow and the number of available places in chambers remains relatively static. However, there is a disproportionately large number of complaints about those practising on their own, confirming the general belief that the experience and practising arrangements of such barristers are prone to be less satisfactory than for those in independent practice generally.

The rule against partnership is largely justified by the relatively small number of barristers in independent practice.[21] Only in exceptional circumstances may a partner take on a case to act for a client when another member of that partner's firm is already acting in the same or a related matter or has previously acted since a professional owes a duty of confidentiality to his or her client in relation to all information obtained in the course of that professional relationship.[22] Because a barrister is not able to practise in any form of professional association with other barristers, he or she can, and frequently

---

[18] The Barristers' Clerks Association administers a training course and has promulgated a code of practice which its members should follow. Most senior clerks are still remunerated, wholly or in part, on a commission basis.   [19] Paragraph 301(d) of the Code of Conduct.

[20] Rule 13(1) of the Solicitors' Practice Rules 1988.

[21] Paragraph 207(a) of the Code of Conduct

[22] See *In re A Firm of Solicitors* [1992] QB 959, CA. The Court of Appeal held that only in a rare case could a solicitor act when the solicitor's firm had previously acted for a client whose affairs were relevant to the later potential instructions. Only if the proposed 'Chinese wall' to be set up within the firm would obviate any risk of the breach of the duty not to communicate confidential information would a court allow a solicitor to continue to act in such circumstances. The law, in two other exceptional cases, is considered in *David Lee & Co (Lincoln) Ltd. v. Coward Chance (a Firm)* [1991] Ch 259 and *Rakusen v. Ellis, Munday & Clark* [1912] 1 Ch 831, CA.

does, act against another barrister or other barristers from the same chambers. Many chambers specialise in specific areas of practice and, in consequence, specialists in many areas are concentrated in a limited number of chambers. The rule against partnership ensures that the choice of barristers available for instruction in any type of dispute is as large as possible. The rule is also justified by the need for a barrister to concentrate on the particular case in hand. The rule encourages such concentration since it ensures that delegation of work and profit sharing are not possible.

Section 66 of the CLSA has opened the way to multi-disciplinary and multi-national partnerships. However section 66(6) allows the Bar Council to make rules prohibiting barristers from entering into any such arrangements and, thus, the prohibition on professional association remains effective.[23] However, the growing moves, in both England and the European Commission, to encourage such practices will put the Bar under great pressure in the future to allow barristers at least limited rights of association with other professionals. The Bar Council is likely to hold out strongly against permitting barristers to associate professionally with solicitors.

2. Referral Status

The referral nature of a barrister's practice evolved from the formal system of pleading required by the courts before considerable changes of practice were introduced in the nineteenth century. Years of practice were required to master the art of pleading. The necessary training was only available in the Inns of Court and the judges, particularly in the sixteenth and seventeenth centuries, prescribed detailed rules of both training and experience in practical exercises and moots organised by the Inns as a pre-condition to exercising rights of audience.[24] As, independently, the professions of attorney, conveyancer and proctor developed, merging to form the Law Society that was granted a charter in 1831,[25] so the functions of preparing a case and presenting it became both defined and discrete. However, the rule requiring a barrister to be instructed by a solicitor and precluding instructions being accepted direct from a lay client was only formalised comparatively recently. For court work, the rule had not become sufficiently recognised to be a rule of law by 1850.[26] In that year, Lord Campbell, the Chief Justice, stated that although there had been an under-

[23] Paragraph (7) of the Overseas Practice Rules allows a barrister to enter into a multi-disciplinary partnership outside the UK which must be with a lawyer other than a solicitor practising in the UK.
[24] These were largely gathered together in Dugdale's *Origines Juridiciales or Historical Memorials*, the third and last edition of which was published in 1680. Dugdale was Garter, Principal King of Arms.
[25] The full title of the Law Society when first established was: 'The Society of Attorneys, solicitors, and others not being barristers, practising in the Courts of Law and Equity in the United Kingdom'.   [26] *Doe d.Bennett v. Hale and Davis* (1850) 15 QB 171.

standing in the profession that a barrister ought not to accept a brief in a civil suit except from an attorney, there was no rule of law to this effect which could be enforced. The conditions and restrictions upon which barristers should be permitted to plead before judges and to have audience before them were matters for the judges and no rule requiring instruction from an attorney had been formulated by them.[27] For opinions, the rule was only introduced in 1955.[28] Until then, a small group of Chancery practitioners regularly accepted instructions from lay clients to advise on and draft conveyances and other related transactions. The rule was introduced, in part, as a trade-off with the Law Society who were concerned about the possible loss of the solicitors' conveyancing monopoly. It is thought that the Attorney-General gave assurances that this would survive in return for understandings from the Law Society not to press for an extension of solicitors' rights of audience. The loss of the right to accept instructions direct from a lay client was a corollary of this arrangement.

In recent years there have been three encroachments on the rule that a barrister's work must be referred by a solicitor. The major encroachment has been to widen the range of those who may instruct a barrister so that many professionals, such as accountants, surveyors, architects and insolvency practitioners may now instruct a barrister in their area of expertise in advisory work and in litigation before arbitrators, tribunals and the Magistrates' courts. This arrangement, seen as a desirable but not significant widening of the referral rules, is enshrined in the Direct Professional Access Rules[29] first introduced in 1989. Many professionals, particularly accountants in the tax field and surveyors in the planning field, already had wide experience in preparing cases in their fields and were therefore regarded as having the requisite experience to instruct a barrister to present such cases.

The second encroachment dates back to 1961 when barristers were first allowed to accept instructions directly from foreigners without the intervention of a solicitor. The relevant rules date back to the first edition of the Overseas Practice Rules[30] introduced in 1973. These have been expanded on a number of occasions since. The rules deal with two situations, barristers accepting instructions from abroad and barristers practising in a jurisdiction other than England and Wales. In order to obtain a share of the considerable volume of overseas work, largely from jurisdictions which do not have a divided legal

---

[27] *Ibid.*

[28] Following a statement made by the Attorney-General, Sir Reginald Manningham-Buller QC, at the AGM of the Bar. This superseded the statement by the Attorney-General, Sir Richard Webster QC, in 1888 (Law Times, 7th July) that generally there was no objection to a barrister seeing and advising a lay client without the intervention of a solicitor on points relating to the lay client's own personal conduct and guidance on the management or disposition of that client's affairs or transactions.

[29] The Direct Professional Access Rules are set out in Annexe E of the Code of Conduct.

[30] The Overseas Practice Rules are set out in Annexe F of the Code of Conduct.

profession, the Bar had to relax its strict rules of access and association. Any barrister may accept instructions to advise on English law from abroad from either a professional client or a foreign lay client direct. Equally, a barrister may accept instructions from a similar source to appear in a foreign court or in an international arbitration in England.[31]

A final, limited, encroachment arises when a barrister is instructed by an employed barrister. Since many in-house legal departments have employed barristers working within them alongside solicitors, the access rules were amended many years ago to allow a barrister to accept instructions from an employed barrister and from the legal department of a Local Authority if that department is headed by either a solicitor or a barrister.[32]

3. Cab-Rank

The third leg of the tripod underpinning independent practice as a barrister is the so called cab-rank rule. This is to barristers what the Hippocratic oath is to doctors. No brief or instructions may be refused, whether to act as an advocate or to advise, unless the barrister is professionally committed already, has not been offered a proper fee, is professionally embarrassed by a prior conflict of interest or lacks sufficient experience or competence to handle the matter. A legal aid brief is deemed to be one offered at a proper fee unless the Bar Council or the Bar in General Meeting otherwise determines.[33]

The purpose of the rule is to ensure that nobody is left unrepresented in court or is unable to obtain advice and other legal services of the type offered by barristers however objectionable that person's views or conduct and however unpalatable the matter. The origins of the rule go back many centuries but custom hardened into a rule of practice when the Bar messes developed at each circuit centre where the assize judge visited and where quarter sessions were held. All criminal jury trials out of London were tried before the assize judge or at sessions before the local recorder, a part-time judge. Complex rules were developed concerning membership of the mess and only those who were members of the relevant Bar mess and circuit had rights of audience at any assize or sessions. All these rules have been abolished. In return for these restrictive practices, the rule developed that any prisoner appearing before the assize judge or the recorder was entitled to representation, even if a proper fee could not be afforded. This also led to the development of the dock brief whereby any unrepresented prisoner could nominate from the dock any barrister in court to represent him or her for a nominal fee without an instructing solicitor. Nowadays, every unrepresented defendant in

---

[31] This is dealt with further in the section concerned with international practice below.
[32] See the definition of professional client in paragraph 901 of the Code of Conduct and see also paragraph 402.1(d).   [33] Paragraphs 501 and 502 of the Code of Conduct.

the Crown Court may be granted legal aid by the judge and, in consequence, the dock brief has become obsolete.[34]

Solicitors are not subject to a similar rule of conduct and an attempt was made to insert a provision into the CLSA requiring every advocate with High Court and Crown Court rights of audience to be subject to a cab-rank rule. A moving speech, introducing the amendment, was made by Lord Alexander of Weedon, Q.C., a former Chairman of the Bar, who identified the merits of the rule as follows:

> The obligation that advocates should accept instructions from all comers provided that the advocate is available, that there is no conflict of interest and that the fee is reasonable, has been the obligation of the Bar for centuries. Sir Thomas Erskine, a distinguished Scot who, having practised at the English Bar for a brief period, became Lord Chancellor and was probably the greatest advocate since Cicero, said in the late eighteenth century that the day when an advocate could discriminate between the causes he accepted according to personal or public sympathies, would be the day on which the liberties of England would come to an end.
>
> I do not seek to put the point so high nor so dramatically, but I suggest that it is a very important principle. Why? It is inevitable that there are some causes which may not be either personally attractive to the advocate or publicly popular: for example, treason trials in the First and Second World Wars; prominent spy trials; trials of terrorists on bombing charges and trials of particularly gruesome rapes or murders. In all such cases it is immensely important that a defendant should have a highly competent advocate to present the defence case. The Bar has recognised this by making what is called the cab-rank rule a fundamental principle of practice. It proposes to retain the rule. I suggest - again not in the spirit of controversy - that it is important that all those who seek the privilege (I emphasize that there is an element of privilege involved) of conducting advocacy in the higher courts should accept this obligation.[35]

All higher court advocates are now subject to a modified cab-rank rule. Section 17(3)(c) of the CLSA requires every relevant authorised body to have in place a non-discrimination rule of practice in relation to the provision of advocacy services. The Bar's cab-rank rule is significantly wider but the statutory provision highlights the public perception that the privilege of being an advocate should be matched by the need to provide adequate representation for all.

Many cynics have argued that the Bar always successfully avoids an unpopular brief by the ruse of invoking a prior commitment when necessary.

---

[34] All criminal courts became Crown Courts by virtue of the Courts Act 1971. Legal Aid in Criminal and Care Proceedings (General) Regulations 1989, regulations 18 and 21 provide for a judge granting a legal aid order. Usually, in criminal trials, this is done by the Magistrates' clerk.

[35] Hansard, House of Lords, 25th January 1990, columns 1190-1191. This speech was made in moving an amendment in committee which was narrowly defeated. Lord Alexander subsequently moved a modified amendment at report stage which was narrowly carried against the government. This amended clause was replaced by section 17(c) of the CLSA when the bill, having been introduced in the House of Lords, was before the House of Commons.

Moreover, some barristers are reputed not to accept instructions in, for instance, rape trials for a defendant or in Rent Act cases for a landlord. However, no-one has been reported in recent years for any alleged infringement of the cab-rank rule and, particularly in the criminal sphere, it is a rule which is zealously observed.

4. Other Requirements

A barrister in independent practice must practise full-time as a barrister,[36] a requirement that goes hand in hand with the requirement that a barrister may not, simultaneously, be a solicitor either by qualification or in practice.[37] However, it is open to question whether a barrister should have to give up his or her qualification on becoming a solicitor rather than merely being precluded from practising as both simultaneously. The rule harks back to the time, in the 1820s, when solicitors were finally excluded from the Inns of Court[38] and to the belief that one who is a barrister should not simultaneously be instructed by a profession of which he is also a member. Since the introduction of Direct Professional Access, this justification is obsolete since a practising barrister may hold a dual qualification with many of those professions entitled to instruct a barrister so long as his or her primary occupation remains that of a practising barrister. If a barrister wishes to transfer to become a solicitor or vice versa, there are transfer regulations facilitating such a move. Former solicitors may be required to pass one or more sections of the aptitude test introduced for EC lawyers and to undertake a period of pupillage but the Joint Regulations Committee may grant an appropriate exemption from either or both stages where previous advocacy experience justifies this.

The reason for the requirement concerned with full-time practice is to seek to ensure that a barrister is able to concentrate exclusively on a case once the preparation for trial, or the trial itself, has started and to retain the necessary cutting edge required of a professional advocate. It is necessary, to maintain high standards, for an advocate to practice advocacy regularly and frequently. The complaint about many American advocates is that they appear in court too infrequently to have obtained the necessary experience of the

[36] Paragraph 208 of the Code of Conduct.

[37] A similar requirement applies to solicitors. Both branches enforce these requirements by ensuring that, on call as a barrister or on admission as a solicitor, the individual has been removed from the roll of solicitors or has been disbarred. The Bar achieves this by requiring an appropriate undertaking to be given as part of the call declaration, see Schedule 5 of the Consolidated Regulations.

[38] The process of excluding solicitors from the Inns of Court was a slow but interesting one. The history is summarised in Halsbury's *Laws of England*, Fourth edition re-issue (1988), Volume 3(1), Title Barristers, paragraph 358. See also M. Birks, *Gentlemen of the Law* (1960) pp 103-8 and H.H.L. Bellot, *The Exclusion of Attorneys from the Inns of Court* (1910) 26 LQR 137.

courtroom.[39] The rule that advocacy must be the primary occupation of a barrister is, however, interpreted in a practical way. Women with young children who remain in practice cannot practise part-time but if their field of practice is, for example, in local Magistrates' courts, they are able to comply with the rule, albeit that their travelling and working day would be lighter than for many barristers.

Compulsory insurance was introduced in 1982. The proposal was controversial and was passed at the AGM of the Bar. The requirement is linked to membership of the BMIF.[40] This Mutual was established in order to provide insurance at a cheaper rate than would be available in the market and it is compulsory that at least the first layer of cover, currently £½ million, should be taken out with the BMIF, all of whose directors are practising barristers. The annual premium is calculated on the claims experience of the relevant area of practice. The cover extends to all types of practice and all work undertaken as a barrister, excluding certain international work such as work in or from the U.S.A. where claims can be prohibitive. The consequences of wasted costs orders are also covered.

A further requirement, of having to be a current subscriber to the Bar Council, is also controversial.[41] The Bar Council is neither a statutory body nor does it have a royal charter. Its powers of enforcement of this requirement are, therefore, unclear. The rule was introduced in 1986, and was passed at the AGM of the Bar and in a subsequent ballot of the Bar by large majorities.[42] The necessity for the rule was that the growing functions and responsibilities of the Bar Council could only be provided if the subscription income of the Bar Council was both maintained and ensured. Opponents, who remain a vocal but small minority of barristers, object largely because of the dislike of a body that is perceived to be a quasi-trade union and because of a general distaste for authority that is a characteristic of independently minded professionals. The Law Society has always been able to levy and enforce a requirement for what are in essence compulsory subscriptions since it has statutory authority to require an annually renewable practising certificate, the income from which is used to run all activities of the Law Society.

The legality of the compulsory subscription rule was soon tested in a disciplinary tribunal whose decision was made public.[43] The barrister in

---

[39] Such advocates are know colloquially as 'oncers', namely advocates who appear in court once a year.

[40] Paragraph 302 of the Code of Conduct. Paragraph 3.9 of the CCBE Code of Conduct requires EC lawyers to be insured to a reasonable extent at all times against claims based on professional negligence.   [41] Paragraph 302A of the Code of Conduct.

[42] Compulsory subscriptions were recommended by the Pearce Report (1974), a report of a committee under Lord Pearce set up by the then Senate of the Bar, by the Royal Committee on Legal Services (1979) and by the Rawlinson Committee (1986), a report of a committee under Lord Rawlinson set up by the then Senate of the Bar.

[43] *S (A Barrister)*, a decision of the disciplinary tribunal of the Council of the Inns of Court, chairman Mr Justice Nolan, 26th July 1990. The decision was reported in the *Guardian* of 9th October 1990.

question had objected to payment as a matter of principle. The tribunal ruled that the rule was lawful but it could not be enforced by disciplinary sanction since that could involve loss of livelihood by the withdrawal of the right to practise by being disbarred or suspended. This was held to be an unjustifiable restraint of trade. More recently, the Bar Council has sought to use the CLSA approval machinery to get round this decision by applying to introduce a rule that anyone in default would, whilst in default, be unable to exercise rights of audience. In that form, the proposed rule was not approved by the designated judges in June 1995 since it was perceived to be similar in its objectionable features to the rule considered by the earlier disciplinary tribunal. However, the Bar Council was, in 1995, considering an adapted version of the rule which would confine the compulsory element of the subscription to the part of its revenue needed to fund Bar Council activities required by the CLSA, namely those associated with conduct, training and discipline. The Bar Council was also considering the introduction of practising certificates. Meanwhile, though there are defaulters, these have remained commendably few in number and the Bar Council's potential subscription income lost by non-payment was, in 1994, about 5% of the total.

EMPLOYED BARRISTERS

An employed barrister is one who, in return for the payment of a salary, provides legal services to his employer and who, if those services include advocacy services, has completed pupillage, at least the first six months of which must have been served with a barrister in independent practice.[44] Barristers have been employed in in-house legal departments of companies and accountancy practices, in government departments and by Local Authorities and the CPS as Crown Prosecutors for many years. The Code of Conduct allows barristers to offer legal services only to a barrister's employer. Thus, a barrister may not be employed by solicitors or accountants to provide legal services to clients of that employer. The legal services that may be provided include advocacy for that employer in the County Court, Magistrates' courts and before tribunals and in arbitrations. These are the courts in which a barrister did not have exclusive rights of audience before the CLSA came into force.

Following the government's requirement for compulsory competitive tendering, that was imposed on Local Authorities in the 1990s, many barristers in local government employment have sought to offer legal services to their previous employer as part of the independent practice of a firm of solicitors. This arrangement clearly offends against the rules concerning

---

[44] Paragraphs 402.1 and 402.2 of the Code of Conduct.

employment and association but the Professional Conduct Committee of the Bar Council has been prepared to grant limited waivers to such barristers.[45]

NON-PRACTISING BARRISTERS

In the late 1980s, a growing number of barristers employed by accountants were offering, or seeking to offer, professional services to clients of their employers. These barristers were unwilling to disbar themselves and to lose their degree and title of barrister. The Bar Council set up a committee in 1989 under Mr Justice Mummery whose principal recommendation was accepted. This was that such employees should not be allowed to hold themselves out as barristers but, if they made it clear that they were non-practising barristers, they could act for their employers or for clients of their employers without having to disbar themselves.[46] They would, thus, be providing legal services without holding themselves out as being a practising member of the profession. In consequence, there are now also a few non-practising barristers working in solicitors' offices, particularly those who have recently failed to obtain a place in chambers, and who have yet to decide upon a full-blown career as a solicitor.[47]

EXCEPTED WORK

Barristers in independent practice may not undertake work involving the receipt or holding of clients' money, or the management, administration or general conduct of a lay client's affairs or of litigation.[48]

There are several reasons for this important rule. Barristers have no training in accounts and no rules or insurance concerned with the handling and conduct of financial transactions. Since a barrister's principal occupation is the conduct of cases in court, it is necessary to insulate a barrister from the

---

[45] Paragraph 104 of the Code of Conduct gives the Bar Council the power to waive the duty imposed by the Code in such circumstances and to such an extent as it may think fit, either conditionally or unconditionally. This function has been delegated to the Professional Conduct Committee. Requirements imposed by the Joint Regulations may be waived by the Joint Regulations Committee which is a committee set up jointly by the Bar Council and the Council of the Inns of Court.

[46] Paragraph 212 of the Code of Conduct. This requires a non-practising barrister, when supplying legal services to the public, to describe himself or herself as 'not practising'.

[47] For disciplinary purposes, such non-practising barristers come under the aegis of the Bar's disciplinary process. The Law Society, which technically also has jurisdiction, since non-practising barristers are employed in a solicitors' office as clerks, refers any complaint to the Bar Council, if such arises.

[48] Paragraph 901 of the Code of Conduct. A barrister may only accept instructions to undertake legal services and, by definition, excepted work is not within the ambit of such services.

distracting and time-consuming work involved in corresponding with third parties and in running the affairs of others. Moreover, barristers lack the facilities to enable them to be involved in administration. The overheads of barristers are very low since they employ in chambers a small number of clerks and office staff in relation to the number of principals. This enables them to retain a competitive edge in cost terms over solicitor advocates. However, the obverse of this is a barrister's lack of resources to do much office work. It is also thought that detailed involvement in the day to day activities of a lay client could compromise the independence and professional integrity required of one whose principal occupation is as a professional advocate.

The rule is more relaxed for employed barristers. An employed barrister, whilst acting in the course of his or her employment, may undertake for an employer any excepted work that does not involve the receipt or handling of the money of third parties and may provide conveyancing services so long as he or she has the requisite training and experience required by the Conveyancing by Employed Barristers Rules[49] which also preclude the handling of clients' money.

There are not many statutory restrictions on non-lawyers undertaking legal work in England. These are in the form of making certain documents, ones that can only be prepared for reward by a solicitor.[50] These restrictions do not apply to barristers and, in consequence, a barrister may draw up a conveyance or administer oaths.[51] These statutory rights are, therefore, circumscribed by the rules precluding the undertaking of excepted work.

INTERNATIONAL PRACTICE

The structure of the profession cannot be considered without also considering international practising rules. These provide for the circumstances and rules whereby English barristers practise abroad or undertake foreign work under the auspices of the Bar's Code of Conduct and also for the circumstances and rules whereby foreign lawyers, particularly from the EC, might qualify as English barristers or work alongside them.

English barristers are able to practise as such in the EC. This is because a barrister in independent practice is defined as one who holds himself or herself out as being willing to render legal services in England and Wales or in relation to the courts of the EC.[52] However, that right is only of practical

---

[49] Paragraphs 402.1(b) and 405 and Annexe G of the Code of Conduct. A register of employed barristers permitted to undertake conveyancing work is maintained by the Bar Council.

[50] Section 22 of the Solicitors Act 1974 makes it an offence for an unqualified person to draw or prepare certain documents for reward. Thus, conveyances, agreements under seal and probate documents must be prepared by a solicitor.

[51] See section 22 of the Solicitors Act 1974 and sections 36 and 113 of the CLSA.

[52] Paragraph 208 of the Code of Conduct.

utility if a barrister may also practise abroad in conditions governed by local practising arrangements and accept instructions in England from foreigners who are not solicitors. Thus, since 1961, an English barrister has been able to practise abroad. The rules are now set out in the Overseas Practice Rules.[53] These rules allow a barrister, subject to the relevant local law and local rules of professional conduct, to practise abroad and to enter into any association, including partnership, with a lawyer for the purpose of sharing any offices or services outside the United Kingdom. They also allow a barrister to accept instructions from a foreign lawyer or a foreign lay client, so long as these instructions do not relate to domestic litigation. If a barrister is also qualified as a foreign lawyer and is practising as such, he or she may, even when practising in England, practise in such a way as that barrister usually and properly conducts his or her foreign practice.[54]

A non-EC national can only practise in England if he or she has been called to the Bar. The Joint Regulations provide that Northern Ireland barristers, Scottish advocates, Hong Kong barristers and Common Law practitioners may be called to the Bar without undertaking the Vocational Course. In the case of Hong Kong and Common Law practitioners, the applicant must show that there are reasonable grounds to expect, upon call, that he or she will be able to practise at the English Bar. In all cases, the Joint Regulations Committee, the appropriate committee dealing with overseas applicants, can require part or all of the aptitude test to be passed. Usually, at least part of the usual period of pupillage will need to be completed, unless an exemption is granted.

For EC nationals a different regime, dictated by two directives, is applicable. These must be considered along with a draft directive that was being finalised by the European Commission in 1995. The two directives in force comprise the Services Directive[55] and the Diplomas Directive.[56] The draft directive, published by the Commission in late 1994, concerns the right of establishment for lawyers.[57]

---

[53] Annexe F of the Code of Conduct. The first edition of these rules was produced in 1973. The initial relaxation allowing overseas practice without instructions from an English solicitor followed a report of the International Committee of the Bar Council under the chairmanship of Michael Kerr, QC, subsequently Kerr LJ. This report expressed a preference for the abolition of the rule precluding partnerships but only pressed for the adoption of rules to allow professional association with foreign lawyers outside the United Kingdom.

[54] The Foreign Lawyers (Chambers) Rules, Annexe K of the Code of Conduct. Paragraph 2(c) provides that a foreign lawyer, namely a person qualified to practise and practising as such, is subject to the same rules of practice as govern a barrister in independent practice except insofar as any such rules conflict with the ordinary or usual way in which the foreign lawyer conducts himself or his practice.   [55] Directive 77/249 EEC ('The Lawyers' Services Directive').

[56] Directive 89/48 EEC ('The Mutual Recognition of Qualifications Directive').

[57] 6293/95 (COM(94)572). The House of Lords Select Committee on the European Communities has produced a detailed report (Session 1994-95, 14th Report, HL paper 82) on this draft which includes an invaluable summary of current EC law concerned with the rights of qualified lawyers to practice law in the EC.

The effect of the Services Directive is that an EC lawyer may advise on the law of his or her home country, on that of the host country or on international and community law.[58] When appearing before the courts of the host country, the EC lawyer may be required to appear in conjunction with a locally qualified lawyer.[59] An English barrister appeared with an eminent Greek lawyer before the Supreme Court of Greece in 1994.[60] A Dutch advocate has appeared with an English barrister before Mr Justice Millett when sitting in the Chancery Division and there have been other appearances by EC lawyers in the English courts, even in the House of Lords.[61]

The Code of Conduct helps to give effect to the requirements of the Services Directive by virtue of the Foreign Lawyers (Chambers) Rules.[62] These permit any foreign qualified lawyer to have his name shown at chambers and to use those chambers for professional purposes. Such a lawyer is then subject to the same rules of practice as govern a barrister in independent practice,[63] although he or she cannot hold himself or herself out as an English barrister and acquires no rights of audience unless and until the provisions for temporary or permanent membership of the Bar have been operated. Interestingly, the Bar Council would be able to discipline such a lawyer for any infringement of the provisions of the Foreign Lawyers (Chambers) Rules, even if that lawyer has not been called to the Bar.

The intention of the Recognition Directive, which is not confined to lawyers, is to allow for a general system for the recognition of higher education diplomas awarded on completion of professional education and training whose length is at least three years' duration. This is achieved by either an aptitude test or a period of adaptation. The United Kingdom, in the case of lawyers, has, like all member states except Denmark, opted for the aptitude test. The Bar Council provides an aptitude test with a maximum length of 11 hours but the Joint Regulations Committee, in conformity with the Directive's requirement that a suitable exemption should be provided for those with appropriate qualifications, frequently relaxes part of the test. In the four years up to April 1995 that the aptitude test has been offered, there have been 36 applicants of which 19 have been granted a full exemption from the test and the majority of the rest of which have been granted a partial

[58] There is a considerable jurisprudence that has been developed by the European Court on the meaning and effect of the Services Directive. This is conveniently gathered in Appendix 5, pages 41–4, of the House of Lords Report.

[59] Regulations 38-40 of the Consolidated Regulations provide for temporary membership of the Bar for this purpose. No express requirement has been imposed requiring an EC lawyer to lead or be led by an English barrister when appearing in an English court.

[60] The Arios Pagos. The court derives its title from the Areopagos, a rock opposite the Acropolis where Athenian justice was dispensed in the 5th century BC. See House of Lords Report at page 26 of the Minutes of Evidence.

[61] House of Lords Report at page 22 of the Minutes of Evidence.

[62] Annexe K of the Code of Conduct.

[63] See footnote 54 *infra* for a limited inroad into this requirement.

exemption. Once the migrant has either passed or been exempted from the test, he or she becomes a qualified barrister, is called to the Bar and may practise as a barrister either in England or in both relevant jurisdictions. In this latter case, the migrant must comply with the Dual Qualification and Foreign Lawyers (Chambers) Rules.[64]

It is to be envisaged that, before long, an Establishment for Lawyers Directive will be in force. The object of this is to allow a lawyer to establish himself or herself in a member state practising under home-country professional title. The period for which this right may be exercised had not, in 1995, been settled. The relevant proposals were controversial since the period was proposed to be limited to one of five years. The Bar Council would need to amend the Code of Conduct to give full effect to the provisions of a directive in the proposed form.

It is also necessary to consider the Code of Conduct for lawyers in the European Community which was finalised by the CCBE in September 1988 and was adopted in May 1989.[65] English barristers are required to comply with this Code so far as it is applicable.[66] The Code consists of five sections that are concerned with general principles, with the relations of a lawyer with clients and the courts and with relations between lawyers. The relevant requirements of this Code are all found, albeit in different language, in the Code of Conduct. Amongst other matters that are prohibited is the making by a lawyer of a 'pactum per quota litis'. This is an agreement between a lawyer and his or her client by virtue of which the client undertakes to pay the lawyer a share of the result of the case. Excluded from this definition is a fee charged in proportion to the value of the matter handled by the lawyer. Fee sharing with non-lawyers is, however, also precluded.[67] The considerable benefit of the Code is that it facilitates the operation and enforcement of the two directives and would also facilitate implementation of the proposed Establishment for Lawyers Directive.

THE CODE OF CONDUCT

The Code of Conduct, is set out in nine parts. The key parts are numbered III, 'Barristers In Independent Practice'; V, 'Briefs And Instructions To Practising Barristers' and VI, 'Conduct Of Work By Practising Barristers'. These are introduced by Part I, 'Preliminary' and Part II, 'Fundamental Principles'. The

---

[64] Annexes I and K of the Code of Conduct

[65] The Council of the Bars and Law Societies of the European Community.

[66] Paragraph 802.1(c) of the Code of Conduct. The Code is set out in Annexe L of the Code of Conduct.

[67] If barristers are allowed to join multi-disciplinary partnerships and share fees and profits, the Bar Council would need to seek an exemption from this provision for English barristers.

Code applies equally to employed barristers, with appropriate amendments to reflect their more limited role as advocates and their employed status. Only the provisions concerned with barristers in independent practice will be considered.

The general purpose of the Code is defined in Part I, as being to preserve and enhance the strength and competitiveness of the Bar by requiring barristers to be completely independent in conduct and professional standing, acting as both sole practitioners and as consultants and to acknowledge a public obligation to act for any client, whether or not legally aided, in cases within that barrister's field of practice. These purposes are underscored by the defined fundamental principles which include, amongst the most important, the definition of a barrister's overriding duty to the court to ensure the proper and efficient administration of justice and the principle that the court is not to be knowingly or recklessly misled. This duty, surprisingly, does not, apparently, preclude a dishonest intention to mislead the court. Evidence that a court was actually misled is required.[68] In addition, a barrister must promote and protect fearlessly, by all proper and lawful means, the lay client's best interests, must act towards the lay client and the professional client at all times in good faith and must never allow his or her absolute independence, integrity and freedom from external pressure to be compromised. The essential requisites of practice as a barrister, already described, are also defined in this introductory part of the Code.

The status of the Code of Conduct is, with certain exceptions with regard to some of its provisions, not part of the general law of England. The exceptions include, by way of example, the rule that a barrister should not mislead the court and should cite all available relevant authority even if adverse to that barrister's lay client's case. Since at least 1850,[69] the power to change the Bar's rules of conduct has lain with the authority recognised by the Bar as having that power. Subject only to the control of the visitors, namely the judges of the High Court acting as visitors to the Inns of Court when hearing appeals by barristers from findings and decisions of disciplinary tribunals. Visitors may decline to enforce any rule and also, some believe, have the power to enforce a rule the Bar has declined to adopt.[70] The CLSA does not alter this structure, it merely adds, as an essential condition which must be fulfilled before any amendment takes effect, the requirement that that amendment should be approved under the approval machinery of the Act.

---

[68] See *Visitors to Inns of Court, ex.parte Calder* [1994] 1 QB 1 at pages 67–8 per Staughton L.J.

[69] The judgment of Lord Campbell CJ in *Doe d. Bennett v. Hale and Davis* (1850) 15 QB 171 which includes this authoritative pronouncement: 'Barristers are at liberty, under the control of the courts, to lay down conditions upon which, for the public good, their services are to be obtained'.

[70] A helpful analysis and account of the history of the status of the Code of Conduct is set out in Staughton LJ's judgment in *Calder's* case at pages 63–5. The suggestion that the visitors can add to the Code of Conduct is found at page 65.

ACCEPTANCE OF BRIEFS AND INSTRUCTIONS

The core of the Code of Conduct divides a barrister's obligations into those associated with the acceptance of briefs and instructions[71] and those associated with carrying out the work required by a brief of instructions. This division is as old as practice at the Bar, being the distinction between the retainer and the instructions given to the barrister retained. The essence of professional practice from earliest times was the retainer, being the formality associated with the giving of instructions and their acceptance. Historically, the retainer of any professional, or any person exercising a common calling, whether a barrister, surgeon, innkeeper or common carrier, carried with it defined benefits and obligations. Professionals could not be sued in contract but, in return, had a limited choice as to whether or not to act. A refusal of a retainer could only occur on recognised grounds such as a prior professional commitment, a professional conflict of interest or the lack of the appropriate skill or calling. In consequence, a barrister had to exercise particular care in considering whether or not to act.[72] Although a barrister's clerk undertook much of the work involved in accepting or refusing instructions, a barrister could not, and cannot nowadays, delegate any responsibility in these matters.

Traditionally, a brief or instructions have always been sent to a barrister with a briefing document known as 'the brief' or 'the instructions' which all the other documents accompany. The documents sent to a barrister are usually tied up with tape. Pink tape indicates a privately instructed case whilst a government department, a local authority or the CPS all use white tape. The difference is explained purely by the fact that government departments economised during the Gladstone era by eliminating dye from their vast consumption of tape.

The most important situations requiring the refusal of a brief or instructions, whether initially or once they have been accepted, will now be dealt with.[73]

1. Experience

A barrister must decide whether or not he or she has sufficient experience or competence to handle the matter in question. This is an onerous requirement since it requires an element of self-assessment. The existence of this rule belies

---

[71] Traditionally, 'brief' was the word given to instructions requiring an appearance in court. The text adopts the modern convention of referring to a brief when advocacy is referred to and to instructions when any other work is referred to.

[72] The cab-rank rule is, in part, derived from the historic professional status of barristers. Solicitors emerged too late in the development of the common law as a separate profession to be subject to the rules associated with those exercising a profession.

[73] Paragraph 501 of the Code of Conduct defines most of these situations.

the conventional wisdom that a newly-called barrister can act in a murder trial. In practice, all barristers will, on occasion, refer work of a specialist kind outside his or her field of practice and will advise that a more experienced barrister should either act with, or in substitution for, the barrister in question.

2. *Professional Commitment*

A brief must be refused if the barrister's other professional commitments preclude adequate time and opportunity to prepare the brief. This should be distinguished from inadequate time or opportunity resulting from the late delivery of the brief. As the Court of Appeal made clear in the wasted costs order case of *Ridehalgh v. Horsfield*,[74] a barrister is required by the cab-rank rule not to let a lay client down. If the preparation time allowed to a barrister by a solicitor is inadequate, a barrister must soldier on and do the best for the client that the circumstances allow. This has given rise to difficulties where a barrister unsuccessfully applies for an adjournment because he or she cannot fairly present a defendant's best case because of excessively late delivery of the brief. Can and should a barrister then advise the lay client to sack him or her and, unrepresented, apply for an adjournment, since a judge is more likely to grant one to an unrepresented defendant? The answer is that a barrister clearly should do so if, in that barrister's professional judgment, a defendant's best interest is served by such a course. However, in order not to leave the court to decide the initial application on an erroneous basis, the barrister ought to make it clear to the judge that he or she will feel obliged to advise the defendant that the client's interests will be best served by sacking the barrister if the application is refused and then re-applying for an adjournment in person. If the trial has started, however, a barrister may only withdraw if the judge accedes to an application to withdraw and, if this is refused, the barrister must continue to act unless relations between the barrister and his or her client have broken down or if continuing to act would cause the barrister to mislead the court.

3. *Conflict*

A conflict can often arise. A barrister may already be aware of a relevant professional confidence as a result of acting for an opposing party in a previous matter, or because he or she has already been instructed in the current matter by an opposing party. A barrister may only present the case that he or she is instructed to present and may not supplement that case from other sources, so that if, for instance, a barrister, having acted for an opposing party previously, is aware of features of that party's case which are both material and are

---

[74] [1994] Ch 206 at pages 267–70.

unlikely to be capable of being made known in any other way, that barrister would be professionally embarrassed in cross-examining representatives of the opposing party. However, the mere fact that a barrister has acted for an opposing party in the past does not create a professional embarrassment although many lay clients mistakenly think that it does. Under retainer rules, now abolished, it was possible for a lay client to 'generally retain' a barrister. This precluded the barrister from accepting instructions from an opposing party. Any instructions within the subject matter of the retainer from the retaining client first had to be offered to the retained barrister. The fee required for such an arrangement was frequently large and the abolition of the general retainer was regarded as a much needed reform of an unacceptable restrictive practice.

A second type of conflict arises when a barrister is representing, or may represent, two or more parties or individuals whose interests may conflict. Most obviously, a conflict of interest arises when two defendants in a criminal trial will be likely to blame each other. However, a conflict will arise in many other circumstances. For example, one will arise if a barrister might learn of the potential evidence of one witness who might be called by another defendant and who might weaken the defence of that barrister's lay client. Since most defences are conducted on legal aid, there is a growing pressure on a barrister to accept instructions for more than one defendant in a criminal trial for reasons of economy. The generally accepted rule of practice is, however, that it is not normally possible to represent more than one defendant.

4. Two Counsel

The role of Queen's Counsel has led to significant changes to the Code of Conduct in recent years. Until 1976, a Queen's Counsel could not appear in court or advise without a junior counsel and could not draft pleadings at all. Hence the popular description of a Queen's Counsel has always been 'a leader' or 'a silk'. The latter term refers to the silk gown traditionally worn in court in comparison to a junior barrister's gown which is made of 'stuff' or woven material. Nowadays, a Queen's Counsel can do anything, including drafting documents and pleadings, either on his or her own or with a junior. However, particularly, but not exclusively, in legal aid cases, it became apparent that, on occasion, two counsel were being instructed when only one was required. This led to Paragraph 503A of the Code of Conduct being introduced in 1991. The rule it provides for is in three parts. Firstly, it requires a barrister to consider whether the interests of the client would be best served by instructing or continuing to instruct that particular barrister. Secondly, when more than one barrister is instructed, each barrister must consider whether it is in the best interests of the client for both or either of them to be instructed. Thirdly, it requires a barrister to advise the client immediately it becomes clear to the barrister that the best interests of the client are no longer best served by that barrister being, or continuing to be, instructed. Once a client is advised of this, it is for the client to decide whether or not to continue to instruct that particular barrister.

These rules are of particular importance in criminal legal aid cases. Many cases, particularly pleas in mitigation, were continuing to have two barristers involved when one, often the junior, could undertake the brief satisfactorily. The Legal Aid regulations now provide a detailed code identifying the situations in which only a Queen's Counsel or one counsel or a counsel without a solicitor will be provided under a legal aid order.[75] Thus, no order for a Queen's Counsel is to be made where there is a reasonable certainty that the indictment will be disposed of by a guilty plea or there are no special circumstances requiring the provision of the services of more than one counsel.[76]

5. *Giving Evidence*

If there is reason to believe that a barrister is likely to be a witness, that barrister must refuse a brief or instructions or, if this situation subsequently occurs, must withdraw. Guidelines have been provided by the Court of Appeal as to the giving of evidence by a barrister[77] in a case in which junior counsel had been called on behalf of his client to rebut a suggestion that the client had only recently invented his defence. The court stressed that a barrister should only give evidence if this was unavoidable. If this happened, the barrister had to withdraw from the case. There is a duty on a barrister to anticipate the circumstances in which such a situation might arise and an experienced barrister ought to be able to envisage even the possibility of this occurring and should then refuse the brief. If the need actually arises during the trial, however, paragraph 504(a) of the Code of Conduct provides that a barrister should only withdraw if he or she can do so without jeopardising the lay client's interests. In consequence, if a barrister gives evidence and there is no other barrister also representing the defendant, an adjournment will invariably arise.

6. *Withdrawal From A Case*

The Code of Conduct, in paragraph 504, contains detailed provisions defining the circumstances in which a barrister may withdraw from a case and return the brief. These include cases where a conflict or a significant risk of a conflict

---

[75] The Legal Aid in Criminal and Care Proceedings (General) Regulations 1989, regulations 45–9.   [76] Ibid regulation 48(6)(a).
[77] *R. v. Jacquith and Emade* [1989] Crim LR 508 and 563.

between the interests of any one or more of a barrister's clients or a risk of a breach of confidence has arisen and all relevant clients do not consent to the barrister continuing to act. The Code of Conduct also requires a barrister to withdraw where the client refuses to authorise him to make a disclosure to the court which his or her duty to the court requires or if he or she becomes aware of the existence of a document which should have been disclosed and which the client fails forthwith to disclose. These rules give rise to the practice that a barrister must follow when defending a client in a criminal case who tells the barrister that he or she is guilty. Thereafter, a barrister can only act if he or she does no more than test the evidence of the prosecution for accuracy and veracity. The barrister cannot act further, and must seek leave to withdraw from the case, if the client wishes to give evidence contrary to the admission previously made to the barrister or to have that barrister pursue a line of questioning inconsistent with that admission.[78]

In legal aid cases, the Bar Council, in 1994, agreed guidelines with the Legal Aid Board.[79] These guidelines are intended to assist barristers to comply with the provisions of the Legal Aid Act 1988 when advising the Legal Aid Board on the merits on behalf of an applicant for civil legal aid or when acting on an assisted person's behalf. Although they are essentially statements of good practice, they may be taken into account when a wasted costs order is being considered against a barrister and they should be read in conjunction with the Code of Conduct.[80]

These guidelines supplement the provisions of the Code of Conduct requiring a barrister to withdraw if it becomes apparent that legal aid has been wrongly obtained or if an abuse of the legal aid fund has become apparent and it is impracticable for the relevant area committee to meet in time to prevent that abuse.[81]

Overriding these duties is the duty on a barrister to withdraw when his or her instructions have themselves been withdrawn by the client. However, once a criminal trial has started, the leave of the court is required.[82] No such leave is required in a civil case. Leave should normally be given if a barrister would be 'forensically embarrassed' by continuing and the defendant should normally be allowed to give his or her reasons to the judge for requesting to be allowed to represent himself or herself.[83]

---

[78] These rules of conduct, which are often misunderstood by the public, are amongst the most difficult to apply.
[79] Reprinted in the Legal Aid Handbook produced annually by Sweet & Maxwell with the approval of the Legal Aid Board.
[80] Particularly paragraphs 203(b), 504(c) and (d) and 802.1(d).
[81] Paragraphs 504(c) and (d) of the Code of Conduct.
[82] *R. v. Lyons* (1968) Cr App R 104.   [83] *Ibid.*

CONDUCT OF A BRIEF OR INSTRUCTIONS

The Code of Conduct defines in some detail what a barrister must do when undertaking a brief or instructions. In conformity with a barrister's overriding duty to the lay client, a barrister must advise that client as soon as he or she becomes aware of a conflict of interest between the lay client and the professional client, including advising, if necessary, that it would be in the lay client's interest to instruct another solicitor. If that occurs, the barrister must, if freshly instructed, continue to act after the change unless that barrister is personally subject to a professional conflict as well. A regularly occurring situation, less common now that standards have risen, is where an action is dismissed for want of prosecution. Clearly, in such a case, the lay client has a potential claim for professional negligence against his or her solicitor which the barrister should ensure that the lay client is aware of.

Outside court, the Code of Conduct deals with two specific situations, drafting pleadings and contact with witnesses. Drafting requirements include: the requirement that a practising barrister must not devise facts which will assist in advancing the lay client's case; that a document drafted by a barrister should not contain any statement of fact or contention unsupported by the lay client, or the barrister's instructions or a contention that the barrister does not consider to be properly arguable; and that no allegation of fraud should be pleaded unless there are clear instructions to make such an allegation and the barrister has credible material in the instructions which, as it stands, establishes a *prima facie* case of fraud.[84]

Contact with witnesses is subject to different rules depending upon whether the case is a civil or a criminal one. Originally, a barrister was not allowed to have any contact with a witness, except the lay client, before that witness entered the witness box. The potential evidence of a witness is usually obtained by interview, conducted by the litigant's solicitor or solicitor's representative and set out in narrative form in a document called a 'proof of evidence'. This document is included with the barrister's brief and forms the basis of examination in chief, conducted by non-leading questions. Frequently, a witness does not 'come up to proof' and a barrister's skill includes the ability to bring the witness up to proof without, if possible, the use of either leading questions or undue repetition.

The rule prohibiting contact with a potential witness has twin origins. It was a means of seeking to avoid the coaching of witnesses and it helped to preserve the referral nature of a barrister's work with its associated need to concentrate on the presentation of a case whilst leaving the preparatory details to the solicitor. A further practical advantage of the rule arises from the fact that barristers have few administrative and office resources and the detailed

[84] Paragraph 606 of the Code of Conduct.

preparation of evidence requires both. Hence, it is in the client's best interests to leave the preparatory work to a solicitor.

A significant development in civil procedure has recently led to an erosion of the rule in civil cases. This was the introduction, in the 1980s, of the use of witness statements as the principal means of adducing evidence in chief,[85] leading to a change to the Code of Conduct in 1990. As a result, a barrister, in the presence of a solicitor, may discuss the case with a potential witness in a civil case if the barrister considers that the interests of the lay client require it and after that barrister has been supplied with a proper proof of evidence of that potential witness. The purpose of the rule is to allow the barrister to have an import in the contents of a witness statement or an expert's report. However, the evidence itself must be that of the witness. Thus, a witness who is being interviewed may not be placed under pressure to provide other than a truthful account of his or her evidence nor may that witness be rehearsed, practised or coached in relation to his or her evidence or in the way in which he or she should give it. It is particularly important that an expert's report is, in its content, the product of the expert. The barrister's role is to advise upon the topics it should cover and the format in which it should be presented.[86]

In criminal cases, a barrister may only interview a witness, other than his client or an expert, in the exceptional circumstances that occur when a barrister is left at court with no proof, no instructing solicitor's representative and no other practical means of ascertaining what the potential witness will say.[87]

There is an undoubted anomaly between the rules governing contact with witnesses by barrister and solicitor advocates, particularly in criminal cases. The latter may interview all witnesses subject to rules prohibiting coaching. Now that solicitors have the ability to acquire rights of audience in all courts, there will be growing pressure on the Bar to relax its rules limiting contact with witnesses. Pressure for change is already evident. Organisations concerned with victims of crime have frequently made clear their objection to rules which forbid even formal contact or an introductory conversation with prosecuting counsel by the victim of a crime, particularly in a rape or child abuse case. The Royal Commission on Criminal Justice regarded the Bar's rules as outmoded and likely to impede both the proper preparation of cases and good human and working relations with witnesses. The report noted that

---

[85] The procedure is set out in Order 38 Rule 2A of the Rules of the Supreme Court. The relevant conduct is set out in paragraphs 607.1–607.3 of the Code of Conduct.

[86] In recent years, courts have frequently stressed that an expert witness owes a duty of impartiality to the court and that any report that an expert presents to the court should not be drafted or influenced by the lawyers of the party instructing and calling that expert as a witness. See, in particular, *Whitehouse v. Jordan* [1981] 1 WLR 246 HL, per Lord Wilberforce at page 256. Lord Woolf's report, Access to Justice (June 1995) recommends that codes of practice providing guidance as to the practice in relation to experts should be drawn up by, amongst other bodies, the Bar Council.   [87] Paragraph 609(b) of the Code of Conduct.

other common law jurisdictions have no such rule and recommended that they should be abolished.[88]

In 1995, the Bar Council resolved in principle to relax its rules in criminal cases to allow formal contact between a barrister and potential witnesses. However, so far, the Bar Council has not sought to implement the wider proposals of the Royal Commission. It is likely that there will be a move in the near future to seek to persuade the two branches of the legal profession to agree upon a common code of conduct for advocates and, no doubt, such a code would deal with the amount of contact that an advocate should be allowed to have with a potential witness.

CONDUCT AT COURT

Usually, a barrister only advises or acts with a representative of his professional client present. This requirement arises from the rule that, ordinarily, a barrister may only be instructed by a solicitor or other professional and, when discussing a case with a witness in a civil case, must do so in the presence of his or her professional client. The requirement is, therefore, a direct corollary of the referral status of a barrister and of the separation of functions between the presentation and preparation of a case. Recently, the rule has been relaxed, as already noted, in criminal legal aid cases and when no representative of the professional client has arrived at court. A more general relaxation is now provided for in paragraph 608 of the Code of Conduct. This allows a barrister to agree to dispense with the attendance at court of the professional client at any hearing in a Magistrates' court or a County Court or in any other court, where the barrister has been supplied with any necessary proofs of evidence. A pre-condition of such a relaxation is that the interests of both the lay client and justice will not thereby be prejudiced. The relaxation was motivated by a wish to reduce costs so far as possible in the interests of the lay client.

The conduct of the trial is regulated by paragraph 610 of the Code of Conduct. This paragraph enshrines eight cardinal rules of conduct. The rules provide, in effect, a code of practice for court work. They are the adjunct of the historic immunity from negligence actions enjoyed by barristers in relation to court work.[89] This immunity has now been extended by section 62 of the CLSA to cover all advocates. The immunity does not cover written work, advisory work or to drafting. However, negligence in court can give rise to a

---

[88] Report of the Royal Commission on Criminal Justice (1993), page 80 and Recommendation 107.

[89] *Rondel v. Worsely* [1969] 1 AC 191 and *Saif Ali v. Sydney Mitchell and Co* [1980] AC 198, both decisions of the House of Lords.

wasted costs order against the barrister in question.[90] The justification for the immunity is threefold. Firstly, the rule precludes the re-litigation of actions by disgruntled litigants. Secondly, it ensures that all litigation is conducted fearlessly and without recourse to the defensive action that professionals, such as members of the medical profession, are thought to be prone to and thirdly, it recognises that most errors made in court are made following necessarily instantaneous decisions which, being taken in the heat of the moment, can be no more than errors of judgment.

It is worth considering each rule of conduct separately.[91]

1. A barrister is personally responsible for the conduct and presentation of his case and must exercise personal judgment upon the substance and purpose of statements made and questions asked.

This rule is a direct corollary of the fact that a barrister is a sole practitioner who may not form a professional association with any other barrister. In cases in which two or more barristers are instructed, each is subject to this rule separately and individually. It is a rule of practice that only one barrister may question any one witness although a different barrister may re-examine a witness from the barrister who examined that witness in chief.[92] The examining barrister alone has professional responsibility for the questions that are asked. This rule also explains the practice whereby any pleading or written submission settled by a barrister must be signed by that barrister. This ensures that the document contains the 'hallmark' of the barrister who has taken professional responsibility for it.

2. A barrister must not, unless invited to do so by the court, or when appearing before a tribunal where it is his duty to do so, assert a personal opinion of the facts or the law.

This rule has two purposes. Firstly, it is intended to maintain the distinction between the functions of the judge or jury who must decide the case from the functions of the barrister who must, and must only, present it. Secondly, it is intended to ensure that a barrister retains objectivity and independence and

---

[90] Sections 4, 111 and 112 of the CLSA. These sections allow an order to be made against a barrister in relation to costs incurred as a result of any improper, unreasonable or negligent act of the barrister in question. Until the CLSA came into force, a barrister could not be made personally liable in costs unlike a solicitor who was always susceptible to personal liability. The difference was that, for historical reasons, a solicitor, but not a barrister was, and still is, an 'officer of the court'.

[91] Paragraph 610 of the Code of Conduct. Paragraphs 610 (a)-(h) are set out verbatim before the commentary in sections 1–8 of the text.

[92] Courts have rules of practice governing the situations in which more than one advocate per party may address them. In the House of Lords, one or two may do so. In the Court of Appeal, one or two may do so in final appeals but, in interlocutory appeals, a second advocate may only 'follow' with leave. Usually, at first instance, one may do so. Until recently, the Chancery Division had, uniquely, a rule that even if the junior examined in chief, the leader had to re-examine.

concentrates on the presentation of a client's case in the most effective way possible. The reference in this rule to tribunals where it is the duty of a barrister to assert a personal opinion is principally a reference to Parliament and, in particular, to the presentation by a barrister of a party's case during the consideration of a private bill. It is the rule and custom of Parliament that all appearances before a parliamentary committee in relation to a private bill are appearances in which the person appearing, even if an advocate, is giving evidence to the committee. It follows that barristers appearing in a private bill presentation need a relaxation of the relevant rule of conduct prohibiting the assertion of opinion.

The technique usually adopted by a barrister in complying with the rule is to preface any legal argument with a phrase such as 'in my submission'. This is a forensic device that attempts to distinguish between the presentation of a case and the expression of personal opinion.

3. A barrister must ensure that the court is informed of all relevant decisions and legislative provisions of which he is aware whether the effect is favourable or unfavourable towards the contention for which he argues and must bring any procedural irregularity to the attention of the court during the hearing and not reserve such matter to be raised on appeal.

This rule enshrines the rule of law requiring all legislative provisions and adverse cases to be cited which has often been stressed by courts at all levels up to the House of Lords. In 1921, the Lord Chancellor, Lord Birkenhead, said this in relation to a barrister's duty in relation to the citation of relevant material to an appeal committee of the House of Lords:

It is not, of course, in cases of complication possible for their Lordships to be aware of all the authorities, statutory or otherwise, which may be relevant to the issues which in the particular case require decision. Their Lordships are therefore very much in the hands of counsel, and those who instruct counsel, in these matters, and this House expects, and indeed insists, that authorities which bear one way or the other upon matters under debate shall be brought to the attention of their Lordships by those who are aware of those authorities. This observation is quite irrespective of whether or not the particular authority assists the party which is so aware of it. It is an obligation of confidence between their Lordships and all those who assist in the debates in this House in the capacity of counsel.[93]

This requirement is placed on a barrister in whatever court or tribunal he or she is acting including arbitrations and inquiries. So far as the requirement concerning procedural irregularities is concerned, this is also a rule of law. An appeal court will usually decline to consider an alleged procedural irregularity unless

---

[93] *Glebe Sugar Refining Company Ltd* v. *The Trustees of the Port and Harbour of Greenoch* [1921] Scots Reports 72. The relevant provision initially not cited was section 23 of the Harbours, Docks and Piers Clauses Act, 1847.

it was raised with the relevant lower court. This rule is grounded in public policy, it being desirable to limit procedural argument and the deciding of litigation by reference to formalities and technicalities. The consequence is that English advocates, unlike their American counterparts, cannot seek 'to build the record' during a trial so as to try to provide the greatest possible scope for appealing.

In criminal cases, the Court of Appeal has frequently stressed the duty of a barrister to draw to the attention of the judge any errors in the summing up so that these can be corrected, to be aware of the commencement date of recent relevant legislation particularly in the sentencing field, to identify to the judge relevant sentencing powers and to be ready and able to draw to the judge's attention any sentencing beyond the powers of the judge. This last duty was succinctly stated by Lawton LJ as follows:

We judge that counsel as a matter of professional duty to the court, and in the case of defending counsel to their client, should always before starting a criminal case satisfy themselves as to what the maximum sentence is.[94]

4. A barrister must not adduce evidence obtained otherwise than from or through his professional client or devise facts which will assist in advancing his lay client's case.

This rule is obvious but is not appreciated by many laymen who regard barristers as the creators of a case and not merely its presenters. This narrower role of a barrister explains various rules of practice adopted by courts. Thus, once a witness starts giving evidence, no one may discuss the case or that witness's evidence with the witness until his or her evidence has been concluded. In a criminal trial, all witnesses are kept outside court and are not allowed to hear any of the evidence until the evidence of that particular witness has been concluded. American advocates are not so circumscribed and will usually coach witnesses before their evidence is given and discuss the evidence with them as it proceeds. Indeed, it is not unknown for an American advocate to discuss with a potentially favourable witness the line in cross-examination to be pursued whilst that witness is giving evidence in chief, having been called by an opposing party.

5. A barrister must not make statements or ask questions which are merely scandalous or intended or calculated only to vilify, insult or annoy either a witness or some other person.

This rule is particularly important when a barrister is conducting a cross-examination. This exercise, as has been often stressed, is not the same as examination crossly. Another purpose of the rule is to prevent a barrister from being the mouthpiece of the client for public relations purposes, an important

[94] *R.* v. *Clarke (R.W.W.)* 59 Cr App R 298 at 301.

consideration given that most trials are conducted in public and many are reported. The function of cross-examination is to test and probe the evidence of a witness. Rarely will it extend to eliciting from a witness an admission that earlier testimony of that witness was false and, thus, it is not permissible to seek to obtain admissions by annoying or bullying the witness.

6. A barrister must, if possible, avoid the naming in open court of third parties whose character would thereby be impugned.

This rule is of particular importance when a barrister is making a plea in mitigation in a criminal case. Obviously, one way of minimising blame is to seek to transfer it to another. However, the interests of the client will often require such a course to be taken. A barrister should not blame another in open court without being satisfied that such a course complies with the clear instructions of his or her client and should, if possible, inform the prosecution in advance of the line intended to be deployed in a plea in mitigation. This allows the prosecution to fulfil its obligation of drawing to the attention of the defence any assertion of a material fact it believes to be untrue and, if necessary, seeking and preparing for a *Newton* hearing,[95] being one that is conducted by the judge before sentence to determine the basis upon which sentence will be passed where the material facts needed to found that sentence are in dispute.

7. A barrister must not by assertion in a speech impugn a witness whom he has had an opportunity to cross-examine unless, in cross-examination, he has given the witness an opportunity to answer the allegation.

This is the extent to which the rule of procedure that a party should put its case to an opposing party is enshrined in the Code of Conduct. There is however, a wider aspect of this rule of procedure. Fairness requires that a party should be able, directly or through a relevant witness, to answer and comment upon any case or version of material facts which conflicts with that party's own case or evidence. Evidence from one party which conflicts with evidence from another is inherently less reliable if it has not been made available in a way that allows the other party to give evidence upon this rival version. However, if this occurs, the evidence is still admissible but is likely to be subject to stringent criticism by an opposing advocate and such evidence may well allow further evidence to be called in rebuttal or by the opposing party being allowed to re-open its case.

8. A barrister must not suggest that a witness or other person is guilty of crime, fraud or misconduct or attribute to another person the crime or conduct of which his lay client is accused unless such allegations go to a

---

[95] *R* v. *Newton (1983)* 77 Cr App R. 13. This case identifies the procedure that a court should follow when a hearing, conducted by the judge without a jury, is ruled to be appropriate.

matter in issue (including the credibility of the witness) which is material to his lay client's case and which appear to him to be supported by reasonable grounds.

This rule is not only intended to protect the witness or other person but also the barrister's lay client since, in a criminal trial, such a line of questioning will put the defendant's own criminal record in issue and will usually allow evidence of that record to be placed before the jury. Unless there is a firm foundation for an attack on a witness or other person of the kind referred to, the attack may well rebound unfavourably on the party whose barrister has initiated it, since the fact-finding tribunal will usually regard such an attack as an example of mud-slinging for the purpose of seeking to divert attention away from the real culprit.

<h2 style="text-align:center">WRITTEN PROFESSIONAL STANDARDS</h2>

Annexe H of the Code of Conduct contains Written Standards for the Conduct of Professional Work. These come in two parts. The first is entitled General Standards and is applicable to all work. The second is entitled Standards Applicable to Criminal Cases. Paragraph 601(d) of the Code of Conduct requires a barrister to have regard to any relevant written standard and the introduction to the Written Standards makes it clear that the contents are to be read in conjunction with the Code of Conduct. They consist, in part, of matters expressly dealt with in the Code of Conduct and, in part, of statements of good practice and they are to be taken into account in determining whether a barrister has committed a disciplinary offence or should be subject to a wasted costs order.

The origin of the written standards is twofold. Firstly, the Royal Commission on Legal Services in 1979, followed by the Civil Justice Review in 1986, suggested that a guide to the standards to be expected of a barrister in court, written in plain English, would be of benefit since it would define best practice and would assist in maintaining a uniformly high quality of service. Secondly, The Standing Commission on Efficiency, set up by the Lord Chancellor's Department in 1986, produced four guides to good practice for the criminal courts, one each for the Lord Chancellor's Department, the Bar Council, the Law Society and the Crown Prosecution Service. The Standards Applicable to Criminal Cases mirrors the relevant guide to good practice produced by The Standing Commission.

Three particular aspects of these standards are worthy of specific mention. The first two are concerned with documents. In both civil and criminal cases there is spelt out in great detail a barrister's duty if he or she comes into possession of a document belonging to another party by abnormal means.

Prompt enquiry of the professional client to ascertain the circumstances in which the document was obtained should be made. Unless the document was properly obtained, it should be returned unread. If it has been read, if possible, the brief should be returned if the barrister would be embarrassed in the discharge of his or her duties by knowledge of its contents and its return would not prejudice the lay client. If this would prejudice the lay client, the barrister should continue with the brief and make such use of the document as would be in the client's interests but only after informing his or her opponent of the knowledge of the document, of the circumstances, so far as known, in which the document was obtained and the intention to use it. In the event of objection, it would be for the court to determine what use, if any, may be made of it.[96]

In criminal trials, a significant duty is placed on prosecuting counsel to ensure that all unused material, being material in the possession of the prosecution which might be relevant to the defence and which has not been served on the defence, is made available to the defence, unless the material falls within one of the narrow exceptions to disclosure. The modern starting point is the Attorney-General's Guidelines issued in 1981.[97] These Guidelines have largely been superseded by case law in which the Court of Appeal has extended the prosecution's duty of disclosure.[98] The prosecution has the principal duty to ensure the disclosure of material documents, namely those which can be seen on a sensible appraisal to be relevant or possibly relevant to an issue in the case, that raise or possibly raise a new issue whose existence is not apparent from the evidence the prosecution proposes to use or to hold out a real, as opposed to a fanciful, prospect of providing a lead or evidence going to the two defined categories.[99] The prosecuting counsel must place before the court material documents for which public interest immunity is sought and the court must rule on that claim for privilege. Material which only goes to the credibility or reliability of defence witnesses, including their previous inconsistent statements and previous convictions, need not be disclosed.

These duties are referred to in the Standards Applicable to Criminal Cases but only by reference to the Attorney-General's Guidelines.[100] The subsequent, far-reaching developments achieved by the case law of the 1990s have not been codified and as such will undoubtedly await the review of the law of disclosure that was being conducted by the Home Office in 1995.

---

[96] Paragraph 7 of the General Standards, Annexe H of the Code of Conduct.

[97] Attorney General's Guidelines (Disclosure of Information to the Defence in Cases to be Tried on Indictment), 74 Cr App R.302.

[98] Particular reference should be made to *R* v. *Saunders and Others*, unreported, 23rd September 1990, a ruling of Henry J. in the 'Guinness Trial', *R* v. *Ward* 96 Cr App R. 1. *R* v. *Preston and Others* [1994] 2 AC 130, *R* v. *Keane* 99 Cr App R 1. and *R* v. *Brown* [1994] 1 WLR 1599.   [99] *R* v. *Brown* supra.

[100] Paragraph 1.4(d) of the Standards Applicable to Criminal Cases, Annexe H or the Code of Conduct.

The other duty placed on prosecuting counsel worthy of mention is that dealt with in the Standards Applicable to Criminal Cases, being the duty imposed as a result of barrister's role as a prosecutor. This duty was reported on, and defined by, a committee under the chairmanship of Mr Justice Farquharson in 1986. The committee was appointed by the Chairman of the Bar to consider and report on the duty and obligations of counsel when conducting a prosecution.[101] This duty, as defined by the report, must be strictly observed, a requirement fully stressed by the written standards.[102] This duty has to be considered in the light of the Code for Crown Prosecutors issued by the Crown Prosecution Service.[103] Both documents identify the appropriate test for determining whether to initiate or continue with a prosecution and the relationship between the prosecution and both the CPS and the judge. The Royal Commission on Criminal Justice noted that the relationship of the CPS with prosecuting counsel was sometimes unsatisfactory because the CPS was said to be reluctant to consult counsel early enough or to take counsel's advice on the discontinuance of weak cases.[104] The Farquharson report provides that where matters of policy fall to be decided after the start of a trial, it is the duty of counsel to consult his or her instructing solicitor or the relevant CPS representative if at all possible, but that the ultimate decision is a matter for counsel. The CPS was, in 1994, working towards an arrangement whereby a qualified lawyer would be present at all Crown Court centres in order to be able to settle matters of policy directly with counsel. The Royal Commission recommended that the Farquharson Committee should be asked to reconvene to see if there was a need for the refinement of its earlier report but this recommendation has not been followed.[105]

The Report by Lord Woolf, Access to Justice, in June 1995, made wide-ranging recommendations for the reform of the justice system. One recommendation was that the Bar Council should draw up guidelines for the pre-proceedings conduct of legal representatives. This would require a further detailed set of written standards to be drawn up if it is to be implemented.

PUBLICITY

The Code of Conduct contains provisions concerning advertising and media comment.[106] These are considerably relaxed from the restrictions applicable until recently. The earlier restrictions precluded any form of advertising or 'touting' as it was popularly known, and media comment. However, nowadays,

---

[101] The Report is reprinted in Archbold, Criminal Practice which is republished annually.
[102] Paragraph 1.6 of the Standards Applicable to Criminal Cases, *Ibid*.
[103] The third edition was issued in June 1994.
[104] The Report of the Royal Commission on Criminal Justice (1993), pages 78–9.
[105] *Ibid*, Recommendation 180.   [106] Paragraphs 307.1 – 307.2 of the Code of Conduct.

a barrister may engage in any advertising or promotion which complies with the British Code of Advertising Practice, namely, that which is honest, decent and accurate. This material may include photographs, statements as to charging rates and the name of any client if the client consents in writing. The only significant restriction is that comparisons or criticisms of other barristers or professionals are not allowed nor may the quality of the individual who is advertising his or her services be commented upon.

Media comment is not allowed in relation to any current case in which a barrister is, or has been, instructed or is to appear, or has appeared, as an advocate. Such comment is defined as comment to, or in, any news or current affairs media upon the facts of, or issues arising in, that case.[107] A solicitor is not so restricted in the media comment that is allowed. Recently, it has been suggested that solicitors should be restricted in the same way as barristers are since many regard it as undesirable that someone appearing in, or concerned with, a current case should comment upon it to the news media. Clearly, it is desirable that advocates from both branches of the profession should be subject to the same rules concerned with media comment but it is not clear whether the Bar will relax its rules or whether solicitors will tighten theirs.

FEES

A barrister may not supply legal services pursuant to any contract entered into with any person other than his or her professional client.[108] Until the CLSA came into force, a barrister could not, as a matter of law, enter into contractual relations at all.[109] This rule of law has now been abolished by section 61 which, however, also allows the Bar Council to make rules prohibiting barristers from entering into a contract. In fact, the Bar Council has published model terms of work by which barristers will offer their services. These provide that the acceptance of a brief or instructions does not give rise to a contract or legally enforceable arrangement.[110] However, a barrister can contract if he or she wants and, in fact, a barrister does so with work instructed under the Direct Professional Access Rules. The reason for maintaining a non-contractual regime with regard to briefs and instructions from solicitors is twofold. Firstly, a solicitor is under a professional obligation to pay a barrister's fee, irrespective of any default by the solicitor's client. This obligation is supported by a scheme that runs in parallel to the model terms of work known as the Withdrawal of Credit scheme. This scheme enforces a

---

[107] Paragraph 804 of the Code of Conduct.   [108] Paragraph 210(b) of the Code of Conduct.
[109] See Halsbury's *Laws of England*, Fourth edition re-issue (1988), Volume 3(1), Title Barristers, paragraph 531.
[110] The Terms of Work on which Barristers offer their Services to Solicitors is set out in Annexe D of the Code of Conduct. The provision defining the status of these terms is paragraph 26.

solicitor's professional obligation to pay fees by providing that, in cases of serious default, no barrister may, until the default has been remedied, accept a brief or instructions from that solicitor or the firm of that solicitor. All barristers are required to comply with directions issued by the Chairman of the Bar with regard to a defaulting solicitor by not accepting a brief or instructions whilst the default continues.[111] Secondly, there are tax advantages in the maintenance of a non-contractual regime. A barrister may never contract with the lay client.[112] Although a barrister could retain his or her referral status even if allowed to contract with the lay client, this is prohibited so as to provide support for the maintenance of a barrister's referral status and to allow for the continuation of the Withdrawal of Credit scheme.

A much-publicised amendment of the law was introduced by the CLSA by allowing conditional fees to be charged.[113] To date, these are only allowed in personal injury cases, insolvency work and cases involving the European Court of Human Rights. The Code of Conduct prohibits such fees to be charged unless allowed by law.[114] A conditional fee is one which is fixed in advance but which only becomes payable if the case is won. A contingent fee goes further and is calculated by reference to the sum obtained. This remains prohibited.[115]

It is too early to determine whether the reform will merely open up the courts to some litigants who would otherwise be unable to obtain legal services, as the supporters of the reform suggest, or whether it will lead to a compromise of the conduct and ethics required of advocates now that they have a stake in the result, as many judges and practitioners suggest. The reform certainly strikes against traditional common law thinking which is to the effect that only if an advocate is completely isolated from the results of a case can that advocate retain the required professional integrity.

EQUAL OPPORTUNITIES

The Bar has been subject to much attention in recent years with regard to its practising arrangements, some of which are alleged to be potentially causative

---

[111] The details of the Withdrawal of Credit scheme are set out in Annexe D of the Code of Conduct. The obligation to comply with the Terms of Work and the Withdrawal of Credit schemes is set out in paragraph 303(c)(iii) of the Code of Conduct. This apparent encroachment on the cab-rank rule is justified by the fact that the lay client can readily instruct another solicitor who can then instruct any barrister on that lay client's behalf.   [112] Paragraph 210(b) of the Code of Conduct.
[113] Section 58.   [114] Paragraph 211 of the Code of Conduct.
[115] The former is allowed by the CCBE Code of Conduct since civilian lawyers have always taken a more relaxed view of what, in English law, is known as maintenance and champerty.

of indirect discrimination.[116] The profession attracts a high proportion of applicants from the ethnic minorities and women as entrants but the proportion of these who are Queen's Counsel or judges remains relatively low. Most judges have previously been barristers in independent practice.

The Bar has done much to ensure that it is a profession which is open to all of ability and to combat indirect discrimination. The impetus for change was section 64 of the CLSA. This section brought pupillages and chambers' practising arrangements within the ambit of the anti-discrimination sections of the Sex Discrimination and Race Relations Acts for the first time.[117] This was followed by the appointment by the Bar Council of two Equal Opportunities Officers and the approval of an Equal Opportunities Code of Practice.[118] A barrister must have regard to the provisions of this Code of Practice.[119]

The Code of Conduct has been amended to deal with discriminatory behaviour. A barrister must not, in relation to any other person, whether in the profession or outside it, discriminate or victimize on grounds of race, ethnic origin, colour, national origin, nationality, citizenship, sex, sexual orientation, marital status, disability, religion or political persuasion. In respect of indirect discrimination, no breach of the Code of Conduct occurs if that barrister proves, on the balance of probabilities, that the act of indirect discrimination was committed without the intention of treating the claimant unfavourably on the relevant prohibited grounds.[120]

The Code of Practice sets out guidance on advertising and interviewing methods for pupillages and tenancies which will, if followed, reduce or eliminate the risk of indirect discrimination. It also recommends the monitoring of applications and gives guidance on how to avoid sexual harassment. Recommended complaints procedures are also identified.

PRACTISING ARRANGEMENTS

Arrangements whereby a barrister practises as a sole practitioner, usually with a group of similarly practising barristers in chambers, are the subject of provi-

---

[116] A report published in November 1992: 'Without Prejudice?' by Lesley Holland and Lynne Spencer, which had been commissioned jointly by the Bar Council and the Lord Chancellor's Department, found substantial evidence of early and continuing unequal treatment between the sexes at many levels of the profession. The proportion of those from ethnic minorities who find a place in chambers remains significantly lower than the proportion who are offered a pupillage and these proportions are significantly lower than the equivalent proportions for white barristers. There also remains an ethnic imbalance so far as success on the Bar's Vocational Course is concerned. The Barrow Report in 1994, concerned with possible indirect discrimination amongst ethnic minority students on the Vocational Course, found no evidence of this but pointed to the greater difficulties those students had in finding pupillages and tenancies.

[117] The Sex Discrimination Act 1975 and the Race Relations Act 1976.

[118] A draft was approved in May 1993 and a revised version, being the Code of Practice itself, was approved in September 1995 and is now a further annexe of the Code of Conduct.

[119] Paragraph 303 of the Code of Conduct.   [120] Paragraph 204 of the Code of Conduct.

sions in the Code of Conduct. In most chambers, a senior member is appointed as head of chambers. This individual, or, where there is no head, all members of chambers, must take, amongst other measures, all steps which it is reasonable to take in the circumstances to ensure that chambers is efficiently administered, that the affairs of chambers are conducted fairly and equitably for all barristers and pupils and that all barristers in chambers are properly insured with the BMIF.[121]

All barristers in independent practice must have regard to the guidelines as to the administration of chambers published by the Bar Council. These, colloquially known as 'Action Pack', give guidance as to good administration in such matters as accommodation, finance, staff, records, communications and insurance.[122] The object of these provisions is to seek to ensure that the quality of service offered by a barrister is efficient, speedy and economical. Practising standards have been the subject of scrutiny by the Legal Aid Board and the arrangements that are to be introduced by the Legal Aid Board, as an attempt to improve legal aid practising standards and reduce financial waste, will require many barristers to improve the quality of their administrative arrangements if they are to continue to be instructed on legal aid.[123]

CONCLUSION

It can be seen that the professional conduct required of a barrister and the ethical requirements of practice are both elaborate and wide-ranging. There is, however, a common theme running through these requirements. This is that the public interest requires the maintenance and preservation of a profession of full-time advocates who are capable of being relied upon to achieve consistently high standards. These standards include the maintenance of both the integrity of the justice system and the best interests of the client. To the extent that these interests conflict, the interests of the justice system must prevail. The profession is small and tightly-knit. The maintenance of such a profession requires detailed practising rules and an efficient and economical service to be provided and many of the provisions of the Code of Conduct are designed to achieve this. In summary, therefore, the Bar's Code of Conduct seeks to achieve six ideals: integrity, justice, service, economy, efficiency and equality of opportunity.

---

[121] Paragraph 304 of the Code of Conduct.

[122] Paragraph 303(b)(i) of the Code of Conduct. The current edition of 'Action Pack' was published in 1992 and relevant extracts are set out in Annexe B of the Code of Conduct.

[123] In particular, proposals for franchising and transaction criteria. These are set out in the Legal Aid Handbook produced annually by Sweet & Maxwell with the approval of the Legal Aid Board. More radical proposals were set out in a green paper produced by the government in June 1995.

4

Professional Rules, Codes, and Principles Affecting Solicitors (Or What Has Professional Regulation to do With Ethics?)

ALISON CRAWLEY & CHRISTOPHER BRAMALL

INTRODUCTION

THIS paper has been prepared in the context of the central theme of the 1993 SPTL conference 'Professional Responsibility and Teaching Legal Ethics'. The authors both work in the Professional Ethics Division of the Law Society. Unfortunately, rather than this meaning that we are at the forefront of academic thinking on the subject, our lives are filled with practical questions concerning the application of the current rules, sometimes in such detail that we may be accused of failing to see the wood for the trees. This paper reflects knowledge gained in the employment of the Law Society, but any opinions expressed are personal to the authors. The invitation to participate in the conference has provided a welcome opportunity to reconsider the underlying principles of professional responsibility. This paper, on the professional rules, codes, and principles affecting solicitors, is largely descriptive and to some extent analytical. However, it is not possible to look at the present rules without being aware of how history has shaped the rules and what present pressures for change exist. While it is arguable that the rules affecting solicitors have kept pace and in some areas have led the legal world, in other areas it is likely that the pace of change in the real world could be leaving the rules behind.

The subtext of the paper is 'what has professional regulation to do with ethics?' Frances Silverman[1] has called the regulation of English solicitors a maze. We would not dispute that it is a maze, but we would assert that, underlying the maze, there are the fundamental principles of legal professional ethics which can be found, in one form or another, in most jurisdictions.

---

[1] *Handbook of Professional Conduct for Solicitors*, F. Silverman, Butterworths 1989.

THE PROFESSION

The Law Society's Research and Policy Planning Unit now produces an annual statistical report providing invaluable information on the evolution of the profession. The latest published report[2] at the time of writing shows that in 1992 there were 76,019 solicitors on the Roll of which 61,329 had practising certificates. 51,017 were in private practice and a little over 8,000 in employed or 'in-house' practice. Of 8,198 private practices (earning more than £15,000 p.a.), 3,167 were sole practitioners. One hundred firms had twenty-six partners or more. Thus less than two per cent of large practices comprise or employ more than twenty-four per cent of all solicitors and fee earners and earn approximately forty per cent of the profession's gross fees from private practice.

These figures probably do little more than confirm the concentration of higher fee paying work in the hands of a few large firms which employ a significant percentage of the profession. However, the number of sole practitioners is far from insignificant. Perhaps one unifying factor for such a disparate profession is that the same regulations apply to all firms, great and small, rich and poor.

CURRENT RULES, CODES, AND PRINCIPLES

The rules, codes and principles of conduct are contained in the 1993 (6th) edition of *The Guide to the Professional Conduct of Solicitors*,[3] updated by subsequent issues of the *Professional Standards Bulletin*.[4] The Guide now runs to 845 pages. The original *Guide to the Professional Conduct and Etiquette of Solicitors by Sir Thomas Lund, 1960*,[5] ran to 173 pages. At that time there were about 20,000 practising solicitors. The 1980s and early 1990s proved to be a time of rapid growth in the size of the profession, the Law Society bureaucracy, and the Guide. It doesn't take long to say 'no you can't do that'. Once de-regulation hit in the 1980s with calls for increased competition and a free market, it took much longer to say 'yes, you can do that *but*, if you do it that way, then . . .'. Even the Bar, with a once enviably concise code of conduct, has realized that when, for example, the rules were relaxed to allow direct access new rules were required to govern that new relationship. So, when a major sea-change happened in relation to the solicitors' rules in the mid-1980s, removing the ban on advertising, touting for business and inviting instructions, and permitting (for the first time, officially) arrangements for the introduction

[2] *RPPU Annual Statistical Report October 1993*, The Law Society.
[3] *The Guide to the Professional Conduct of Solicitors* Sixth Edition 1993, the Law Society.
[4] *PSD Professional Standards Bulletin*, the Law Society, Aug. 1993 et seq.
[5] *A Guide to the Professional Conduct and Etiquette of Solicitors*, Sir Thomas Lund CBE, the Law Society 1960.

of work, new codes of practice were required to regulate the activities that were previously prohibited.

The regulation of the Bar is largely derived from one source. Unaffected by statutory regulation until very recently, the Bar could make rules fairly quickly and put them into force with comparatively little fuss. The Law Society's authority to regulate solicitors derives largely, but not entirely, from statute: the Solicitors Act 1974, the Administration of Justice Act 1985, the Financial Services Act 1986, and the Courts and Legal Services Act 1990. While the Council of the Law Society make the rules they must generally have the concurrence of the Master of the Rolls. Rules affecting investment business also require the agreement of the Securities and Investments Board.

The 1989 Green Paper, *The Work and Organisation of the Legal Profession*[6] proposed that rule-making powers should effectively be passed to the Lord Chancellor. This attack on a self-regulating profession was strongly resisted. The outcome of the debate was an attempt at a compromise. All rules relating to the education of solicitors and any rules ('however they may be described') relating to the conduct of litigation and advocacy are now required to be approved under the Schedule 4 procedure set out in the Courts and Legal Services Act 1990. This requires the Society to seek the advice of the Lord Chancellor's Advisory Committee on Legal Education and Conduct on proposed new rules or amendments to rules. The Lord Chancellor is also required to seek the views of the Advisory Committee and of the Director-General of Fair Trading prior to seeking the approval of the four 'designated judges'. The new rules require the approval of all four designated judges and the Lord Chancellor. The new process, introduced, ironically, in an Act which was heralded as deregulating legal services, is complex, leads to delays and frustrations, and could lead to regulatory stagnation in some areas. The quickest time so far between a new rule being approved by the Council of the Law Society and finally made under Schedule 4 is eight to nine months. The longest is two years nine months.

Statutory Rules and Codes

The Solicitors Act 1933 first gave the Society power to make rules relating to solicitors' accounts and rules 'for regulating in respect of any other matter the professional practice, conduct and discipline of solicitors'. Similar powers are now contained in sections 32–4 of the Solicitors Act 1974, and are supplemented by powers in relation to establishing a Compensation Fund and providing for professional indemnity cover.

[6] *The Work and Organisation of the Legal Profession*, Lord Chancellor's Department, CM 570, 1989, paras. 4, 11–4. 13.

The first Practice Rule was made in 1936 to deal with the problem of touting and 'ambulance chasing'. It said 'simply':

A solicitor shall not directly or indirectly apply for or seek instructions for professional business or do or permit in the carrying on of his practice any act or thing which can reasonably be regarded as touting or advertising or as calculated to attract business unfairly.

In the first 'Guide' in 1960, twenty-seven pages were devoted to what would and would not breach Rule 1. It included a paragraph on 'lectures', and when the description 'solicitor' could be used when giving lectures.

By 1975 there were only five more Practice Rules, dealing with acting for both parties in conveyancing transactions; fee-sharing; contingency fee agreements and acting in association with claims assessors; firm names; and the supervision of offices. Now the position is more complex:

- The *Solicitors' Practice Rules 1990* contain sixteen substantive rules with three accompanying codes, the Publicity Code, the Introduction and Referral Code, and the Employed Solicitors Code. Table 1 (see paragraph 3.3) shows that the Practice Rules are something of a mixed bag, many dealing with regulatory issues, ie mode of practice, rather than ethical issues.
- The first *Accounts Rules* were made in 1934. The Solicitors' Accounts Rules 1991 and Accountant's Report Rules 1991 show surprising similarity to their predecessors. The principles behind these rules are straightforward. Clients' money should be kept separately from the solicitor's own money, and records should show accurately what money belongs to which client. Compliance with the rules is monitored at the first level by requiring solicitors to seek an accountant's report in a form specified by the Society—and requiring the *solicitor* to submit the form to the Law Society. The Society can refuse to issue a practising certificate if an accountant's report is outstanding.
- The present *Solicitors' Indemnity Rules* date from 1987 when the profession, in effect, became its own underwriter, with the setting up of the Solicitors' Indemnity Fund. Before that rules had required mandatory compulsory insurance under a Master Policy scheme but only since 1976. The present scheme indemnifies solicitors against civil claims arising in the course of practice as a solicitor up to a limit of £1 million per claim. It does not indemnify a solicitor against his or her own dishonesty.
- The *Solicitors' Investment Business Rules* 1990 have their origin in the Financial Services Act 1986, and are subject to the supervision of the Securities and Investment Board. They aim to subject solicitors involved in mainstream investment business to the same degree of regulation as others in the field, while recognizing that many solicitors' only involvement with investment business is incidental to a legal transaction. Compliance with these rules is directly monitored by the Law Society.
- *The Solicitors' Incorporated Practice Rules* 1988 (which came into force in 1992) stem from the Administration of Justice Act 1985 which permitted solicitors to practice in incorporated form. These Rules permit solicitors to practice through

either unlimited or limited companies (with a share capital) provided the company has been 'recognised' by the Law Society. The time-lag between 1985 and 1992 has meant that very few practices are incorporated as the previous favourable tax position of companies no longer exists.

- The biggest block of statutory rule changes recently arose from the provisions of the Courts and Legal Services Act 1990 relating to multi-national practice. Foreign lawyers, after becoming registered with the Law Society, can now enter into partnership with solicitors. This does not give foreign lawyers the same powers as solicitors to provide 'reserved' legal services. Multi-national practices are regulated by the Law Society, and the main sanction against foreign lawyers is removal from the register.

Non-statutory Principles and Codes

If a foreign lawyer were to come to England for the first time and, looking to understand the codes of ethics that affect solicitors, read only the sets of statutory rules referred to above we may be thought a strange profession. While some of the Practice Rules will be seen to be based on familiar concepts common to legal professional ethics world-wide the majority appear to be technical regulations having little to do with the real ethical dilemmas faced by lawyers. The complication for the solicitors' profession is that much of its ethical code of conduct either predates the statutory rules referred to earlier, or developed concurrently but not under statutory authority as such. While the increasing bulk of the Guide is largely due to the recent proliferation of statutory regulation, the core of the Guide is its principles and commentaries. Some of these have changed little since 1960, others have moved with the times. The splitting of the text into principles and commentaries was first effected in 1986—a flexible method of guidance which is also used by the Institute of Chartered Accountants in England and Wales. The idea is that the principle is the most important and fairly immutable statement of professional conduct but is often stated in fairly general terms. The commentaries give guidance as to how the principles can be applied (or even ignored) in particular circumstances. The commentaries do not and cannot cover all circumstances.

It is perhaps an occupational hazard that some solicitors read the Guide as they would other law books. If a particular circumstance is not mentioned in the commentaries, it is argued that the principle cannot apply to that circumstance.

However, the codes of conduct represented by the principles and commentaries should not be treated as if they are tax statutes to be scrutinized for loopholes. They establish rights and responsibilities that must be viewed broadly and in the spirit. Perhaps it is that spirit, or the ideals of legal ethics, that need more emphasis in the current training of lawyers?

Until 1888 only the Court had power to discipline solicitors. The Supreme

Court retains an inherent jurisdiction over its own officers and many of the principles and commentaries have their origins in court decisions, whether of a disciplinary nature or relating to the fiduciary relationship between solicitor and client. Agency law, as applied to solicitors, has had a significant effect on the development of principles of professional conduct, yet is itself often taught only as an 'add on' to other legal subjects.

A good example of the impact of agency law is the regulation of deposit interest earned on clients' money, and Practice Rule 10 on commissions. Both these rules derive from the solicitor's fiduciary duty not to make a secret profit. The landmark case *Brown* v. *IRC*[7] clarified the fact that interest earned on clients' money—even small amounts—belongs to the client. Because of administrative difficulties, the government (in s.33 Solicitors Act 1974) gave the Society power to make rules requiring solicitors to pay 'the equivalent' of interest to clients, and disapplied the common law duty—thus enabling the Society to set *de minimis* levels in rules that would not have been possible at law. Practice Rule 10, which requires solicitors to account to clients for commission, stems from the same fiduciary duty. However, statute has not disapplied the common law. While Rule 10 contains a *de minimis* of £20 to the *conduct* rule, it is not clear whether the common law would accept the same *de minimis*.

Peter Bird and Bruce Weir in their book *The Law, Practice and Conduct of Solicitors*[8] analysed the principles as they appeared in the 1987 Guide. They concluded that while thirty derived their authority from statute, ninety-one were based on decisions of the courts, giving ninety-five per cent of the principles in the Guide a basis of statute or case law. That analysis, they felt, justified the need for a book which dealt with both the law and conduct of solicitors. In other cases the principles are derived from the case law of disciplinary proceedings within the Law Society or the Solicitors' Disciplinary Tribunal. In either case they reflect a judgment as to what constitutes conduct unbefitting a solicitor. The findings of the Tribunal are public and so can set precedent. However, most of the cases referred to the Tribunal are extreme, involving serious breaches of the accounts rules and a combination of other breaches. The cases therefore highlight the need for good business organization, and give a good warning as to how letting one or two 'little things' slip can build into chaos. Occasionally a case will have something to say on for example conflict of interest, and such cases may lead to a change of emphasis in the commentaries to the Guide, but rarely to a complete change.

Government criticism of the Guide in the Green Paper, *The Work and Organisation of the Legal Profession*, January 1989,[9] together with the

---

[7] [1965] AC 244.

[8] *The Law, Practice and Conduct of Solicitors*, Peter M. K. Bird and J. Bruce Weir, Waterlow Practitioners Library 1989.   [9] paras. 4, 6–4 and 10.

questioning by solicitors of the authority for some of the principles in the Guide, led the editorial board of the 1993 Guide radically to revise the order of the Guide's contents.

A new Chapter 1 was included, explaining the derivation of the principles and other contents. This includes a statement that non-statutory guidance on conduct is treated as authoritative by the Adjudication and Appeals Committee, the Solicitors' Disciplinary Tribunal, and the Court. Chapter 1 also states that 'the requirements of professional conduct should not be confused with the requirements of the general law . . . even though the requirements of conduct may in some cases follow or closely parallel the general legal requirements.' The advantage of the principle and commentary system is that the principles do not stand still. They, like the common law, are able to move with the times and be a flexible tool. Perhaps rigid adherence to a statutory code—particularly one which requires a great deal of time and effort to change—would be less attractive.

Alfred Philips in his thought-provoking book *Professional Ethics for Scottish Solicitors*[10] doubted the value of an increased codification of the rules of professional conduct. In the preface, referring to the 1989 Green Papers, he anticipated a pressure 'for an all-round drop in the ethical level of the lawyer's professional attitudes and behaviour and for the substitution of lip-service adherence to codes of conduct . . .' which, he argued, are incapable of being formulated in any sensible way. His argument is that the more that is reduced to rules, the more distanced will become the ideals of legal ethics. In that regard Mr Philips contrasts Scotland's paucity of written rules favourably with England's 'maze'. While this argument has a philosophical attraction, it is based on preserving professional mystique, which, in an increasing number of professions, is being replaced by notions of openness and accountability—led by demand from the consumer of the professional service.

Distinguishing Mere Regulation from Core Ethics

It is hoped that our hypothetical foreign visitor, given the full Guide, and not just the statutory rules, would recognize that solicitors are a profession faced with the same dilemmas as lawyers all over the world. Given that the conference giving rise to this paper mainly concerns the teaching of legal ethics it is important to distinguish those rules that require thought and understanding—the core moral or ethical dilemmas affecting lawyers—from regulations which, rather like VAT regulations, require knowledge and implementation but may sometimes be beyond understanding! Any lawyer undergoing professional legal education in whatever branch in this country should be equipped to understand and follow the technical regulation. Therefore, it

---

[10] *Professional Ethics for Scottish Solicitors*, Alfred Philips, Butterworths, Edinburgh 1990.

perhaps warrants little as part of legal education. Teachers surely want to teach something that is interesting and which gets to the heart of some of the problems that students may face in their future professional life.

Which of the statutory rules have that interest? Practice Rule 1 states:

A solicitor shall not do anything in the course of practising as a solicitor, or permit another person to do anything on his or her behalf, which compromises or impairs or is likely to compromise or impair any of the following:
(a) the solicitor's independence or integrity:
(b) a person's freedom to instruct a solicitor of his or her choice;
(c) the solicitor's duty to act in the best interests of the client;
(d) the good repute of the solicitor or of the solicitors' profession;
(e) the solicitor's proper standard of work;
(f) the solicitor's duty to the Court.

The deregulation in the 1980s appeared to some solicitors to threaten the profession's very existence. That provoked a prolonged debate within the profession on questions of principle—leading to the decision to set out the principles as a Practice Rule. There was a wide consensus in favour of the principles.

The principles speak for themselves. The main interest lies in when the principles themselves clash and it is the realization that there are those inherent dilemmas which will help students of professional ethics avoid treating rules of conduct as black letter law. Not infrequently the best interests of the client will conflict with the solicitor's duty to the court or the reputation of the profession—the most clear example being where a client has confessed guilt to the solicitor, then decides to plead not guilty, but wants the solicitor to put forward a defence on false facts.

The solicitor's independence or particularly impartiality can often appear to conflict with the best interests of the client, although in many of these cases the best interests of the client are distinguishable from the wishes of the client. It is not uncommon for a solicitor to be prevented from acting for a client because of a conflict of interests with another (possibly former) client but then to be subject to considerable pressure from the client to act. Sometimes the interests of the client—when calculated in cost or speed terms—clashes with the solicitor's duty in relation to a proper standard of work. Full discussion and analysis of the principles in Practice Rule 1 and their interrelationship should certainly equip any trainee solicitor with the thought processes that will help in the ethical dimension of his or her future professional life.

An analysis of the Practice Rules shows that many of them deal with matters of regulation rather than core ethics. Of sixteen substantive Practice Rules, how many go to the heart of professional ethics? Table 1 comprises a suggested analysis.

While it can be said that the mode of practice rules depend on core

TABLE 1.

Rule 1 (basic principles)	*core legal/ethical duties*
Rule 4 (employed solicitors)	*relate to mode of practice ie*
Rule 5 (offering services other than as a solicitor)	*regulatory rather than*
Rule 7 (fee-sharing)	*ethical*
Rule 11 (name of firm)	
Rule 13 (supervision and management of an office)	
Rule 14 (structural surveys and formal valuations)	
Rule 2 (publicity)	*seek to preserve professional*
Rule 3 (introduction and referrals)	*status post-deregulation—*
	regulatory rather than
	ethical
Rule 6 (acting for seller and buyer)	*based on common law/*
Rule 8 (contingency fees)	*fiduciary duties relating to*
Rule 9 (claims assessors)	*conflicts of interest and the*
Rule 10 (commissions)	*administration of justice—*
Rule 12 (investment business)	*restatements in conduct*
	terms of legal/fiduciary
	duties
Rule 15 (client care)	*recognition of consumer*
	interests
Rule 16 (cross-border activities within the EC)	*recognition of increasing internationalism*

principles such as independence, it is difficult to think what moral content Practice Rule 11 really has. Some of the rules are merely statements of common law or fiduciary duties. Possibly for political reasons, it was felt that these should also be matters of professional conduct and were therefore restated as such.

As indicated above, the 'core' ethical rules are more likely to be found in the principles and commentaries in the Guide. The chapters on conflicts of interest, confidentiality, and professional undertakings are, in the authors' view, the most important chapters in terms of teaching professional responsibility.

To a certain extent that view is backed up by the statistical evidence that we have from the type of enquiries received in the Professional Ethics Division. Table 2 shows the number and type of queries over a twelve month period. The statistics are significant as they reflect the matters that cause concern to solicitors rather than clients. They highlight the dilemmas the profession actually has.

Given increasing technicality and the fact that the profession has to address its mind annually to accountants' reports and renewal of investment business certificates—and that firms receive monitoring visits in relation to both—it is perhaps not surprising that a total of sixteen per cent of enquiries relate to accounts and investment business regulation. These rules are complex, technical, and not in plain English. Many enquiries about the accounts rules are from book-keepers and accountants. However, the biggest 'block' of calls—about twenty-six per cent—relates to Practice Rule 1, conflicts, confidentiality, and undertakings—that core of professional responsibility.

It is also reassuring that so many solicitors do call for advice as it shows a general wish within the profession to do the right thing. If a solicitor is under pressure from a client—for instance, to act where there is a conflict of interests—it helps for the solicitor to say that he or she has been advised not to act by the Law Society. All enquiries are treated confidentially, and the Professional Ethics Division is distanced by Chinese walls from the policing and disciplinary processes in the Society.

While many of the queries are answerable by reference to the principles and commentaries in the Guide or to the Practice Rules, the complexity of questions is increasing. New regulations always lead to an increase in calls—in the past few years mortgage fraud, and more recently money laundering, have been of concern.

WHAT SHAPES THE RULES?

With the recent increase or explosion in statutory regulation and the pressures for change, it is important to remember the ambit within which the Society exercises its regulatory powers. Self-regulation must operate within bounds defined by a wider public interest. Lord Diplock made this point in relation to the rule making powers of the Law Society in *Swain* v. *the Law Society*.[11] He said:

The purpose for which these statutory functions are vested in the Law Society and the Council is the protection of the public or, more specifically, that section of the public that may be in need of legal advice, assistance or representation. In exercising its statutory functions the duty of the Council is to act in what it believes to be the best interests of that section of the public, even in the event (unlikely though this may be on any long term view) that those public interests should conflict with the special interests of members of the Law Society or of members of the solicitors' profession as a whole.[12]

However, the nub of the problem is not only that there may be differences in the interests of the profession and of the public, but that there is no consensus as to where either the public's or the profession's interests lie.

Neither the profession nor the representatives of the public interest speak

[11] [1983] 1AC 598.   [12] at p. 608. E.

TABLE 2. *Professional ethics statistics 1993*

Category of Work	Written	Telephone	Totals
Rule 1 The Five Principles	66	2811	2877
Rule 2 Publicity Code	290	1823	2113
Rule 3 Introduction and Referral Code	115	648	763
Rule 4 Employed Solicitors Code	105	645	750
Rule 5 Hiving Off and Other Business	53	368	421
Rule 6 Acting for Vendor/Purchaser	50	1006	1056
Rule 7 Fee-sharing and Mixed Partnerships	28	300	328
Rule 8 Contingency Fees	70	338	408
Rule 9 Claims Assessors	12	16	28
Rule 10 Commissions	70	363	433
Rule 11 Name of Firm	59	307	366
Rule 12 Investment Business and FSA[A]	406	2314	2720
Rule 13 Supervision of Offices	138	765	903
Rule 14 Structural Surveys	3	6	9
Rule 15 Client Care	26	435	461
Rule 16 CCBE[B] Code	0	17	17
Accounts Rules	604	4617	5221
Setting up in/Retiring from Practice	96	1551	1647
Lien	101	1248	1349
Retainer Accepting/Terminating	64	1408	1472
Undertakings	339	1135	1474
Contract Races	22	639	661
Oaths, Statutory Declarations	4	414	418
Privilege and Confidentiality	480	2215	2695
Pastoral, including Death of SP,[C] Complaint Disciplinary Procedures, Interventions, SAS[D]	245	1981	2226
Financial Problems	25	535	560
Solicitors Act and Admin. of Justice Act	247	1739	1986
Counsel's Fees and Joint Tribunal	21	183	204
Agent's Fees	37	212	249
Conflict Generally	474	4063	4537
Documents Handed Over	32	961	993
Incorporation Rules	27	242	269
Costs	168	1663	1831
Miscellaneous	2060	4859	6919
Other International Aspects including Overseas Practice Rules	35	304	339
MNPs[E] and RFLs[F]	14	289	303
TOTALS	6586	42420	49006

A   Financial Services Act 1986
B   Council of the Bars and the Law Societies of the European Community
C   Sole Principal
D   Solicitors' Assistance Scheme
E   Multi-national partnerships
F   Registered foreign lawyers

with a clear and consistent voice on these issues. Not only internal but also external pressures push both ways—towards deregulation and towards increased regulation. Furthermore, even deregulation has, paradoxically, the effect of adding to the maze of regulation.

Pressures Internal to the Profession

It would seem likely that pressures to change rules of conduct would have little effect on those core principles relating to conflicts of interest and confidentiality. However, even those principles are open to debate in today's changing world. The English (and Welsh) solicitors' profession is noted for its entrepreneurship. This has led to some pressure to relax even the conflict of interest rules, especially to permit solicitors to compete on a level playing field with other providers of services (for instance, from solicitor property sellers, who may wish to give financial advice to purchasers; from solicitors advising on life policies, who may wish to retain commissions; and in the City where there are pressures for a more wide-spread acceptance of Chinese walls).

It is interesting to note in Harry Kirk's *Portrait of a Profession*[13] that it was an exceptional number of solicitor frauds that led the Law Society's Council in 1938 to seek the powers to require an accountant's report as a condition for the grant of a practising certificate. The Compensation Fund was established in 1942, again an apparently inevitable step after the number of solicitor frauds in the 1930s. In 1965 the Law Society was given the power to make a special levy in case of an emergency in addition to the fixed annual contribution. This was because in 1957 it was realized that a solicitor named Eichholz had systematically defrauded clients to the extent that the claims finally paid out totalled over half a million pounds.

The recent staggering rise in the number and amount of claims on the Compensation Fund, requiring the Law Society to impose substantial special levies on the profession, has led to calls for more effective regulation to prevent fraud taking place, including calls for new restrictions on acting for mortgagor and mortgagee, and for solicitors to be licensed to hold clients' money. Conversely, increasing claims have also led to calls for the abolition of the Compensation Fund.

The recession has led to a number of deregulatory pressures particularly where the regulations impose a cost on the profession. However, the recession has also given impetus to the more entrepreneurial members of the profession in their call for deregulation to enable them to compete on a level playing field with other providers of services.

Permitting multi-national practice was essentially deregulatory, yet

---

[13] *Portrait of a Profession. A History of the Solicitor's Profession, 1100 to the Present Day,* Harry Kirk, London, Oyez Publishing 1976.

required sixty pages of amendment rules to cope with the idea of a non-solicitor partner. Permitting solicitors to practise in incorporated form, also deregulatory, led to a complex set of rules, the Solicitors' Incorporated Practice Rules, which seek to ensure that an incorporated practice offers the same client protections as a partnership. More recently, deregulating rights of audience in the Higher Courts has led to the codification of the principles and commentaries that apply to solicitor-advocates in the form of an advocacy code, as well as two new Practice Rules (16A and 16B).

Pressures External to the Profession

In the last thirty years or so pressure from the Office of Fair Trading, the Department of Trade and Industry, and the Monopolies and Mergers Commission have had a significant deregulatory influence. In the early years this led to the abolition of scale fees. However, that deregulation, as usual, led to new regulation in the form of the Solicitors' Remuneration Order 1972, Practice Rule 6 (acting for seller and buyer), and, later, to the written professional standards on information on costs for clients.

In the mid 1980s the end of the anti-touting/advertising rules led to the introduction of a new Publicity Code, an Introduction and Referral Code, the Employed Solicitors Code, and an entirely new rule—Practice Rule 5—known as the rule against hiving off, as well as the formulation of Practice Rule 1.

During this time there has also been pressure for multi-disciplinary practice in some form. If that were to come about it would probably result in at least as many amendment rules as were required to encompass multi-national practice.

While deregulatory in conception it is clear that proposals relating to conditional fee agreements will be governed by statutory regulation and may lead to the development of new principles of conduct.

External pressures which have increased regulation notably include the Financial Services Act, which led to the Solicitors' Investment Business Rules. More recently we have had new directives from the EC Commission which will lead to new requirements to control money laundering and to new Law Society guidance which will be seen by some as an attack on solicitor/client confidentiality. Pressure from the Commission for Racial Equality has led to an anti-discrimination code and a new Anti-Discrimination Practice Rule.

Media pressure and bad cases have led in the past to the setting up of the Compensation Fund and the Solicitors' Indemnity Fund. More recently it has contributed to the creation of the Solicitors' Complaints Bureau with new compensatory powers relating to inadequate professional services. Level playing fields might suggest the removal of some of the restrictions on non-contentious costs, but the Legal Services Ombudsman has proposed (and the

Law Society has agreed) an extension of the right to call for a remuneration certificate. The Ombudsman, whose powers include the right to exercise pressure through the media, continues to advocate new rules to make advance costs disclosure mandatory. The call from consumer groups for a better standard of work (particularly in relation to client care issues) has led to a reconsideration of standards for the profession. The legal aid franchise exercise has arguably been beneficial in requiring many firms to adopt practice management standards—but they remain voluntary for the rest of the profession. Conveyancing standards are also under discussion but as a voluntary scheme. Inevitably, however, the adoption of any form of standards leads to consumer pressure to make those standards mandatory. In practice, solicitors may feel more acutely the direct pressure from consumers to reduce their fees, especially for conveyancing. Some in the profession interpret this as meaning that consumers are happy with reduced standards if this means lower costs.

WHAT SHOULD BE THE OBJECTIVES AND PRINCIPLES OF FUTURE CHANGE?

The following are the principles adopted by the Law Society at the last major review of the Practice Rules in 1990:

1. to maintain and safeguard the unique position of solicitors as officers of the Court and as trusted professional advisers;
2. to enable solicitors to compete in the market place for the provision of legal and allied services;
3. to eliminate unjustified restrictive practices;
4. to take into account the points made by the government in the white paper on legal services in connection with conveyancing by authorized practitioners;
5. to take into account the Code of Conduct for Lawyers in the European Community adopted by the Council of the Bars and the Law Societies of the European Community (CCBE);
6. to clarify where needed;
7. not to molly-coddle the public or the profession.[14]

Again the difficulty is finding the balance between principles that pull in different directions. Looking at those principles now, deriving as they do from the deregulatory fervour of the mid to late 1980s, are there any we should change? Is a new moralism creeping through the profession embodying a reaction against deregulation? In the 1980s, an important part of the profession accepted that we are businessmen and women. There are signs of a reassertion of traditional professional values. For instance, in the apparently

[14] *Report of the Standards and Guidance Committee to Council on Revision of the Practice Rules,* July 1990.

endless debate on multi-disciplinary practice, there seems to be a hardening of opinion against MDPs, whereas in the mid-1980s there may have been a bare majority in favour.

It may however be questioned what headway such a reassertion of traditonal values can make if it implies higher costs, given

1. the public revulsion at high legal fees at the upper end of the market;
2. the threat to high street conveyancers from competition and recession; and
3. the reduction in the scope of and eligibility for legal aid.

Are there new developments in regulation that can help to achieve the balancing act necessary to meet the needs of the public for access to legal services and the need of solicitors to make a living? Can we at the same time safeguard what is the best of professionalism? That does not necessarily mean reverting to the time (as recently as the 1960 *Guide to the Professional Conduct and Etiquette of Solicitors*) when Sir Thomas Lund could assert that the only sanction for breach of professional manners in an extreme case would be:

The exclusion of the offender from membership of The Law Society on the ground that he did not conform with the accepted conduct and traditional behaviour of solicitors, who are gentlemen.[15]

---

[15] *op cit.*, p. 1.

5

Confidence, Public Interest, and the Lawyer

MICHAEL BRINDLE & GUY DEHN

ACROSS the whole legal spectrum there is a deeply established and wholly justified concern that confidence should be preserved, whether it be confidence flowing from contractual relationships or otherwise. The reasons for this are obvious, and it has been recognized that the preservation of confidence is not merely a private matter, but is also a matter of public interest.[1] The problem addressed in this chapter is the way in which this public interest clashes with other public interests which militate against confidence being respected and in favour of disclosure. There are clearly situations where the preservation of confidence is capable of preventing proper and important concerns as to health and safety, or as to dishonesty or corruption in commercial or civic life, from coming to light. We address the general legal position as to the interrelation between these competing public interests, and then proceed to consider the special legal position of the lawyer in connection with this controversy. We believe that there are both special dangers and special opportunities which arise in this connection, some of which are explored below. The extent to which the courts have to date been involved in working out the complexities which arise where lawyers become involved in this clash of public interests is limited, but we anticipate that problems of this type are likely to arise more frequently in future.

THE GENERAL LAW

We do not dwell upon the basis for the public interest in the preservation of confidence. Our concern is to explore the circumstances in which a person, *prima facie* subject to an obligation of confidence, is nevertheless entitled to breach that confidence. It is worthy of note that for as long as the law of confidence has itself existed, there has existed alongside it a public interest exception. Thus it was stated in 1743 that 'no private obligations can dispense with that universal one which lies on every member of the Society to discover every design which may be formed, contrary to the laws of the Society, to destroy the public welfare'.[2] This came to be known as the rule that 'there is no

---

[1] *W* v. *Edgill* [1990] 1 All ER 835 at 848 per Bingham LJ.
[2] *Annesley* v. *The Earl of Anglesea* 17 State Tr. 1139 (noted at LR 5 QB 317N).

confidence as to the disclosure of iniquity'.[3] Unfortunately, this formulation tended to attract too much attention to what does or does not count as 'iniquity' and in *Weld-Blundell* v. *Stephens*,[4] Bankes LJ defined the 'iniquity' exception very narrowly as being limited to the proposed or contemplated commission of a crime or a civil wrong. Fortunately, this very narrow formulation does not represent the modern law, as has been clear since the decision of the Court of Appeal in *Initial Services Limited* v. *Putterill*.[5] The 'iniquity' exception in fact extends to any misconduct of such a nature that it ought in the public interest to be disclosed to someone having a proper interest to receive it. Even that formulation may be too narrow, in that it seems that there need not necessarily be any 'misconduct' as such at all. The important decision of the House of Lords in *Attorney-General* v. *Guardian Newspapers* (the *'Spycatcher'* case)[6] supports the view that the public interest in the maintenance of confidence may be overridden wherever there is a countervailing public interest in disclosure which is sufficient to override it.

We believe that under the modern law it is preferable no longer to speak about there being no confidence in iniquity, but rather to recognize that there is always a balance to be struck between competing public interests.[7] The circumstances in which there may be a countervailing public interest defeating the obligation of confidence are so many and varied that it is wrong to seek to limit them by reference to any particular rubric. Passing well beyond the immediately apprehended commission of a crime or serious civil wrong, breach of confidence has been justified in order to reveal serious concerns about the Intoximeter equipment used for roadside breath testing, a case in which the Court of Appeal was explicit in stating that the public interest exception is not limited to misconduct or iniquity.[8] The Court of Appeal has even held to be justifiable revelations about the private lives of popular singers who were said to have courted publicity and thus to be in no position to complain if the wholesome picture which they sought to present to the world was corrected.[9]

Two decisions of the House of Lords perhaps deserve special mention. The first is the *Spycatcher* case, in which the House of Lords upheld the trend of the recent authorities supporting the general public interest exception, but did not find that the revelations of Mr Peter Wright fell within that exception. The two particular features of that case which merit attention are firstly the consideration of the appropriate remedy for breach of confidence where the confidential matters have already come into the public domain and secondly the observations of the House as to the special position of government secrets. Lord Goff of Chieveley stressed in his speech that whereas in an

[3] *Gartside* v. *Outram* [1856] 26 LJ Ch 113.   [4] [1919] 1 KB 520.
[5] [1968] 1 QB 396.   [6] [1988] 3 WLR 776.
[7] This approval has recently been adopted by laws J. in *Hellewell* r. *Chief Constable of Derbyshire*, The Times 13th January 1995.
[8] *Lion Laboratories* v. *Evans* [1985] QB 526.
[9] *Woodward* v. *Hutchins* [1977] 1 WLR 760.

ordinary private case of confidentiality it is not incumbent upon the party seeking to preserve confidence to show that it is in the public interest that publication should not occur, it is a requirement in the case of government secrets that the government should positively show that the public interest lies in publication being prevented. The reason for this additional requirement is that in a free society there is a continuing public interest that the workings of government should be open to scrutiny and criticism.

Lord Goff's remarks about the workings of government give rise to the question of their applicability to quasi-governmental bodies and to those parts of the public sector which have been privatized. In many cases the function or service provided remains no less public than that of the government itself. The Courts have yet to work out how far such bodies can invoke private confidence without first showing that there is a public interest in the prevention or inhibition of scrutiny of their conduct. The extent to which they are accountable to Parliament may well be a significant factor in evaluating this question.

The other decision of the House of Lords, namely the *Granada* case,[10] represents a salutary warning against too ready an application of the public interest in disclosing confidential information. In that case, the British Steel Corporation (which was accountable to Parliament through the Secretary of State for Energy) sought disclosure of the identity of the 'mole' within their organization who had approached Granada with allegations of poor management and bad practices within the Corporation. Despite strong arguments adduced as to the importance of the freedom of the press and despite the trenchant dissent of Lord Salmon, the House found in favour of the Corporation. The key to the view of the majority seems to lie in the remark of Lord Wilberforce that 'the most that it is said the papers reveal is mismanagement and government intervention'. In other words their Lordships were saying that there was nothing approaching misconduct in what the 'mole' had revealed and that therefore, even on the modern more liberal public interest approach, the confidence which the corporation sought to enforce was paramount.

On the face of it, this decision stands in somewhat uneasy contrast with cases such as *Lion Laboratories* v. *Evans* and makes it difficult to predict how the Courts will react in individual cases as to what does or does not suffice as a matter of public interest to override the public interest in the preservation of confidence. However, two points should be made. Firstly, there seems to be a distinction between mere mismanagement on the one hand and serious illegality, fraud, risk to health and safety or the environment on the other. This is understandable, since management is an art, not a science, and most employees at some time or other will form the view that they are on the receiving end of mismanagement of some sort. Secondly, the decision in *Granada* was dependent upon a concession by Counsel that there was no

---

[10] *British Steel Corporation* v. *Granada Television Ltd.* [1981] AC 1097.

misconduct sufficient to release the 'mole' from his duty of confidence; the point which was really pressed in argument was that there was nevertheless a public interest in the media being entitled to protect its sources. Whilst their Lordships gave some recognition to this, it is not surprising that in the circumstances of the case it did not prevail over the duty of confidence which the Corporation was invoking.

One point which does emerge clearly from the cases considered above is that the application of the public interest in disclosure is likely to vary depending upon the person to whom disclosure is contemplated.[11] It will take a very strong case to justify disclosure of confidential information to the press, but a much less strong case to justify disclosure to an appropriate regulatory authority. This seems to us to be of very considerable importance in considering practical problems arising in this area. Somebody who is subject to an obligation of confidence but who feels pressed in the public interest to make some form of disclosure should consider carefully the extent of disclosure which is necessary. In the first instance, it will usually be appropriate that the matter is raised internally when possible. For instance, an employee of a large organization who wishes to blow the whistle on some undesirable activities within the organization should, where possible, first of all approach the organization itself. The problem may lie at an intermediate level of management, and there may be reasonable grounds for believing that disclosure to senior management may be quite sufficient to deal with the mischief of the case.

The real problem in the *Granada* case was that the employee in question went straight to the press, where that appeared to the judges to constitute excessive exposure in the context of the public interest exception. But some disclosure outside the employment relationship will, in many cases, be justified and appropriate. Where there is wrongdoing in the financial services sector, an employee or other person bound by confidence should consider disclosure to the Securities and Investments Board or one or other of the self-regulating organizations established under the Financial Services Act 1986. In other cases (although not usually in the employment field), a complaint to one of the increasing number of Ombudsmen may be appropriate and sufficient. It will only be rarely that disclosure to the press can be justified as an appropriate reaction.

Thus, the test in practice is one of the minimum necessary disclosure to fit the circumstances of the case. In the *Lion* case, it is unlikely that the Court would have taken the view which it did if it were not for the fact that there was already a lively public debate about the Intoximeter, at a time when the police were seeking to crack down on drink driving and where the Home Office was

---

[11] See *Lion Laboratories* at 537D per Stephenson LJ and *Spycatcher* at 807D per Lord Goff of Chieveley.

already 'an interested and committed party'.[12] Anyone going straight to the press and breaching confidence will have to be able to justify to the Courts why some lesser and less damaging form of disclosure was not sufficient and appropriate.

THE RÔLE OF THE LAWYER

We deal first with legal advisers as a class, but make certain distinctions below as to the position of a solicitor, a barrister and other forms of legal adviser. The first point to consider is whether and to what extent disclosure made **to** a lawyer is wrongful or could give rise to complaint. We envisage the situation where someone in whom confidence is reposed is considering whether or not to disclose it, but first takes legal advice as to what he should do or can do. Here, it seems obvious that the relationship between client and lawyer will be a matter covered by legal professional privilege, such that what passes between client and lawyer cannot in general be revealed to any third party. But it is not simply a question of legal professional privilege. The right to legal advice is a fundamental right, and is recognized as such by the European Convention.[13] It is plainly in the public interest for those who are considering whether or not to disclose confidential information to be able to have full and free access to legal advice without fear that this will of itself place them in difficulties. From the point of view of the law of defamation, it has been held that solicitor/client communications are absolutely privileged,[14] and, although some doubt has been cast on this,[15] problems are only likely to arise in the vary rare case where it can be demonstrated that the client has been motivated by express malice in reporting the matter in question to the lawyer.

While we believe that the proposition put forward in the previous paragraph is clear, it is not quite so easy, as a matter of analysis, to decide whether or not disclosure to a lawyer is (a) not a disclosure at all or (b) not a breach of confidence or (c) though a breach, not unlawful. It seems to us that (a) is certainly not the answer, but that there is some difficulty in choosing between (b) and (c). As a matter of principle, we prefer (c), since this seems to us to be simply another (and very clear) example of a public interest overriding what is *prima facie* a breach of confidence. In her detailed analysis of the relationship between the obligation of disclosure and the public interest, Dr Yvonne Cripps points out that the analysis based on (c) gives the Court much greater flexibility in the choice of remedies available in the case of *prima facie* breaches of confidence than does (b).[16] The decision of the House of Lords in

---

[12] Per Stephenson LJ at 539F, and Griffiths LJ at 553B.   [13] Cmd. 8969, at Article 6.
[14] *More* v. *Weaver* [1928] 2 KB 520.   [15] *Minter* v. *Priest* [1930] AC 558.
[16] Yvonne Cripps, *The Legal Implications of Disclosure in the Public Interest* (1994) 2nd ed., esp at pp. 25–32.

the *Spycatcher* case, seems to us to support (c) and to be a good illustration of the flexibility of remedies in its practical application.

We now turn to consider disclosure **by** the lawyer as a result of instructions received from his client. Such disclosure will of course be disclosure by the client, and its legitimacy will stand or fall on the basis of the general considerations already discussed above. But what of the lawyer himself? Is he exposed if he makes disclosure on behalf of his client in circumstances which turn out not to be justified?

In the law of defamation, there is specific authority that the solicitor is not liable in defamation in respect of publication made by him as agent acting on his client's instructions.[17] This is obviously of great importance to solicitors in connection with a tort such as defamation, which is based upon strict liability. As for breach of confidence, there does not appear to be direct authority on the situation, but as a matter of general principle it is clear that the solicitor does not become liable for breach of confidence if he is merely acting as agent for his client, and no more. To be liable in tort, he would have to be aiding or abetting the breach of confidence with knowledge that a breach of confidence was occurring. If he is merely acting as agent for his client, he is no more liable for breach of confidence than is any solicitor liable for inducing a breach of contract when he writes on his client's behalf to repudiate a contract.

Difficulties do, however, begin to arise in so far as the lawyer does anything by way of contact with the outside world beyond merely carrying out his client's instructions. In the case of the ordinary solicitor or barrister, this is unlikely to arise, except inadvertently. It is a greater problem in the case of a legal adviser which has, as part of its *raison d'être*, a fundamental interest in assisting in the raising and addressing of matters of genuine public concern. It is important, however, to stress that although the law is very jealous to protect the lawyer/client relationship, such tenderness rapidly disappears where the solicitor or other legal adviser ventures out on his own. Here, the problem of confidence presents itself at a different level. The problem now becomes not the confidence which it is the *prima facie* duty of the client to preserve, but the confidence which the client himself reposes in the lawyer and the lawyer's duty to respect that confidence. While the lawyer, in giving advice and dealing with the outside world as the agent of his client, does not risk personal liability and is concerned simply with the general principles discussed above, so soon as he departs in any way from the strict adherence to his client's instructions he enters a different and more dangerous world. He then not only risks attack from the proprietor of the confidence which the client has revealed to his lawyer, but also risks action by the client himself for acting beyond his instructions or a charge of professional misconduct. It is these problems which are considered below.

[17] *Gatley on Libel and Slander*, 8th ed, para. 518.

The Solicitor

The solicitor in the course of his practice will rarely have any wish to go beyond his client's instructions, but from time to time difficult situations will arise. In principle, it may be argued that the solicitor's scope for disclosing his client's confidence (against his interest) involves the same broad balancing exercise as considered in general terms above. It is not clear, however, that the solicitor's scope for acting against his client's wishes is so great. In *Parry-Jones* v. *The Law Society*,[18] it was held that a solicitor's duty to his client could not preclude him from his duty to produce documents (confidential to the client) pursuant to the Solicitors Accounts Rules. This was because there was a specific legal duty on the solicitor to comply with the law embodied in those Rules, and it is obviously trite law that a duty of confidence cannot preclude compliance with the law of the land (see the *Tournier* case discussed below).

But how much further can the solicitor go? It must be open to serious doubt whether a solicitor can arrogate to himself a discretion as to whether or not disclosure of confidence reposed in him by his client can be justified on the basis of broad grounds of public policy. The Law Society's Guide to Professional Conduct of Solicitors[19] states that the duty to keep a client's confidences can be overridden in certain exceptional circumstances. What the scope of those exceptional circumstances might be is not entirely clear. Plainly the *Parry-Jones* case would be covered, as would any situation in which, by maintaining confidence, the solicitor is in any way assisting in any criminal or fraudulent conduct. But the notes to paragraph 16.04 of the Law Society's Guide justify only a very narrow scope to the exceptional circumstances referred to in the rule, and do not appear to justify a wider exception based simply upon countervailing public interest. This narrow approach may be influenced by the attitude of the law to legal professional privilege. What passes between solicitor and client is sometimes treated as having a sanctity similar to that of the confessional. That comparison extends not only to unwillingness to look into what passes within the relationship but also to reluctance to allow the solicitor, any more than the priest, to reveal what he has been told to any stranger to the relationship.

It is interesting to compare this position with the familiar rules relating to the obligation of a banker to maintain confidence, as laid down in the *Tournier* case.[20] Bankes LJ classified the situations in which a banker may disclose in breach of confidence to his customer under four heads:

1. Where disclosure is under compulsion of law;
2. Where there is a duty to the public to disclose;
3. Where the interests of the bank requires disclosure;
4. Where the disclosure is made by the express or implied consent of the customer.

---

[18] [1968] 1 All ER 177.   [19] 6th ed, para. 16.04.
[20] *Tournier* v. *National Provincial and Union Bank of England* [1924] 1 KB 461.

The interesting head is (2), and Bankes LJ goes on to cite the language of Lord Findlay in *Weld-Blundell* v. *Stephens*[21] in which he speaks of cases where a higher duty than the private duty is involved, as where 'danger to the state or public duty may supersede the duty of the agent to his principal'.

It is not at all clear whether in the case of solicitors there is such a wide exception. The matter may be tested by an example. What is a solicitor to do if he discovers in the course of acting for a client that there exists a very real danger to public safety? Assume that he is consulted by the owner of a fairground, who is in financial difficulties. It becomes clear to him that the owner has neglected the proper maintenance of the fairground, such that several of the rides are dangerous, and that it is unlikely anything is going to be done by the owner to remedy the situation. Serious personal injury or death is only a matter of time. What is he to do? A reading of the Guide to Professional Conduct does not immediately appear to confirm that the solicitor would be justified in contacting the Health and Safety Executive, who might take action to safeguard public safety, but might well also take action against the solicitor's client. Surely, as a matter of public policy, however, the solicitor ought to be entitled, without either being liable to action by his client or to a charge of professional misconduct, to take the necessary steps in the public interest to prevent death or serious injury. It seems to us that the Professional Guide does not do enough to recognize the strength of the public interest which can require disclosure. While no doubt situations differ between different principal/agent situations, and while there may be good grounds for allowing a wider scope for disclosure on the part of the banker than on the part of a solicitor, this should simply be a matter of degree, and the yardstick as to what disclosure is or is not permissible by a solicitor against his client's interest should be flexible. In short, there is no real reason why the general principles governing the balancing of public interests in the maintenance of confidence, and disclosure in the public interest, should not be applied, no doubt with the caveat that in the case of a solicitor revealing his client's confidence the countervailing public interest in disclosure must be a particularly strong one.[22]

---

[21] [1920] AC 596.

[22] It may be worth comparing the recent case-law in the family courts, recognizing that the welfare of the child overrides legal professional privilege: see *Oxfordshire CC* v. *M* [1994] 2 All ER 269A: see also *R* v. *Barton* [1972] 2 All ER 1192, dealing with legal professional privilege and the criminal defendant.

The Barrister

The distinction between the rôle of solicitor and the rôle of barrister is of course rapidly being blurred by the advent of the solicitor-advocate. However, for the moment different codes of practice govern solicitors and the Bar. The Bar's Code of Conduct adopts a very rigid rule to deal with the situation of the barrister who has a duty of disclosure to the Court, where the client refuses to sanction disclosure. In those circumstances the Bar's Code envisages that the duty of the barrister is to withdraw from the case, not to make the disclosure which the client refuses to permit.[23] This is a very striking provision, and reflects the importance which the Bar's Code attaches to the requirement that the barrister should fearlessly advance his client's interests at all times and the need for the client to be able to repose complete confidence in his advocate. In the event of unavoidable conflict, the only remedy is withdrawal. Thus if one returns to the example of the fairground owner, the barrister in the situation posited above would, as it appears from the code, not be entitled, contrary to his client's instructions, to reveal the danger to public safety, although his instructing solicitor may be, and an employee of the barrister's client almost certainly would be entitled to break the confidence of his employer.

In our view it is very difficult to justify these differences. In each case the fairground owner has imparted confidential information, whether it be to employee, solicitor, or barrister. In each case, the same public interest, namely the preservation of public safety, has precisely the same weight. Any justification for the disparity must lie in the peculiar position of the barrister as the fearless exponent of his client's case. Because of the need to ensure that barristers are not deflected from defending their client's interests, however unpopular, save in so far as the barrister is required not to mislead the Court, it is the orthodox view that the barrister should not be given any element of discretion as to whether or not to make disclosure against his client's wishes. Also, provided that the solicitor is able to act in the public interest, then in practical terms the added restriction on the barrister may not actually operate against the public interest favouring disclosure.

How convincing this is may be open to question. We would prefer that the law and rules of professional conduct should be restated so as to make clear that in all cases there exists a balance to be struck between the public interest in the preservation of confidence and the public interest meriting disclosure. As Atkin LJ said in the *Tournier* case[24] the extent of the exceptions which may exist to the duty of confidence must vary with the special circumstances peculiar to each type of situation. Thus, in the case of bankers there are now many well recognized exceptions to the duty of confidence, and these are being

---

[23] The General Council of the Bar, *Code of Conduct of the Bar of England and Wales* (1990: loose-leaf), at 504(e). [24] At p. 486.

further extended as measures are being taken to inhibit money laundering and drug trafficking.[25] In the case of a solicitor, a good case can be made that the exceptions to the duty of confidence should be less extensive, in view of the special importance the law attaches to the lawyer/client relationship and the superimposition of the law of legal professional privilege upon the law of confidentiality.[26] As for the Bar, it is arguable that the exception to the duty of confidence should be even narrower, at least so long as barristers continue to be a referral profession instructed by solicitors or other professionals who can themselves make disclosure in the public interest where appropriate.

But these are differences of degree. What is important is that the codes for solicitors and barristers should explicitly recognize the public interest exception. It is hard to believe that more explicit recognition of this principle will lead solicitors and barristers too readily to compromise the interests of their clients. On the contrary, such recognition would be concordant with the fact that solicitors and barristers are officers of the Court and have an important rôle to play in the administration of justice. This is and should be more than simply ensuring that the advocate does not actively mislead the Court. If the principle is more clearly recognized, there is no reason to believe that the proper ambit of the public interest exception cannot be adequately evolved, as has occurred in the case of the employer/employee or banker/client relationship. This evolution, we believe, is better handled by the professions and the judiciary than by legislative intervention; this will ensure a measured approach to the development of public interest disclosure by lawyers.

If we return for one last time to the case of the fairground owner, let us imagine that in his meeting with his solicitor he has not revealed the imminent danger which the public faces. He is charged with minor offences to which he intended to plead guilty at the Magistrates' Court. He is represented by a young barrister, whom he instructs to say little or nothing by way of mitigation. When asked by the barrister for the reason for this, he states that the true position is very much worse than the Health and Safety Executive had discovered, and that he does not wish actively to mislead the Court by indicating that the minor transgressions for which he is charged have been or will be remedied. On the day of the hearing, all the rides are operating and the owner tells the barrister precisely how much money he is making out of them. When the barrister asks him whether he is not concerned someone might be killed, he simply laughs. The instructing solicitor is not at Court, but has simply sent a clerk to hold the file. What is the barrister to do? He can follow his client's instructions without misleading the Court. He can withdraw from the case. Neither of these reactions seem at all appropriate. Surely he should be entitled to tell his client the matter is so serious that he feels bound to inform the Health and Safety Executive immediately of the public danger and he should proceed to do so, doing his best to preserve his client's interest by minimizing publicity? Under the present Code it seems that this option is not available. We find that hard to justify.

Power or Duty

So far, we have concentrated on the question as to whether or not there is a power, in appropriate circumstances, to disclose a *prima facie* confidence. Nevertheless, the example of the fairground owner considered above evokes the question as to whether or not there might be a duty to disclose. In most situations, it does not seem to us that the law recognizes a duty, as opposed to a power, to make disclosure, although the money laundering regulations affecting bankers provide an example of an obligation to disclose. Misprision of felony is no longer an offence, and in general there is no recognized legal duty to reveal misconduct. However, while there will rarely be a specific obligation to disclose, the exercise of the lawyer's power to do so must be looked at in the context of his obligations as an officer of the Court. In other words the exercise of the power must be governed by the lawyer's general professional obligations. It is, of course, of considerable practical assistance to a lawyer to be convinced that his obligations require him to make disclosure, rather than leaving him with a discretion as to how to balance conflicting pressures. In practice, we doubt whether there will be many situations where the balancing exercise can be easily avoided.

The Opportunities

So far we have stressed the dangers and difficulties in which a lawyer may find himself when caught between the duty to honour confidence and the public interest in disclosure. However, where there are dangers there are also opportunities, and it seems to us right to stress that lawyers can play a helpful and positive role in resolving the conflicts which we have been considering. Looking at the competing public interests which need to be weighed in the balance within, for instance, an employment contract, the lawyer/client relationship may well be the most effective way in which these interests should first be evaluated. In doing this, legal advisers are bound to take into account broad ethical considerations. Clients often seek advice about matters which *prima facie* fall within their express or implied duties of confidence to their employer. In many cases if the concerns were raised elsewhere the client would risk discipline or dismissal by his employer for breach of that confidence. As we have explained, because of the nature of the lawyer/client relationship, an employee can seek legal advice about such a concern without breaching the duty to the employer and in strict confidence. Any action by an employer to discipline or deter an employee from seeking such legal advice would be unlawful and would be treated seriously by the courts.

By contrast, if an employee contacts his MP about something which is worrying him at work, he can be dismissed for breach of confidence, even if the MP does nothing with the information other than put the matter to the employer. Whilst raising a concern with a regulatory body is at least lawful, the statutory responsibilities of the regulator will dictate its response to the concern, and the interests or involvement of the employee will at best come a poor second. Most people consider bringing a regulator into their workplace as an act of disloyalty to their employer. Equally, many employees would be reluctant to bother a regulator with something which was only a concern, as opposed to something they were sure was correct or they felt able to prove.

For these reasons many employees who come across dangers to the public or serious malpractice in the workplace choose not to contact the regulator. Where they do, many choose to raise the matter anonymously. Anonymity in these matters is not desirable for two reasons. Firstly it is the preferred vehicle of the malevolent and vexatious and secondly it does not facilitate an effective or efficient investigation by the regulator. Even though contacting a regulator is lawful, it is not at present clear that an employee who is dismissed for this reason is entitled to anything beyond his statutory entitlement—even if his concern is well founded and he is acting in good faith. With current maximum awards from Industrial Tribunals at £11,300 for such a dismissal[27]—even in a case where the High Court has found the disclosure to be in the public interest—this statutory provision can be scant recompense even to a low-paid employee if he is unable to work again because of his action. This contrasts with the position in the United States where, despite the doctrine of employment at will, employees who are dismissed for blowing the whistle can receive substantial damages.

Against this background it is not surprising that many employees will lack the courage or wherewithal to raise a concern (however serious) in the first place, either internally or with an appropriate authority. Equally, without independent advice there is a real risk that those who do speak up will raise the concern in an inappropriate way, exposing themselves to criticism or worse. Lawyers are in a unique position. Advice can be sought from them without the employee breaching the confidence or loyalty he owes to his employer. The wider public interest in this application of the lawyer/client duty of confidence is clear. Not only can employees seek legal advice about their rights and responsibilities, and the risks and opportunities they may face should they raise their concern, but also they receive an independent perspective and a helping hand. Proper legal advice obtained early enough allows the

---

[27] Unfair Dismissal (Increase of Compensation Limit) Order 1995 (SI 1995 No. 1953).

employee to see the wood for the trees and to make an informed and responsible decision about whether and how he should raise his concern.

On occasions where the employee decides to raise the concern internally, the advice can help to ensure that the employer responds by dealing with the message rather than the messenger. Without independent advice, employees in such circumstances can be confused about where and how any legal and practical responsibility they have can be discharged. The result is all too often that the employee—even where the concern is well founded and raised in good faith—ends up usurping management functions and in the process alienating colleagues and undermining his own position.

Where it is appropriate, the lawyer can actually assist an employee in raising the matter internally (or do so on his behalf) without undermining the fidelity or confidentiality of the employment contract. However, one must recognize that intervention by a lawyer can prompt an adverse reaction from the employer, who may instinctively assume that there is a serious dispute or imminent litigation. Thus, subtlety of approach can be of very great importance. Where the lawyer makes clear to the organization at the outset that his involvement is no more than to assist the client in seeing that his concern is addressed, his intervention should not cause any over-reaction by the employer and need not require the involvement of the organization's own lawyer. Indeed, the intervention may be positively welcomed by the organization's management, or at least from individuals within it. Where there is nobody with whom the employee can safely raise the matter internally, and the lawyer is satisfied that the matter is such that it should be raised with a regulator, the lawyer can advise how to do this. One further advantage the lawyer offers is that he can—where instructed by the client—raise the matter with the regulator on the employee's behalf in such cases and (even where the employee is reluctant that his identity is disclosed to the regulator) the lawyer can liaise with and respond to the regulator's enquiries on behalf of his client.

If anonymity is necessary, then use of a lawyer may make this possible, although it has been held that legal professional privilege does not as such protect a solicitor from disclosing the name of his client (*Bursill* v. *Tanner*[28] and *Pascall* v. *Galinsky*[29]). In the *Granada* case discussed above, there was some muted recognition by the House of Lords that, in some circumstances at least, there is a public interest in the protection by the media of its sources, and if (unlike in *Granada*) an anonymous disclosure of information were held to be in the public interest, the *Granada* decision indicates (albeit without total clarity) that the courts would not compel, or would not necessarily compel, disclosure of the name of the informant.[30]

---

[28] [1885] 16 QBD 1. [29] [1970] 1 QB 39.
[30] Per Lord Wilberforce at 1174H–1175D, per Lord Fraser at 1201A–1202A.

The Public Interest Legal Adviser

There is of course no such thing as a public interest legal adviser. It is, however, possible for legal advice to be given by a lawyer who is particularly concerned to promote ethical conduct in compliance with the law in the public, private, and voluntary sectors, and in the professions. The ordinary solicitor or barrister in practice has comparatively little scope (particularly with the professional codes in their present shape) to promote a proper awareness of the correct balance between the competing public interests in confidence and in disclosure. He or she will always err heavily on the side of caution. There is, however, no reason at all why legal advice should not be available in a broader context nor why it should not be sensitive to the public interest. To this end, Public Concern at Work, a charity established in 1993, provides free legal advice, primarily to those in employment, as to how to handle conflicts between duties of confidence and loyalty to the employer, and wider considerations of the public interests in disclosure. The main impetus behind the establishment of the charity has been the various recent official inquiries into major disasters and abuses.[31] These inquiries have thrown up cases where employees had suspected malpractice but were too afraid to speak, where they had raised concerns but nothing had been done in time, where employees were victimized for speaking up against malpractice, and where employees saw the relevant danger but did not wish to rock the boat. A common message has come from all of these inquiries, namely the inadequacy of communication within the workplace. Without doing any damage to the law of confidence, much greater use can and should be made of internal avenues of complaint and inquiry, and legal services can assist greatly in promoting this type of communication.

These inquiries have also recognized that in many cases raising the matter internally has not ensured that the problem has been properly addressed. Without the benefit of hindsight the extent to which external disclosure of confidential matters is appropriate or wise is of very great difficulty, but there is much to be said for the merits of the view that such advice should be given by lawyers who are particularly attuned to the significance of wider public interests. Thus, there is a very important rôle for lawyers who have this added dimension to add to their concern for the narrower interests of their individual client.

Of course there are difficulties and conflicts involved in this. If, as is essential, the lawyer must act as a genuine legal adviser to a client who is consulting him, then he cannot altogether escape from restrictions such as those which impede barristers and solicitors in going beyond the four corners

---

[31] eg *Bingham Inquiry into Supervision of BCCI* HC, 198, 1992; *Blom-Cooper Inquiry into Ashworth Special Hospital*, Cm 2028, 1992; *Hidden Inquiry into Clapham Rail Disaster*, Cm 820, 1989, *Sheen Inquiry into Zeebrugge Ferry Disaster* Ct 8074, 1987.

of their client's instructions. To venture out too far into the public interest risks destroying the essential basis of the status of legal adviser without which no useful job can be done. None the less, and difficult though the balance is to strike, we believe that there is a rôle, consistent with genuine legal advice, for the lawyer who is concerned to promote the public interest.

To what extent should lawyers promote compliance with the law and ethical behaviour to their clients? Lawyers are not evangelists and are instructed by clients to advise on, or assist with, certain tasks, or to represent their interests. It is rarely any part of their job to go beyond the scope of their instructions and to inquire generally into their client's affairs. However, once instructed to advise on a contentious or non-contentious matter lawyers will naturally strive to ensure that their client's actions are lawful. On occasions it may appear that a client is more interested in compliance with only the letter and not the spirit of the law. Where a business client is seeking general advice on a matter lawyers can and should properly consider and advise on the spirit of the law (and to that extent ethical conduct). This is not only because of possible liability or culpability on the part of the lawyer, such as was alleged in the *Blue Arrow* case, but also because such conduct is most likely to be in the long term best interests of the client or business organization seeking advice.

One of the themes of Professor Cranston's introductory chapter is the extent to which current legal ethics are rooted in the rôle of the defence lawyer in criminal cases protecting the liberty of the individual against an overbearing State. We are not convinced that this should be a universal touchstone for all ethical problems. Where, as in the developing law of confidence, broad and conflicting public interests have to be weighed against each other, it is debatable whether, and to what extent, the lawyer's freedom to weigh such competing interests should be more strictly limited than his client's liberty to do so. In its own back yard, the Law Society has recently announced the introduction of a confidential hotline to the Society's Investigation Unit when a solicitor or employee suspects that fraud may be being perpetrated by someone in his firm or by another member of the profession.[32] This is very much to be encouraged, and, in our view, should be extended by The Law Society so as to recognize that solicitors, advising clients as to the extent to which it is justifiable to breach *prima facie* confidence, should have regard to the full scope and ambit of the public interest exception to the law of confidence, extending if necessary to justifiable disclosure despite the wishes of a particular client.

The Bar also needs to rethink its guidance in this area, especially in so far as it differs from the guidance given to solicitors. With the advent of the solicitor-advocate doing work similar if not identical to that of the barrister, serious divergence between applicable rules of conduct may become difficult

---

[32] *Law Society Gazette*, 13 Apr. 1994, pp. 3 and 10.

to defend. More fundamentally, we believe that there is a strong case for shifting the emphasis of the lawyer's duty, especially in civil cases, from the fearless and single-minded pursuit of the interests of his client some way towards the overriding duty owed to the court, to the standards of the lawyers' profession, and to the public. We would wish to echo the words of Lord Reid in *Rondel* v. *Worsley*,[33] cited by Professor Cranston, to the effect that these public or quasi-public duties must in the end prevail if the legal profession is to retain credibility as a public service. In the context of the problems surrounding breach of confidence and the public interest, we believe that legal advisers of all sorts should not shrink from venturing into the comparison and indeed conflict between countervailing public interests, even if this means giving advice to the client which ultimately is of an ethical or quasi-ethical nature. We further believe that this should be pressed, where necessary, into situations, naturally somewhat rare, where the lawyer should feel that it is his duty to reveal facts given to him by his client in confidence, even though such revelation is contrary to his client's wishes.

Other than as a matter of emphasis, it is difficult to justify any fundamental distinction between situations in which it is legitimate for a lawyer to disclose contrary to the wishes of his client, and similar situations involving other confidential and professional agents or advisers. In the difficult waters which lie ahead for the legal profession, it is essential that the lawyer's own concepts of what is or is not ethical or professional do not become too far removed from public perceptions. The image of the lawyer as no more than a 'hired gun' is becoming very damaging, however impeccable may be the arguments based upon the rôle of the defence lawyer in a criminal trial. We do not believe that this is an adequate basis for coping with the difficulties of conflicting public interests.

[33] [1969] 1 AC 191, at 227.

6

Professional Responsibility When Dealing with Parental Irresponsibility

SIR ALAN WARD

NOT often enough do busy practitioners pause to reflect, as having to prepare this chapter has required my pausing to reflect, on their professional responsibility as they go about their daily tasks as lawyers and judges, asserting, defending, or deciding the irresponsibility of parents in bringing up their children. To recognize that irresponsibility is not usually difficult: parents are irresponsible when they fail in the trust and duty which nature and society impose upon them to promote and safeguard the well-being of their children. Recognizing professional irresponsibility is not always that obvious.

I would define professional responsibility as the fulfilment of that trust and duty which is imposed by one's calling to be morally accountable for one's actions in the practice of that department of learning in which one professes to have special knowledge and skill. One is morally accountable when a choice has to be made between courses of action which drive one in different directions. A theme of this chapter will be to consider the extent to which, if at all, the child's welfare dictates the path which professionals are bound to follow.

The paramountcy of welfare is certainly the bed-rock of the Children Act 1989. The challenge of this paper is to consider whether that bed-rock is always rock solid, or whether it is a water-bed changing its shape according to the pressure put upon it. If policy considerations are pressure points, what matters of policy weigh more heavily than the child's welfare?

JUDICIAL RESPONSIBILITY

1. The Lord Chancellor

The Lord Chancellor commands high praise for his commitment to the Children Act. He continues to have considerable responsibility for the manner in which it is operated. Among the matters reserved to him, and in which he takes a keen interest, is the allocation of the judiciary approved by him to hear children's cases. There is a public interest which demands that the work be done by a selected cadre of judges, limited in number, temperamentally suitable, and trained for the job. The balance the Lord Chancellor has to strike is to appoint enough judges to get the work done, but not so many as to devalue the specialization. There are other pressures upon him. Section 1(2) of the Act requires the court to have regard to 'the general principle that any delay in determining [any question with respect to the upbringing of the child] is likely to prejudice the welfare of the child'. By Section 1(1), welfare is the court's paramount consideration. Sadly, across the country at present, there are delays up to and not infrequently in excess of six months between the case being ready to be set down and its being heard. Many think such delays are scandalous. In part, these delays are due to the cases taking too long, creating a back-log. In part, the delay is caused by there simply not being enough judges and court rooms available to dispose of the work load. The welfare of the children who are kept waiting cannot, it would seem, be the Lord Chancellor's only consideration, for the obvious resource implications must weigh more heavily. That the Lord Chancellor cannot satisfy these conflicting interests illustrates the dilemma that afflicts many practitioners in this class of work, from the top to the bottom.

2. *The Judges*

Do the judges always give first place to the welfare of the child? I fear not. For example:

(1). Appeals

The most important Family Law case to reach the House of Lords in the past decade may not be *Gillick* v. *West Norfolk & Wisbech Area Health Authority*[1], seminal though these speeches are, but a case less frequently cited in academic writing namely, *G* v. *G*.[2] The issue there was whether appeals in custody cases were subject to special rules of their own in that the Court of Appeal had itself to decide a question with respect to the child's upbringing which would have imposed upon it the duty set out in section 1 of The Guardianship of Minors Act 1971 to give paramount consideration to the child's welfare. That contention was 'entirely' rejected. One can but speculate whether the true reason for limiting the rôle of the Court of Appeal in these cases is the need to prevent the system being overloaded with work, ie a policy decision based upon cost effectiveness. One has to ask if a custody case is so finely balanced as not to admit of any answer which one could confidently assert to be right, may not 2, 3, or 5 judges collectively have a better chance of identifying the least detrimental solution for the child rather the single judge whose unhappy lot it is to find some solution?

[1] [1986] 1 AC 1112.   [2] [1985] 1 WLR 647.

(2). Leave to Apply for Section 8 Orders

In *Re A & Ors (minors) (Residence: Leave to Apply)*[3] Balcombe LJ held that in granting or refusing an application for leave to apply, the court was not determining a question with respect to the upbringing of the child concerned and so welfare was not the paramount consideration. I am not sure that I understand why refusing to give granny the opportunity to offer her home to little Johnny is not determining whether granny should be permitted to bring him up. I do understand that some filter has to be imposed on the number of parties who wish to be heard because too many make the case too long and too expensive, and create the very delays which make more judges necessary. The policy is unspoken (cut down the parties!) but the child's welfare may suffer.

(3). Press Publicity

Recently in *Re H (minors) (Injunction; Public interest)*[4] the issue was what publicity should be given to the family when the father, to whom custody had been given, had undergone a 'gender reassignment', which is more easily understood as a sex change operation. I found myself giving the judgment at the Court of Appeal and saying: 'More than a question of upbringing arises for determination by the court. The freedom of the press is in issue'. (Some have apparently commented that I was really saying that freedom **from** the press was in issue!) So the welfare of the children came second.

Thus it is certainly true that I and others have not always made the welfare of the child our paramount consideration. We would all be horrified if it were suggested that we were professionally irresponsible so to have decided.

(4). Judicial Control of the Proceedings

The extent to which the litigation should be under the control of the judge is one of the matters on which Lord Woolf will report to the Lord Chancellor. Meanwhile, there is ample exhortation from on high to be more interventionist. In his speech to Bar Conference in October 1993, Lord Taylor said this:

[The judges'] duty in the interests of justice is to secure a fair, and efficient and expeditious trial. That may require them to intervene to avoid irrelevance, to curb prolixity and to protect witnesses. . . . A tendency has . . . developed to regard tolerance and patience as the ultimate judicial virtues. That they are judicial virtues, no one doubts; but to make them paramount can all too easily lead to a court process in which almost everything goes and goes for a very long time . . . Without being unpleasant or talking excessively, a judge can and should intervene to confine advocacy to the issues, to stop repetitive or oppressive cross-examination and to discourage long windedness.[5]

---

[3] [1992] Fam 182.   [4] [1994] 1 FLR 519.
[5] Opening Speech by the Lord Chief Justice of England, Bar Conference, 2 Oct. 1993, pp. 3–4.

The Master of the Rolls has been no less explicit. In *Arab Monetary Fund* v. *Hashim & Ors No(8)*[6] he said:

A judge did not act amiss if, in relation to some feature of [a] party's case which struck him as inherently improbable, he indicated the need for unusually compelling evidence to persuade him of the fact. An expression of scepticism was not suggestive of bias unless the judge conveyed an unwillingness to be persuaded of a factual proposition whatever the evidence might be. . . . Above all [the judge] had to try to press the hearing firmly but fairly to a conclusion, conscious one man's six months in court might be the next man's denial of justice. . . . Judges were constantly urged to be robust and interventionist to mitigate the blemish on the legal system which protracted trials, civil as well as criminal, had become. In responding to that call judges had to be true to their judicial oaths.

I try to respond to that call—some would say with enthusiasm. I am, however, conscious that it can be taken too far. There are two dangers. Firstly, weak counsel and overawed litigants may capitulate under fierce judicial onslaught and injustice may be done. Sometimes the evidence from the last witness can totally change the judge's preliminary view of the case and fair opportunity to call that last bit of evidence should never be denied. Secondly, the balance of conflicting public interest is delicately poised if one has to risk an occasionally rushed and wrong decision in one case in order more quickly and more cheaply to give access to justice to many more cases. The challenging question is: should justice be resource driven? I feel distinctly uneasy about the prospect that it will be.

PROFESSIONAL RESPONSIBILITY

1. The Duty to the Court

There is no more forthright exposition of this than Lord Templeman's speech in *Ashmore* v. *Corpn. of Lloyd's*[7]:

The parties and particularly their legal advisers in any litigation are under a duty to co-operate with the court by chronological, brief and consistent pleadings which define the issues and leave the judge to draw his own conclusions about the merits when he hears the case. It is the duty of counsel to assist the judge by simplification and concentration and not to advance a multitude of ingenious arguments in the hope that out of ten bad points the judge will be capable of fashioning a winner. In nearly all cases the correct procedure works perfectly well. But there has been a tendency in some cases for legal advisers, pressed by their clients, to make every point conceivable and inconceivable without judgment or discrimination.

---

[6] *The Times*, 4 May 1993.   [7] [1992] 1 WLR 446, 453.

The duty of the profession to promote within their own sphere the cause of justice is higher than their duty to their client. That must be the golden rule of professional conduct and if in any situation there is a queasy feeling of unease in the pit of the stomach then the profession must always remember that honour must on no account be sacrificed for any client, however important he may at the time seem to be. The reputable client will accept the constraints of professional responsibility; the client who urges even the slightest bending of the rules is a disreputable client and he should be shown the door.

2. *The Duty to the Legal Aid Fund*

This is, I fear, more honoured in the breach than in the observance. Most practitioners will know that regulation 67(1) of the Civil Legal Aid (General) Regulations 1989 provides that:

Where an assisted person's solicitor or counsel has reason to believe that the assisted person has—

(a) Required his case to be conducted unreasonably so as to incur an unjustifiable expense to the fund or has required unreasonably that the case be continued . . . the solicitor or counsel shall forthwith report the fact to the area director.

I doubt whether more than a handful will be aware how much further regulation 67(2) goes. This provides that:

Where a solicitor or counsel **is uncertain** whether it would be reasonable for him to continue acting for the assisted person, he shall report the circumstances to the Area Director. (Emphasis added.)

Some of the profession seem slow to recognize their responsibility to the Legal Aid Fund which is not a bottomless well of money which practitioners can expect to draw up by the bucket load. Greed and inefficiency of a few will kill the goose laying their golden eggs.

I make this stricture on the few, not unmindful of how difficult it always is to tell the client that he has no reasonable prospect of success. Especially where the object of the litigation is a child, the more disadvantaged the client, the greater his feeling of having been steam-rollered by the Social Services juggernaut or by his spouse, the harder it becomes to deny this client his day in court. The tendency for the sympathetic practitioner is not to shut the client out, but to leave it to the judge. I must challenge that attitude and ask whether it is not an abdication of professional responsibility. Which causes the greater afront to justice, the trusted adviser patiently telling the client that the case is hopeless, or the judge so robustly intervening that the unhappy client leaves the court with the feeling that the judge was against him throughout and that he has not had a fair trial? I am coming to the view that there is a heavy burden on the profession to take control and to be compassionate in their advice, but none the less dispassionate in assessing the prospects of eventual success. I do not forget the speech of Lord Pearce in *Rondel* v. *Worsley*:[8]

It is easier, pleasanter and more advantageous professionally for barristers to advise, represent or defend those who are decent and reasonable and likely to succeed in their action or their defence than those who are unpleasant, disreputable and have an apparently hopeless case. Yet it would be tragic if our legal system came to provide no reputable defenders, representatives or advisers for the latter.

In the *Ridehalgh* case,[9] Sir Thomas Bingham MR said this:

Pursuing a hopeless case
A legal representative is not to be held to have acted improperly, unreasonably or negligently simply because he acts for a party who pursues a claim or a defence which is plainly doomed to fail . . . Legal representatives will, of course, whether barristers or solicitors, advise the clients of the perceived weakness of their case and of the risk of failure. But clients are free to reject advice and insist that cases be litigated. It is rarely if ever safe for a court to assume that a hopeless case is being litigated on the advice of the lawyers involved. They are there to present the case; it is (as Samuel Johnson unforgettably pointed out) for the judge and not the lawyers to judge it.

It is, however, one thing for a legal representative to present, on instructions, a case which he regards as bound to fail; it is quite another to lend his assistance to proceedings which are an abuse of the process of the court. Whether instructed or not, a legal representative is not entitled to use litigious procedures for purposes for which they were not intended, as by issuing or pursuing proceedings for reasons unconnected with success in the litigation or pursuing a case known to be dishonest, nor is he entitled to evade rules intended to safeguard the interest of justice, as by knowingly failing to make full disclosure on *ex parte* application or knowingly conniving at incomplete disclosure of documents. It is not entirely easy to distinguish by definition between the hopeless case and the case which amounts to an abuse of the process, but in practice it is not hard to say which is which and if there is doubt, the legal representative is entitled to the benefit of it.

That case concerned the liability of the practitioners personally to pay a party's costs wasted through the improper, unreasonable, or negligent conduct of the practitioner. Conduct which would be regarded as improper according to the consensus of professional (including judicial) opinion can be fairly stigmatized as such whether or not it violates the letter of a professional code. The acid test for unreasonable conduct is whether the conduct permits of a reasonable explanation and if so the course adopted may be regarded as optimistic, and as reflecting on a practitioner's judgment, but it is not unreasonable. Negligent is understood in an untechnical way to denote failure to act with the competence reasonably to be expected of ordinary members of the profession.

---

[8] [1969] 1 AC 191, 275 B.   [9] [1994] 3 WLR 462, 479–80.

3. The Duty to Give Full and Frank Disclosure

This is a responsibility well known to family lawyers and the performance of the duty creates a tension between the profession and the client who is never too eager to give ammunition to the enemy. It is, however, an important duty, failure to perform which will be regarded as an abuse of the process of the court and condemned accordingly. The rule is stated by Lord Brandon of Oakbrook in *Jenkins* v. *Livesey* as follows:[10]

Each party concerned in claims for financial provision and property adjustment (or other forms of ancillary relief not material in the present case) owes a duty to the court to make full and frank disclosure of all material facts to the other party and the court. This principle of full and frank disclosure in proceedings of this kind has long been recognised and enforced as a matter of practice.

Surprisingly there does not appear to be the same clear statement with respect to children's cases. In *R* v. *Hampshire CC ex parte K*, Watkins LJ said:[11]

Local authorities therefore have a high duty in law, not only on the grounds of general fairness but also in the direct interests of a child whose welfare they serve, to be open in the disclosure of all relevant material affecting the child in their position or power (excluding documents protected on established grounds of public immunity) which may be of assistance to the natural parent or parents in rebutting charges against one or both of them of in any way ill-treating the child.

Although that case is limited to the duty imposed on local authorities, I can see no reason why it should not apply to all parties before the courts. An analysis of *Jenkins* v. *Livesey* shows how the duty arose in that case. Lord Brandon said:[12]

The scheme which the legislature enacted by sections 23, 24 and 25 of the Act of 1973 was a scheme under which the court would be bound, before deciding whether to exercise its powers under sections 23 and 24, and, if so, in what manner, to have regard to all the circumstances of the case, including, *inter alia*, the particular matter specified in paragraphs (a) and (b) of s25(1). It follows, in proceedings in which parties invoke the exercise of the court's powers under sections 23 and 24, they must provide the court with the information about all the circumstances of the case including, *inter alia*, the particular matters so specified. Unless they do so, directly or indirectly, and ensure that the information provided is correct, complete and up to date, the court is not equipped to exercise, and therefore cannot lawfully and properly exercise, its discretion in the manner ordained by s25(1).

The scheme enacted in the Children Act 1989 likewise places the court under certain duties. By section 1(5):

[10] [1985] 1 AC 424, 437.   [11] [1990] FLR 330, 336.   [12] [1985] 1 AC 424, 436.

Where a court is considering whether or not to make one or more orders under this act with respect to a child, it shall not make the order or any of the orders unless it considers that doing so would be better for the child than making no order at all.

Under section 1(1) when a court determines any question with respect to the upbringing of the child, the child's welfare shall be the court's paramount consideration and under section 1(3) the court shall have regard to the so-called check-list factors there set out. It seems to me, therefore, that the court is not equipped to exercise and cannot therefore lawfully and properly exercise its discretion in the manner ordained by section 1, unless the parties have directly or indirectly ensured that all material information impinging upon the child's welfare is before the court, correct, complete, and up to date. In the exercise of its inherent jurisdiction, the court has been accustomed to moulding and adapting its procedures to attain the end of protecting the child's best interest. Thus Lord Devlin in *Re K (infants)*[13] cited the judgment of the judge below, Ungoed-Thomas J, with approval:

In the ordinary lis between parties, the paramount purpose is that the parties should have their rights according to law, and in such cases the procedure, including the rules of evidence, is framed to serve that purpose. However where the paramount purpose is the welfare of the infant, the procedure and rules of evidence should serve and certainly not thwart that purpose.

In *D v. NSPCC*[14]—a case which, for the richness of its prose, is pure delight to read—Lord Hailsham of St Marylebone referred to:

The general importance of the principle that, in all cases before them, the courts should insist on the parties and the witnesses disclosing the truth, the whole truth, and nothing but the truth where this would assist the decision of the matters in dispute.[15]

Although these cases proceeded under the court's inherent jurisdiction, the whole basis of the decisions is the principle of the paramountcy of welfare and since the court is required by Section 1 of the Children Act to apply the same principle, the same result should follow.[16]

I incline to the view, therefore, that the rule of full and frank disclosure is of universal application in children's cases as well as in claims for ancillary relief.

4. Legal Professional Privilege

Lord Simon of Glaisdale eloquently explains the public interest which compels relevant evidence being excluded from forensic scrutiny. He says in *D v. NSPCC*:[17]

---

[13] [1965] AC 201, 240.   [14] [1978] AC 171.   [15] At p. 225.
[16] Cf *In re B* [1993] Fam 142.   [17] [1978] AC 171.

Nearer the heart of the argument in the instant appeal lies another class of relevant evidence which the public interest in the administration of justice itself demands should be withheld from the courts. This is evidence excluded by legal professional privilege. Our national experience found that justice is more likely to ensue from adversary than from inquisitorial procedures—Inquisition and Star Chamber were decisive, and knowledge of recent totalitarian methods has merely rammed the lesson home. To promote justice the adversary procedure involves advocacy of contrary contentions by representatives with special gifts and training. In the words of Dr Johnson:

> 'As it rarely happens that a man is fit to plead his own cause, lawyers are a class of the community, who by study and experience, have acquired the art and power of arranging evidence, and applying to the points at issue what the law has settled. A lawyer is to do for his client all that his client might fairly do for himself if he could.'

This process would be undermined if the trained advisers were compelled to divulge weaknesses in their cases arising from what they had been told by their clients. Indeed, the adversary system, involving professional assistance, could hardly begin to work effectively unless the client could be sure that his confidences would be respected. And a legal representative with only partial knowledge of his case would be like a champion going into battle unconscious of a gap in his armour.[18]

That privilege is not extended to care cases under the Children Act 1989. In *Oxfordshire CC* v. *M*[19] the President, with whom Steyn LJ and Kennedy LJ agreed, justified it in these terms:

The proceedings under the Children Act 1989 are not adversarial, although an adversarial approach is frequently adopted by various of the parties. However, so far as the court is concerned, its duty is to investigate and to seek to achieve a result which is in the interests of the welfare of the child . . . Children's cases . . . fall into a special category where the court is bound to undertake all necessary steps to arrive at an appropriate result in the paramount interests of the welfare of the child. If a party . . . were to be able to conceal or withhold from the court matters which were of importance and were relevant to the future of the child, there would be a risk that the welfare of the child would not be promoted as the Children Act 1989 requires . . . The court must have power to override legal professional privilege in these circumstances.[20]

Steyn LJ balanced the conflicting public interests. He held that the general legal professional privilege attaching to an expert's report must yield to the greater value to be attached to the particular legislative purpose of making the child's welfare the sole criterion in care proceedings.

I see no reason why this should be confined to care proceedings and why it should not be extended to all proceedings under the Children Act. There is a caveat, namely that the promotion of the welfare of the child does not require all communications between a client and a lawyer should be disclosed: advice is not material which could arguably affect the judgment of the court.[21]

---

[18] At p. 231.   [19] [1994] 2 WLR 393.   [20] At pp. 401–2.
[21] *Ibid.*, at p. 405 *per* Steyn LJ.

Unresolved, as yet, is the question whether legal professional privilege should also yield in ancillary relief proceedings. While there is a growing initiative especially by the Family Law Bar Association and the Solicitors' Family Law Association to adopt a conciliatory approach, the administrative and inquisitorial rôle of the judge in the exercise of the *parens patriae* jurisdiction cannot easily be imported into the resolution of financial disputes between husband and wife. The ordinary rules of the adversarial system would, therefore, seem to apply and under those rules privilege can be claimed.[22] That, may, however, be too narrow a view of the position, if, as Lord Wilberforce suggests in *Waugh* v. *British Railways Board*[23] the more powerful argument for legal professional privilege is to encourage anyone who knows the facts to state them fully and candidly and to bear his breast to his lawyer. In the special nature of this litigation candour is not merely encouraged but required. It is a duty to the court to give full and frank disclosure. The public interest in ensuring that all facts are laid before the court in order that it may properly perform its duty thus outweighs any public interest arising from the exigencies of the adversarial system of litigation. I would give the court power to override legal professional privilege in this area as well.

This view places the profession in a difficult and potentially embarrassing position. If the client will not permit disclosure of all facts material to welfare or to the Section 25 Matrimonial Causes Act 1973 factors, then the legal representative may have no option but to seek leave to withdraw. The professional conduct rules will need to be amended to take account of these developments.

5. Privilege in Conciliation

Re D[24] has confirmed that there is a separate category of privilege where a third party (whether official or unofficial, professional or lay) receives information in confidence with a view to conciliation. This new classification has been developed out of an already recognized public interest in the stability of marriage which promotes the need to encourage reconciliation wherever possible. There is now another public interest. As Sir Thomas Bingham MR notes:

The practice of conciliation has grown and evolved in various ways over the last ten years, in court and out of court, voluntary or directed, and extends over many parts of the country. Resolution of disputes over children by parents locked in acrimony and controversy has gradually but perceptibly taken over from efforts to preserve the state of the marriage of the parents. Conciliation over parental or matrimonial disputes does not form part of the legal process but as a matter of practice it is becoming an important

---

[22] See *Causton* v. *Mann Egerton (Johnsons) Ltd* [1974] 1 WLR 162.
[23] [1980] AC 521, 531.   [24] [1993] Fam 231.

and valuable tool in the procedures of many family courts. This underlies the great importance of the preservation of a cloak over all attempts at settlement of disputes over children. Non-disclosure of the contents of conciliation meetings or correspondence is a threat discernible throughout all in-court and out-of-court conciliation arrangements and proposals.[25]

Thus the courts have recognized that unless parties can speak freely and uninhibitedly, without worries about weakening their position in contested litigation, if that becomes necessary, conciliation will be doomed to fail. So the judgment of the Court of Appeal was that: 'Evidence may not be given in proceedings under the Children Act 1989 of statements made by one or other of the parties in the course of meetings held or communications made for the purpose of conciliation save in the very unusual case where a statement is made clearly indicating that the maker has in the past caused or is likely in the future to cause serious harm to the well being of the child.'

The court was careful to state that it is necessary to balance the public interest in protecting the interests of the child against the public interest in preserving the confidentiality of attempted conciliation. Moreover the law as there stated was appropriate to cover that particular case and no other, and no more general statement of the law was thought to be desirable. If and when cases arise not covered by that ruling, they will have to be decided in the light of their own special circumstances. I welcome this opportunity further to develop this area of the law. There are matters which need to be clarified. Why, for example, is it only harm caused **by the maker** of the statement which can be revealed? What if the maker of the statement admits that his or her partner has abused the child? Why limit disclosure to **serious** harm when withholding evidence of any material fact impinging upon the welfare of the child could lead to the 'spectre . . . that judges will sometimes decide cases affecting children in ignorance of material facts and in a way detrimental to their best interests'.[26] Moreover, if there is a duty of full and frank disclosure, is not the public interest in the truth being known greater than the public interest in securing settlements of disputes? How does the professional adviser deal with the dilemma that, if adverse information is given to him by the client on the way to the conciliation appointment, he is bound to disclose it, but he will not be bound if it is given in the course of the conciliation process itself? I tend always to believe that honesty is the best policy. The protection of children from neglect or ill-usage has been recognized by an existing head of public policy.[27] I believe that the vital public interest in the protection of children demands that if the court has to make the decision, attempts to conciliate having broken down, then the court must have all material facts before it to perform its duty.

---

[25] At p. 240.   [26] *Oxfordshire CC* v. *M* [1994] 2 WLR 393, 404 per Steyn LJ.
[27] *D* v. *NSPCC* [1978] AC 171, 240, per Lord Simon.

I see no reason why a similar position should not be adopted for the conciliation of claims for ancillary relief. I would protect the negotiations and would not permit evidence to be given of the offer and counter-offer, of the willingness or unwillingness genuinely to negotiate, but I would not protect from disclosure facts which it is the parties' duty—and the advisers' duty—to lay before the court.

6. Privilege From Without Prejudice Negotiations

This is a privilege in aid of litigation. It is founded upon the public policy of encouraging litigators to settle their differences rather than litigate them to a finish. The rule is no more clearly expressed than in the judgment of Oliver LJ in *Cutts* v. *Head*:[28]

That the rule rests, at least in part, upon public policy is clear from many authorities, and the convenient starting point of the inquiry is the nature of the underlying policy. It is that parties should be encouraged so far as possible to settle their disputes without resort to litigation and should not be discouraged by the knowledge that anything that is said in the course of such negotiations (and that includes, of course, as much the failure to reply to an offer as an actual reply) may be used to their prejudice in the course of the proceedings. They should . . . be encouraged fully and frankly to put their cards on the table . . . The public policy justification, in truth, essentially rests on the desirability of preventing statements or offers made in the course of negotiations for settlement being brought before the court of trial as admissions on the questions of liability.

This protection extends so far as to prevent a litigant being embarrassed by any admission, even of the most central fact in dispute in the litigation, being made known to the court if that admission is made in an attempt to achieve a settlement. In *Rush & Tompkins* v. *GLC* Lord Griffiths said:[29]

It[30] should not be allowed to whittle down the protection given to the parties to speak freely about all issues in the litigation both factual and legal when seeking compromise and, for the purpose of establishing a basis of compromise, admitting certain facts. If the compromise fails, the admission of the facts made for the purpose of the compromise should not be held against the maker of the admission and should therefore not be received in evidence.[31]

I do not see that the rule can be so rigorously applied in family cases, whether children's cases or money cases. I do not see how under the cloak of without prejudice negotiations a party can seek to prevent facts being disclosed to the court which that party is under a duty to lay before it. I would again elevate the public policy interests of protection of the children, and disclosure of material facts relating both to welfare and financial matters, above the public policy

---

[28] [1984] Ch 290, 306.   [29] [1989] AC 1280.
[30] *Waldridge* v. *Kennison* (1794) 1 Esp 142.   [31] At p. 1300.

interest in the cost effectiveness which underlies the need to encourage compromise.

The duty of the academic is to expand the sum of knowledge and to instruct not only their undergraduates but the judges whose judgments they so gleefully dissect and criticize. It is an academic's right to do so. Their responsibility is, however, just occasionally to have sympathy for the poor old judge who may have had inadequate help from the advocates appearing before him and who certainly, as certain as certain can be, never has enough time to think as deeply as he would wish, being ever aware of the clamour of the throng in the corridor outside his court, urging him to get on with it and deal with the next case sooner rather than later.

For six happy years early in my career, I was an academic *manqué*, supervising family law over the week-ends in Cambridge. Any tendentious views in this chapter are to be read in that light and if ever I am called upon to give judgment in respect of any matter on which I have expressed these entirely personal opinions, then it is a bold advocate who cites them to me, for it will give me perverse pleasure to excoriate them!

7

Ethics and Criminal Justice

ANDREW ASHWORTH*

THERE has been no shortage of criticisms of English criminal justice in recent years, whether from the media, victims, practitioners, academics, judges and magistrates, or even Royal Commissions. It has been described as inefficient, unfair, prone to mistakes, and so on. The concern of this chapter is with one particular kind of criticism—that certain conduct in criminal justice is unethical. If this criticism is to be sustained it will be necessary to argue that some ways of dealing with victims or suspects are morally wrong. The focus here is on the pre-trial stages of criminal justice, leaving aside the substantive criminal law and sentencing.

Much discussion of ethics in criminal justice takes the dilemma of the individual lawyer as the central issue. What are the ethics of defending a client one knows or believes to be guilty? Is it ethically defensible to question a witness, particularly a victim, in a way that is likely to cause extreme distress to that witness? How strongly should the lawyer advise a guilty plea to a defendant who maintains innocence but against whom the evidence appears incriminating? Important as these issues are,[1] they tend to draw discussions of ethics towards the particular decisions that confront the individual lawyer. The tendency then might be to undervalue, or even to overlook, the structural and cultural dimensions of ethical and unethical conduct. The lawyer is subjected to the forces of socialization or acculturation in her or his profession—whether as counsel, prosecutor, defence lawyer, magistrate, justices' clerk, judge, or whatever. Moreover the lawyer, certainly in the field of criminal justice, takes decisions within a system constituted by various procedures and process, and within a framework provided by the decisions of others. Particularly powerful in the last respect are the decisions of the police, which is one reason why a considerable amount of the discussion below concerns the conduct of the police. The net is cast wide, so as to take in both written rules and actual

* Much of the material in this chapter is developed at greater length in chapters 2, 3, and 4 of my *The Criminal Process: an Evaluative Study*, 1994. I was assisted by comments on drafts from Brian Bix, Sionaidh Douglas-Scott, Andrew von Hirsch, and Lucia Zedner.
[1] For general surveys, see David Luban, *The Good Lawyer*, 1983, and J. G. Haber and B. H. Baumrin, 'The Moral Obligations of Lawyers', (1988) 1 *Canadian Journal of Jurisprudence* 105. Cf also the discussion by Charles Fried, 'The Lawyer as Friend: the Moral Foundations of the Lawyer-Client Relation', (1976) 85 *Yale L.J.* 1060. I am grateful to Dr. Andrew Phang, of the National University of Singapore, for directing me to a great deal of reading in this field.

practices, and particular attention is paid to the terms in which practitioners justify their approaches, often by reference to 'the public interest' or some wider concept of justice.[2] The chapter concludes by reconsidering the implications of codes of ethics for the practice of criminal justice.

ETHICS AND CRIME

It is important to begin with the affirmation that committing a crime may itself be regarded as unethical or morally wrong behaviour. This is not a self-evident proposition—much depends on the contents of the criminal law, the political system in which it is situated, and even the method by which it was created[3]— but it will be assumed for the purpose of the discussion that follows. Doubts about the ethical status of strict liability crimes, victimless crimes, and certain other offences will be left for another day, in the belief that there is a sufficient core of crimes proscribing behaviour that is morally wrong beyond a peradventure.

I will further assume that it is the State's duty, or at least a rightfully exercised power, to render those who commit crimes liable to conviction and punishment, and liable to compensate their victims.[4] For similar reasons the State may properly create a police force (or police service), and give appropriate powers for law enforcement to the police, prosecutors, courts, the probation service, and the prison service. To refer to the whole institutional apparatus as the 'criminal justice system' may be euphemistic, in implying a degree of co-ordination and shared objectives that do not exist, but it is a convenient phrase that has passed into common usage. It is certainly apt to describe a catalogue of mistakes at different stages that lead to a wrongful conviction: one can say that it is the criminal justice system that has failed.

RULES AND ETHICS

What of the argument that there is no need to discuss ethics when there are so many legal rules, codes, and guidelines impinging on the work of law enforcement agents? Is there really any room for additional disputation of a

---

[2] For a treasury of examples, see Andrew Rutherford, *Criminal Justice and the Pursuit of Decency*, 1993.

[3] For a developed argument, see Nicola Lacey, *State Punishment* (1988), chs. 4 and 6.

[4] This leaves out of account the call for a restorative orientation of criminal justice, which must be argued separately. For a variety of views, see eg Lucia Zedner, 'Reparation and Retribution: are they reconcilable?', (1994) 57 *Modern Law Review* 228; Daniel Van Ness, 'New Wine and Old Wineskins: Four Challenges of Restorative Justice', (1993) 4 *Criminal Law Forum* 251; Andrew Ashworth, 'Some Doubts about Restorative Justice', (1993) 4 *Criminal Law Forum* 277; and Daniel Van Ness, 'A Reply to Andrew Ashworth', *ibid* 301.

moral or ethical kind when we have such documents as the Police and Criminal Evidence Act 1984 and its Codes of Practice, the *Code for Crown Prosecutors*, the *Victim's Charter*, guideline judgments on sentencing, and the Criminal Justice Acts 1991–93? Three good reasons may be offered for pressing ahead with ethical enquiries.

Firstly, ethical principles should apply to those who make rules and guidelines as well as to those who are subject to them. Thus there should be no suggestion that ethical issues affect only the lower ranks: the decisions of members of the legislature, the Home Secretary, the Director of Public Prosecutions, and the Lord Chief Justice should be equally subject to appraisal on ethical grounds. However, there should be no confusion between legal rules and moral or ethical principles. It is good that legal rules should be based on ethical principles, even though on many occasions they are shaped by short term pragmatism or other political forces. The distinctive function of ethical principles is to supply strong reasons for adopting a particular rule. In that sense they are more fundamental, many of them being found in the European Convention of Human Rights and Fundamental Freedoms.

Secondly, there is no warrant for the view that the criminal justice system is entirely covered by rules and clear-cut guidance. Recent years have seen greater efforts to introduce various forms of guidance and accountability, but there are still vast tracts of discretion, some of it left deliberately so as to enable flexibility, some eked out by practitioners in order to allow them to follow their preferred practices. Wherever there is discretion, there may be choices between following ethical principles and following other policies or preferences.

Thirdly, it is well known that there are strong occupational cultures among the various professional groups in the criminal justice system. The evidence is clearest in relation to the police. For example, a recent study of detectives for the Royal Commission on Criminal Justice concluded that a necessary step towards improving the situation would be 'raising CID officers' awareness of the faults in the traditional "detective culture" ("macho" and "elitist" attitudes, belief that "rules are there to be bent", excessive secrecy and suspicion of outsiders, and so on) and the ease with which young officers are sucked into it, almost without realising it'.[5] In its report, the Royal Commission refers to 'the culture and approach of the Criminal Bar' as a possible obstacle to the success of some of its proposals for stream-lining pre-trial procedure.[6] In the face of such well-entrenched cultures—the 'Spanish

---

[5] Mike Maguire and Clive Norris, *The Conduct and Supervision of Criminal Investigations*, Royal Commission on Criminal Justice Research Study No. 5 (1992).
[6] Royal Commission on Criminal Justice, *Report*, (Cm 2263 of 1993). hereinafter cited as RCCJ, para. 7.36, on preparatory hearings.

customs', the 'Ways and Means Act', the judgments of moral character[7]—
what are the prospects for rules, let alone guidelines or unfettered discretion?
In practice these cultures are often direct competitors with ethical principles,
partly because they tend to put sectional interests first. However, as we shall
see, professional cultures do have some ethical content, and often embody a
challenge to the values of those who argue for the recognition of rights.

DEVELOPING ETHICAL PRINCIPLES FOR CRIMINAL JUSTICE

What kind of principle may be described as ethical? It should be a principle
that is impartial as between persons and for which reasons can be given. Thus a
principle may not properly be described as moral or ethical if it tends to be
justified by reference to its benefits for a particular person or group. Impartiality as between persons may be linked to respect for the separateness or
autonomy of individuals, as we shall see. But this emphasis on the individual, appropriate as it is in the context of a system in which someone cloaked
with State authority and supported by considerable organizational power may
be dealing with a person who is suspected of a crime, should not lead us to
overlook the justification for having some form of system in the first place. The
general public benefit supplies the major reason for having criminal law,
police, courts, and other parts of the system. Without such a system, life
would be chaotic and insecure, and the weak would be even more at the
mercy of the strong. On balance, and on the available evidence, it is clearly
more beneficial to have a criminal justice system than to have no criminal law
and no official means of law enforcement.

If the system is justified by reference to its general social consequences, is
there any reason to recognize the rights of individuals, rather than allowing all
arrangements to be made purely on the utilitarian ground of calculating the
greatest happiness of the greatest number? One answer to this would be to
consider the position of the victim of a crime. Does he or she not have a right
to be treated fairly and with respect by law enforcement agents, and to receive
compensation either from the offender or from the State for the harm done? On
a factual level it is well documented that victims have in the past felt that the
criminal process operates as a kind of secondary victimization, with all its
demands and pressures.[8] Surely we ought to recognize the right of victims to
respect for their dignity: correspondingly it should be a duty upon State
officials to avoid or minimize these secondary effects so far as possible. It is

---

[7] On judgments of moral character, see eg K. Hawkins, *Environment and Enforcement*, 1984 on
pollution inspectors, and H. Parker, M. Sumner and G. Jarvis, *Unmasking the Magistrates*, 1989,
on magistrates. This use of 'moral' is a good reason for keeping to the term 'ethical' elsewhere.
[8] eg J. Shapland, J. Willmore and P. Duff, *Victims in the Criminal Justice System*, 1985, pp.
176–8.

wrong to treat victims in a way that leaves them in ignorance about the progress of the case, or forces them to wait in court with supporters of the defendant, or fails to prepare them for the possible strains of giving evidence in court, etc.[9]

Are the arguments different when we come to consider the rights of criminals? If someone is convicted of a serious offence such as rape, child abuse or grievous bodily harm, why should they be treated with any respect? These questions are hinting at the conclusion that a person who has committed a crime forfeits all rights and can thereafter be subjected by the state to whatever form of punishment or treatment may be ordained. Are there any good reasons for rejecting this conclusion? The strongest argument is that a person who commits a criminal offence should not be laid open to whatever sanction a court chooses to impose, for whatever reason. Surely there should be a right not to be punished more than is proportionate to the seriousness of the offence: in principle, sentences should be related to the comparative seriousness of offences (rather than, say, to their predicted deterrent effects),[10] since this shows respect for the offender as a rational and autonomous being.[11] However, rights such as the right not to be punished disproportionately may be advanced as *prima facie* rights rather than absolute rights.[12] This reflects the practical point that individual rights may conflict and that, in resolving these conflicts, it will sometimes prove necessary to curtail a right or to subordinate it to another. Thus it could be adjudged that a particular offender remains a danger to members of the community in general or to one particular citizen, and might well commit a further serious offence if released after the proportionate sentence. In such a situation of 'vivid danger', the probability of serious harm to other citizens might suffice as a justification for detaining the offender beyond the proportionate sentence, although the fallibility of such predictions is well documented.[13]

It has been argued that convicted offenders should not forfeit all their rights: their essential humanity ought to be recognized, and they ought not to be treated as mere pawns but should in general be punished no more than is

[9] For detailed accounts of the impact on victims of court-room procedures and lawyers' practices, see Paul Rock, *The Social World of an English Crown Court*, 1993.

[10] Considerations of space make it difficult to develop these arguments fully here. For a fuller version, with further references, see A. von Hirsch and A. Ashworth (eds), *Principled Sentencing*, 1993, pp. 56–7 and ch.2 generally.

[11] In the present context, 'autonomy' is being used merely as a restraining idea which can generate various limits on the treatment of individuals, particularly by the State. To argue for the attainment of autonomy as an ideal state would be a separate enterprise: cf J. Raz, *The Morality of Freedom*, 1986, pp. 154–7.

[12] J. L. Mackie, 'Can there be a Right-Based Moral Theory', in Jeremy Waldron (ed), *Theories of Rights*, 1984.

[13] For this argument, see A. E. Bottoms and R. Brownsword, 'Dangerousness and Rights', in J. Hinton (ed), *Dangerousness: Problems of Assessment and Prediction*, 1983, developing remarks by R. Dworkin, *Taking Rights Seriously* 1977, ch.1.

proportionate to the seriousness of their offence. A related issue is how they should be treated, if imprisoned. Do they deserve any minimum standards of facilities, or is it sufficient that they be kept alive as cheaply as possible? This is another awkward question, particularly at a time when so many citizens who have not been convicted of serious offences find themselves living in dreadful conditions, often without sufficient money for decent housing, heat, clothing, and food, and possibly homeless. On an ethical plane it should be affirmed that citizens living in conditions of poverty have no less a claim that the State should treat them with respect and dignity.[14] But that should not alter the rightful claims of imprisoned offenders that the State should treat them with respect in terms of sanitation, food, clothing, and so forth. The increasing disquiet about prisoners 'slopping out' shows how conceptions of decent treatment can alter, and how the notion of a right to certain minimum standards begins to take root.

In describing ethical arguments in favour of proportionate sentences and decent treatment in prison, emphasis has been placed on the morality of the State acting in this way towards people who are rational autonomous beings. In practice, there are also pragmatic arguments running in the same direction that may be no less powerful—the spectre of miscarriages of justice, and the prospect of greater prison stability. The former argument has become more prominent in recent times, as several major miscarriages of justice have been uncovered, with people who have been wrongly convicted spending many years in prison. Few systems can claim to be error-proof, and the possibility of convicting and punishing innocent people makes it all the more fitting that the basic rights of convicted persons should be respected. The argument about prison stability received strong endorsement from the Woolf Inquiry into the prison disturbances of 1990. Indeed, it was argued not merely that degrading prison conditions are contributing factors to prison disturbances, but also that they may contribute to further lawbreaking on release.[15] The Royal Commission on Criminal Justice similarly argues that 'the fairer the treatment which all the parties receive at the hands of the system, the more likely it is that the jury's verdict . . . will be correct'.[16] These pragmatic considerations may be powerful in practice, but pulling in the same direction is the argument in favour of maintaining the integrity of the criminal justice system: since it

---

[14] For the Victorian concept of 'less eligibility'—the argument that conditions in prison should be no better than those for the lowest in society—see L. Radzinowicz and R. Hood, *The Emergence of Penal Policy*, 1986, pp. 146–7, 381–2.

[15] 'The conditions which exist at present in our prisons cause a substantial number of prisoners to leave prisons more embittered and hostile to society than when they arrived. They leave prison, then, in a state of mind where they are more likely to re-offend.' Home Office, *Prison Disturbances April 1990*, 1991, para. 10.27.   [16] RCCJ, para. 1.27.

performs a moral function in punishing wrongdoers, the system and its officials should show proper respect for moral values.[17]

If it is now accepted that behaving ethically requires public officials to observe certain restraints in their dealing with convicted offenders, it would surely apply *a fortiori* that these restraints should operate in the pre-trial stages. Until a person has been convicted by a court, he or she should be treated as if innocent. Now to some people, particularly to some practitioners and politicians, this sounds the sirens of pretence and misplaced sympathy. Most of the people who are prosecuted acknowledge their guilt by pleading guilty. Some of them, even, were caught red-handed or readily confessed at the earliest stage. It hardly makes sense to treat them as innocent and to constrain the processes of investigation and arraignment by reference to a presumption that is manifestly inapplicable in their case. This argument, however, should not be accepted. At a factual level it draws attention to the frequency of guilty pleas but ignores the many pleas of not guilty; on its own premise it could only apply to guilty plea cases. Even at that, it overlooks the possibility of confessions and guilty pleas by the innocent,[18] thus ignoring the case for safeguards. One of the reasons for the criminal trial is to provide a forum for the issue of guilt or innocence to be examined openly. Even if the belief in the suspect's guilt is held strongly by police officers or tax inspectors or prosecutors or others, there are two reasons why this should not alter the presumption of innocence: first, how is the official's judgment to be tested, or is it to be left merely as a matter of subjective belief? and second, what if it is found that the defendant has based his indication of a guilty plea on a misconception about the law or the evidence? I conclude, therefore, that there is insufficient reason to abandon the presumption of innocence, even in guilty plea cases, until there has been a determinative court hearing.

One of the principal reasons for having a criminal trial is to require the prosecution to prove its case in open court, if it can, and to allow the defendant the opportunity to contest that case. Few would contemplate a system in which decisions on guilt or innocence were taken behind closed doors without a proper opportunity to make a defence (even though aspects of the English criminal process, in which guilty pleas and negotiated pleas of guilty play such a large part, suggest that we almost have such a system now). Allied to this, but far more controversial in its ambit, is the presumption of innocence at trial. Perhaps most would agree, without the need for elaborate argument, that the prosecution should bear the burden of proof. A system in which the onus lay on the defendant to establish innocence would be oppressive. Beyond that there is

---

[17] For statements of the integrity principle, see the famous dissenting judgments of Justices Holmes and Brandeis in *Olmstead v. United States* (1928) 277 US 438, 484–5, and A. A. S. Zuckerman, *Principles of Criminal Evidence*, 1989, p.344. For a critical appraisal, see A. Ashworth, *The Criminal Process: an Evaluative Study*, 1994, ch.2.

[18] The former, at least, was recognized by the Royal Commission: RCCJ, paras. 4.31–4.32.

room for much dispute—whether the prosecution should have to prove guilt beyond reasonable doubt, whether the defence (as well as the prosecution) should have a duty to disclose its case, whether the defendant should have the right to remain silent in pre-trial investigations and/or at the trial, without adverse inferences, whether there should be exceptions for particular types of case, and so forth. These weighty issues, on which the British Government has declined to follow the recommendations of the Royal Commission on Criminal Justice,[19] cannot be argued to a conclusion here.[20]

What can be done is to set out some principles that have the authority of the European Convention on Human Rights. This Convention has been in force since 1953. The United Kingdom has ratified it and individuals have the right to petition the Commission, which will, if the application is held admissible, pass the case to the European Court of Human Rights for adjudication. The Convention has been incorporated into the domestic law of several European countries, and the case for it being so incorporated in the United Kingdom has recently been argued by senior members of the judiciary.[21] The articles of the Convention cover a range of matters relevant in civil or criminal proceedings. Commentators have concluded that 'the Convention is at its best when it is operating as a charter for procedural fairness',[22] and it is in this connection that certain principles are extracted from it here:

- a person should not be subjected to torture or inhuman or degrading treatment (Article 3);
- a person should only be liable to detention on reasonable grounds until a court appearance or trial (Article 5.1(c));
- anyone arrested or detailed should be brought before a court promptly in order to review the grounds (Article 5.3);
- there should be a right to a fair and public hearing within reasonable time (Article 6.1);
- there should be 'equality of arms' between prosecution and defence in the criminal process (Article 6.1, as interpreted by the Court);
- 'everyone charged with a criminal offence shall be presumed innocent until proved guilty according to law' (Article 6.2);
- a person charged with a criminal offence should have adequate time and facilities for the preparation of a defence (Article 6.3(b));

---

[19] See the Criminal Justice and Public Order Act 1994 sections 34–37.

[20] See further Ashworth, The *Criminal Process*, and M. McConville (ed), *Criminal Justice in Crisis*, 1994.

[21] Sir Harry Woolf, *Protection of the Public: A New Challenge*, 1990; Sir Nicolas Browne-Wilkinson, 'The Infiltration of a Bill of Rights', [1992] *Public Law* 397; Sir John Laws, 'Is the High Court the Guardian of Fundamental Constitutional Rights?', [1993] *Public Law* 59; Sir Thomas Bingham, 'The European Convention on Human Rights: Time to Incorporate', (1993) 109 *LQR* 390.

[22] C. Gearty, 'The European Court of Human Rights and the Protection of Civil Liberties: An Overview' [1993] *Camb LJ* 89, at 98. For a fuller commentary, see P. van Dijk and G. J. H. van Hoof, *Theory and Practice of the European Convention on Human Rights*, 2nd ed, 1990.

- a person's privacy should be respected (Article 8);
- all rights should be secured without discrimination on any ground such as sex, race, colour, language, religion . . . or other status (Article 14).

The European Convention on Human Rights contains no specific references to victims' rights, but the Council of Europe has approved a number of recommendations designed to ensure proper respect and support for victims in the criminal process.[23] All these rights may be said to impose correlative ethical duties on law enforcement agents towards individual suspects and defendants.[24] Some of the rights have been gaining recognition rather slowly: for example, the principle of non-discrimination embodied in Article 14 has made only an oblique appearance in criminal legislation in England and Wales,[25] and the identification of discriminatory practices at various stages of the criminal process is proceeding slowly.[26] Other rights have been developed by English law in much greater detail than in the Convention or many other European countries: for example, the Police and Criminal Evidence Act and its Codes of Practice refine certain general rights in order that they have a much more consistent and meaningful impact in practice. On the other hand, the European Court of Human Rights has recently held that the presumption of innocence can be construed as supporting a right to silence, a decision that conflicts, in spirit at least, with the new English legislation.[27]

The distinctively ethical approach is to promote the moral values themselves, and to understand the reasons for doing so. This is why the ethical approach is particularly relevant to the exercise of discretion and to face to face dealings between officials and individuals, both of which are wide-spread in criminal justice. This, too, is where the conflict with occupational cultures becomes apparent. If an ethical approach is to be developed, it must be constructed upon the rights of victims, suspects, and defendants so as to yield principles for the proper motivation of those who administer criminal justice.

IDENTIFYING 'UNETHICAL' PRACTICES

The discussion so far has been concerned broadly with establishing some general ethical principles applicable to pre-trial criminal justice, particularly

---

[23] Council of Europe, *The Position of the Victim in the Framework of Criminal Law and Procedure*, 1985.

[24] J. Feinberg, 'In Defence of Moral Rights', (1992) 12 *OJLS* 149, at p. 155, argues in favour of starting with 'rights' rather than 'duties' on the ground that rights can be waived by their holders.

[25] Criminal Justice Act 1991, s.95; the monitoring envisaged by this section now seems to be taking shape.

[26] See Roger Hood, *Race and Sentencing*, 1992, and Marion Fitzgerald, *Ethnic Minorities and the Criminal Justice System*, RCCJ Research Study No. 20, 1993.

[27] *Funke, Cremieux and Miailhe* v. *France*, A.256 (1993); cf note 19 above.

in dealings between public officials and citizens. The importance of the subject, however, lies in its practical relevance. Now is the time to move away from abstract theorizing, and to test some actual practices. What unethical practices in criminal justice can be identified? Exactly why might it be right to describe each one as unethical? What motives typically lie behind unethical practices?

Some ten presumptively unethical practices will be identified. Each will be discussed fairly briefly, so as to enable a spectrum of practices to be mentioned. Whether the practices can properly be termed 'unethical' will not be determined until we have discussed the explanations for them, but they are discussed here because they appear unethical. There is no suggestion that all the practices are wide-spread, but it is believed that they occur on some occasions, and references are given to support this belief.

i) The Necessity Principle of Detention:

One of the purposes of introducing new rules on detention in police stations in 1986 was to ensure that persons brought to police stations under arrest are only detained if it is necessary to do so, and if there is sufficient evidence for a charge.[28] Research by McKenzie, Morgan and Reiner shows that custody officers routinely authorize detention, without an examination of the sufficiency of evidence, and do so by reference to the need 'to secure or preserve evidence or to obtain evidence by questioning'.[29] This practice is unethical because it deprives suspects of protection against being detained unless that is absolutely necessary, a protection that Parliament intended to give them.[30] The reasons behind the unethical practice emerge fairly clearly: detention makes it easier for the police, and a custody officer who insisted on the necessity principle would be seen as failing to support the judgment of the officers who brought the suspect into the police station.

ii) The Principle that Questioning Should be Regulated According to Proper Standards of Decency:

Since the early part of this century there were 'Judges' Rules' to guide the police in the conduct of questioning, so named because they indicated the circumstances in which the courts might exclude evidence on account of the

[28] Police and Criminal Evidence Act 1984, s.37.
[29] I. McKenzie, R. Morgan and R. Reiner, 'Helping the Police with their Inquiries: the Necessity Principle and Voluntary Attendance at the Police Station', [1990] Crim LR 22; see, to the same effect, M. McConville, A. Sanders and R. Leng, *The Case for the Prosecution*, 1991, ch.3.
[30] The Home Secretary at the time stated the principle that detention must be necessary, 'not desirable, convenient or a good idea but necessary': cited by McKenzie, Morgan and Reiner, *ibid*, p. 23.

manner in which it was obtained. A stream of cases over the years revealed individual incidents of unfair or oppressive questioning by the police. The Police and Criminal Evidence Act and its Codes of Practice were designed to lay down standards of fair treatment and to reinforce the courts' discretion to exclude evidence obtained in contravention of the standards.[31] The reason behind these protections is to spare defendants intimidation, not to mention violence, and to enhance the reliability of any evidence that is obtained. Yet the years since 1986 have seen a spate of cases in which police officers have been found to have departed from the Code of Practice on Questioning:[32] these cases do not yield a statistical estimate of the frequency of departures, since firstly there may also be numerous unreported trial rulings that exclude evidence on these grounds, and secondly there will be some guilty plea cases where the departures from the Code are not challenged, but the reported cases do provide concrete evidence of unethical conduct. Though some of the early cases might be explained by police officers' lack of familiarity with the Codes of Practice, that certainly cannot be claimed in the relatively recent case of the Cardiff Three,[33] and many others suggest an intention to deprive the suspect of the protections provided by Parliament. The reason for doing this is probably the belief that the Code makes the work of the police too difficult, and erects barriers in the way of seeking the truth by the most effective means. This point—which in reality represents a challenge to the ethical position of the Code—will be developed later. A linked form of unethical behaviour is the falsification of the record of an interview by the police, such as was revealed in the cases of the Birmingham Six[34] and the Tottenham Three.[35] That is unethical beyond a peradventure.

iii) The Principle that Questioning should be Mechanically Recorded:

During the 1980s experiments with the tape recording of statements by suspects to the police appeared to succeed, and tape recording is now widely used. Although English law has not yet embraced the principle that only mechanically recorded statements are admissible,[36] and indeed the Police and Criminal Evidence Act itself does not provide for mechanical recording, experiments have pressed ahead with the video-recording of statements

[31] For discussion, see Peter Mirfield, *Confessions*, 1985, and Andrew Sanders, 'Rights, Remedies and the Police and Criminal Evidence Act', [1988] Crim LR 802.
[32] See, for example, *Samual* [1988] QB 615, *Alladice* (1988) 87 CrAppR 380.
[33] *Paris, Abdullahi and Miller* (1993) 97 CrAppR 99.
[34] *McIlkenny et al* (1991) 93 Cr.App.R. 287.
[35] *Silcott, Braithwaite and Raglip, The Times*, 6 Dec. 1991.
[36] Cf RCCP, paras. 3.14 and 4.50, declining to introduce such a principle and underplaying the risk that police officers may falsely attribute unrecorded oral remarks to a suspect. Cf S. Moston and G. Stephenson, *The Questioning and Interviewing of Suspects outside the Police Station*, RCCJ Research Study No. 22 1993.

made at certain police stations. Here, the principle is that all questioning of the suspect by the police should be recorded on a video camera. However, unauthorized practices were brought to light by the making of a television programme in which television cameras were welcomed into a police station by the police but, accidentally, left on when the television crew had departed. On a few occasions police officers were seen to return to question the suspect, without switching on their own video camera, with the connivance of the custody officer, and then proceeded to adopt a far stronger line in questioning than they had been prepared to do on camera.[37] This was clearly unethical, since it deprived the suspect of the protection from unfair and oppressive questioning which mechanical recording is supposed to give. The reason for thus circumventing the rules was that the rules were thought to stand in the way of efficient investigation and to inhibit the police in obtaining from the suspect the admissions they believed they should obtain.

iv) Reading the Defendant's Rights:

One of the innovations of the Police and Criminal Evidence Act was to require the police to inform each suspect/defendant of certain rights—the right to make a telephone call from the police station, the right to have someone informed of the detention, and the right to have legal advice that is free, independent, and given in a private consultation. After the implementation of the new law in 1986 it was found that not all suspects were being informed of these rights.[38] The relevant Code of Practice was altered in 1991, and Home Office research has shown that the rate of informing suspects has increased but is still less than complete: almost all suspects were told of the right to legal advice, but only 73 per cent were told that it is free, 56 per cent were told that it is independent, and hardly any were told that the consultation would be private.[39] No less significantly, in over a quarter of cases where information was given, it was spoken in an unclear or unduly rapid fashion. There was also evidence that some police officers emphasized the possible problems (such as delay) in summoning legal advice, presumably in order to encourage a suspect to waive the right. Whether these practices can be described as unethical depends to some extent on the motives for them. It is quite possible in some cases that officers simply forgot, in the heat of the moment, to inform the suspect of all or any rights; or that statements of rights spoken rapidly were directed at people who knew their rights from previous visits to the police

[37] M. McConville, 'Videotaping Interrogations: police behaviour on and off camera', [1992] Crim LR 532.

[38] See, eg A. Sanders and L. Bridges, 'Access to Legal Advice and Police Malpractice', [1990] Crim LR 494.

[39] D. Brown, T. Ellis and K. Larcombe, *Changing the Code: police detention under the revised PACE codes of practice*, Home Office Research Study No 129, 1993; to similar effect see M. Zander and P. Henderson, *Crown Court Study*, RCCJ Research Study No 19, 1993, pp. 8–10.

station. But it is also possible that in some cases the information was not given, or was given in incomplete or garbled form, because the police officer resented the 'rights' and thought that lawyers would inhibit the smooth progress of the investigation. Indeed, that would often be the explanation for trying to persuade a suspect to waive the right or to cancel a request.[40] In those cases, the practice would be unethical, as well as seeking to deprive the suspect of a right provided by Parliament for his or her protection.

v) Disclosure of Unused Evidence:

Whatever the strength of the prosecution's duty to investigate claims of exculpation, alibi, or other lines of defence, there is also the question of what they should do with information favourable to the defence that happens to come into their possession during the investigation. This may be evidence from a forensic scientist,[41] or evidence from any witness, or real evidence. Since the Attorney General issued guidelines in 1981, it has been clear that the Crown has a duty to disclose to the defence any material that is not to be used as part of the prosecution case, subject to certain exceptions.[42] Critical to the performance of this duty are the police, since they are the people most likely to acquire this information in the first place, and, unless they notify the Crown Prosecution Service, both that Service and Crown counsel are unlikely to discover its existence. Thus the failure by the police to disclose to anyone certain evidence in favour of the defence was a reason for quashing the convictions in the cases of the Maguire Seven,[43] the Birmingham Six,[44] and Judith Ward.[45] The Attorney General's guidelines were not in force at the time of the original trials in these cases, but the principle of disclosure did exist. Whether or not these are classified as cases of the unethical suppression of evidence, the years of imprisonment served by those who were unaware of the evidence bears testimony to the power of information.[46] If they were cases of suppression, the motivation can only be a belief that the 'inconvenient' evidence would muddy the waters and perhaps jeopardize the conviction of someone the police believed to be guilty. One problem with this motivation, as has become apparent subsequently, is that if the police assumption of guilt is hasty and ill-founded, the very purpose of crime prevention is undermined because the real offenders remain free.

[40] See Sanders and Bridges, *supra*, at p. 506.
[41] To be dealt with separately below: para. (vi).
[42] Attorney General's Guidelines, 'Disclosure of Information to the Defence in cases to be Tried on Indictment', (1982) 74 CrAppR 287.   [43] *Maguire et al*, (1992) 94 CrAppR 133.
[44] *McIlkenny et al*, (1991) 93 CrAppR 287.
[45] *Ward* (1993) 96 CrAppR 1; cf the Court of Appeal's change of direction in *Johnson et al* [1993] Crim LR 689, and the recommendations in RCCJ, paras. 6.50–6.53.
[46] See P. O'Connor, 'Prosecution Disclosure: principle, practice and justice' [1992] Crim LR 464. Cf. the Government's proposals for a new disclosure system, more favourable to the prosecution, in *Disclosure: a Consultation Document*, 1995.

vi) Disclosure of Expert Findings:

The Forensic Science Service is contacted by the police at an early stage in many important enquiries, and asked to report on various matters. In some cases a whole variety of scientific tests will be carried out. However, in the case of the Maguire Seven the results of certain tests favourable to the defendants were not notified to the defence; similar non-disclosure occurred in the cases of the Birmingham Six and Judith Ward. This can be regarded as unethical, unless it is supposed that the Forensic Science Service is intended to be an adversarial organization on the side of the prosecution—and, even then, the application of the same duty of disclosure as applies to the prosecution generally (see (v) above) would require the Service to inform at least the prosecution of all findings. The Royal Commission concluded that the Service has become more impartial in its outlook since the 1970s when those cases were decided,[47] but one of its research studies found continuing evidence of an adversarial approach among some forensic scientists, excluding certain items from their reports and arguing that it is for the defence to expose the limitations of their findings.[48] The cause of this is a belief that forensic scientists should be on the side of the police, not impartial seekers after scientific truths or probabilities. It is that belief, which diverges from the official aims of the Service,[49] that renders non-disclosure unethical.

vii) Securing the Individual's Rights at the Police Station:

We have already seen that the Police and Criminal Evidence Act gave to suspects the right to consult a legal adviser when brought to a police station. One of the reasons for this is that a lawyer, particularly if he or she remains present throughout the police interview(s), should be able to ensure that the conduct of the police towards the suspect is scrupulously fair. However, two research studies have found that legal advisers rarely intervene to protect their client, in some cases allowing hostile and hectoring modes of questioning to pass without comment.[50] In gross cases this is unethical conduct by the legal adviser in failing to protect the client from questioning that does not show respect for the suspect (and may contravene the Code of Practice). There is dispute about where the boundary lies between the ethical and the unethical, between allowing certain pressure to be exerted by the police and preventing

---

[47] RCCJ, paras. 9.27 and 9.47.
[48] P. Roberts and C. Willmore, *The Rôle of Forensic Science Evidence in Criminal Proceedings*, RCCJ Research Study No. 11, 1993.   [49] RCCJ, pp. 150–51.
[50] J. Baldwin, *The Rôle of Legal Representatives at Police Stations*, RCCJ Research Study No. 3, 1992. M. McConville and J. Hodgson, *Custodial Legal Advice and the Right to Silence*, RCCJ Research Study No. 16, 1993. Both studies also confirmed that most 'legal advisers' attending to give advice at police stations are not qualified solicitors but clerks, articled clerks, or former police officers on retainers. The Law Society is working to improve this situation.

unfairness to the suspect. But perhaps the important point for the present discussion is the finding that legal advisers may fail to protest to the police about unfair tactics in the hope of currying favour with them. Indeed, one of those who drew up the Law Society's guidance for solicitors at police stations has stated that 'interviews run better if the solicitor is able to establish a working relationship with the interviewer based on mutual respect, which has to be earned, of two professionals trying to do a proper job and co-operating to do it'.[51] If this means that the solicitor should earn respect by strenuously objecting to unfair questions, then the research shows that this is not occurring. If, on the other hand, it suggests that solicitors should allow the police some leeway so as to show they are 'good chaps' and 'prepared to do business', this is unethical because it means that some legal advisers are compromising the very rights they are supposed to protect.

viii) Prosecutorial Review of the Decision to Prosecute:

One of the key points made by the Royal Commission on Criminal Procedure in 1981 was that weak cases should be removed from the system as early as possible. This is partly a question of management (ensuring that the system's resources are used in the most effective and economical way), and partly a matter of respect for the defendant in not subjecting him or her to the anxiety of a prosecution without proper foundation. One of the primary tasks of the Crown Prosecution Service (CPS) was to bring professional prosecutorial review into the system, to prevent weak or inappropriate cases from going to court,[52] and for this they were given a power of discontinuance.[53] However, the history of the office of Director of Public Prosecutions revealed a tendency towards 'prosecution inertia', which sometimes led to the continuance of a case or a charge simply because it had been commenced on that basis.[54] Research in the early years of the CPS suggested a similar pattern, with few cases dropped on 'public interest' grounds and some cases where the police had brought a prosecution on inadequate evidence being pursued by the CPS in order to support the police.[55] In more recent years, as the CPS has become established, the rate of discontinuance has risen markedly, from 4.5 per cent of cases in magistrates' courts in 1989 to 11 per cent in 1991.[56] However, it is noteworthy that the House of Commons Home Affairs Committee went so far as to recommend that the CPS should 'act co-operatively with the police' in

---

[51] D. Roberts, 'Questioning the Suspect: the Solicitor's Rôle', [1993] Crim LR 368; cf the reply by J. Baldwin, 'Legal Advice at the Police Station', [1993] Crim LR 371.

[52] Royal Commission on Criminal Procedure, *Report*, Cmnd 8092 of 1981, para. 7.6.

[53] Prosecution of Offences Act 1985, s.23.

[54] G. Mansfield and J. Peay, *The Director of Public Prosecutions*, 1986.

[55] M. McConville, A. Sanders and R. Leng, *The Case for the Prosecution*, 1991, ch.7.

[56] *Information on the Criminal Justice System in England and Wales: Digest 2*, 1993, p. 33.

supporting local police initiatives in charging people following incidents of public disorder.[57] If, despite the rising rate of discontinuances, there are still cases in which the CPS fail to discontinue a case where they know that there is insufficient evidence, this may be unethical behaviour.[58] The motivation is probably to 'support' the police, a position that may consist either of supporting them in order to achieve smooth working relationships or of supporting them because of a belief that it is in the interests of 'justice' to do so. But in both types of case this would imply that suspects have no right not to be prosecuted on inadequate evidence.

ix) Deciding on Mode of Trial:

A large number of offences of intermediate gravity are triable either way, that is, either at the Crown Court or in a magistrates' court. For these offences the defendant has an absolute right to elect Crown Court trial; if no such election is made, it is the magistrates' court, after hearing representations from the prosecutor, that takes the decision. The Royal Commission, in one of its more controversial proposals, has recommended that the defendant's right to elect should be removed.[59] However, under the existing law various cases have arisen in which the prosecution has preferred an either-way charge, the defendant has elected Crown Court trial, and the prosecution has thereupon dropped the either-way charge and brought a charge that is triable summarily only, in a magistrates' court. Defendants have challenged these tactics by means of judicial review, and the Divisional Court has held that in general the choice of charge lies within the discretion of the prosecutor so long as the substituted charge is not inappropriate and there is no bad faith, oppression, or prejudice.[60] Substituting a lesser charge may therefore be lawful, but is it ethical? Much depends on the motivation, and here the Divisional Court seems to have been naive. Judges have repeatedly commented that it is 'Gilbertian' for a defendant to complain of being charged with a **less** serious offence than he or she should face.[61] Yet the reason for the complaint emerges clearly from surveys of the opinions of defendants and their lawyers about the quality of magistrates' justice: they believe that trials are fairer in the Crown Court, whereas magistrates' courts are more hurried, less thorough, and more police-

[57] Home Affairs Committee, Session 1989–90, *The Crown Prosecution Service*, H.C. Paper 118, 1990, para. 27.
[58] This refers to cases where there is clearly insufficient evidence. Where there is doubt, it may be reasonable to continue with the case.   [59] RCCJ, ch.6.
[60] *R* v. *Liverpool Stipendiary Magistrate, ex p. Ellison* [1989] Crim LR 369; however, where the magistrates have decided that a charge should be tried summarily, it would be an abuse of process for the prosecutor to drop that charge and prefer one that is triable only on indictment: *Brooks* [1985] Crim LR 385.
[61] *Ibid.*, repeating the words of Lord Lane, CJ, in *R* v. *Canterbury and St. Augustine JJ., ex p. Klisiak* (1981) 72 CAR 250.

minded.[62] Acquittal rates tend to be lower in magistrates' courts, too,[63] and this may be one reason why the CPS prefer to have many cases heard in those courts. The ethical argument is complex, because no one can tell which acquittal rate is the more accurate—ie whether it is magistrates who favour the prosecution unduly, or juries that favour defendants unduly. But so long as Parliament allows defendants a choice, and so long as official prosecution policy remains as stated in the Code for Crown Prosecutors, it may be argued that it is unethical for the CPS to drop an either-way charge once a defendant has elected Crown Court trial and prefer a summary-only charge, if they do so chiefly in order to enhance their prospects of conviction. It is believed that there is now an internal CPS circular aimed at preventing such practices.

x) Complying with Pre-Trial Procedures:

Over the years there have been several attempts to ensure that a significant number of Crown Court cases should be preceded by a form of pre-trial review, that identifies the issues and enables an informed estimate of the length of the case to be made. Most recently a pilot study has been taking place in three Crown Court centres, instituting a 'plea and directions hearing' before trial, supported by a Practice Direction from the Deputy Chief Justice. The Royal Commission reports that the Practice Direction is being breached by defence lawyers on a considerable scale,[64] and it goes on to make various recommendations for preparatory hearings, and other procedural requirements aimed at ensuring that cases are prepared at an earlier stage. But the Commission is moved to refer to the doubts of some lawyers that any such changes would succeed, since 'the defence lawyers called upon to make it work will in practice ensure that it fails, both because delay and obfuscation usually operate in favour of the defendant and because the culture and approach of the Criminal Bar is based on last-minute preparation of cases'.[65] The Commission proposes a system of sanctions to prevent the culture from prevailing, whereas the dissenting commissioner thinks the culture so strong that it is pointless even to try.[66] It is plain from this that there is a culture of taking advantage of delay, and refusing to alter working practices, that might be described as unethical in the sense that it has little systematic regard for the legitimate rights of defendants—sometimes veering towards the illegitimate, in lengthening delays where possible, and occasionally veering towards the incompetent, in leaving insufficient time for proper preparation of briefs. Barristers them-

---

[62] D. Riley and J. Vennard, *Triable-Either-Way Cases: Crown Court or Magistrates' Court?*, Home Office Research Study No. 98, 1988, ch.3.

[63] J. Vennard, 'The Outcome of Contested Trials', in D. Moxon (ed), *Managing Criminal Justice*, 1985, finding acquittal rates of 57% in the Crown Court and 30% in magistrates' courts.

[64] RCCJ, para. 7.15.   [65] RCCJ, para. 7.36.

[66] RCCJ, Note of Dissent by Professor Zander, para. 37.

selves, however, tend to deny that late delivery of briefs and last-minute preparation place anyone at a disadvantage.[67]

UNDERSTANDING 'UNETHICAL' BEHAVIOUR

The preceding section has set out some examples of behaviour that might be described as 'unethical', in the sense that it fails to show proper respect for citizens and often removes, circumvents, or weakens certain rights of the suspect or defendant. There may be other practices that lead to miscarriages of justice because of mistakes or casualness within the system, but the focus here is on conduct that may be said to involve some conscious circumvention of the rules. Suspending final judgment on whether these practices are to be termed unethical, we must first enquire into the reasons for them.

Lawyers have tended to regard practices of this kind as the product of individuals, exercising a discretion unconstrained by context or by colleagues, whereas in fact they tend to form part of a process in which several influences such as organizational and occupational rules operate.[68] The culture of the Bar may be mentioned in this connection, and other agencies from the Forensic Science Service to some of the 'regulatory' inspectorates may have their own culture or cultures.[69] A great deal of empirical research has focused on the police, who have such a central rôle in criminal justice. The research has often concluded that much police behaviour is influenced by a 'cop culture' that is spread widely through the organization. There is no need here to enter into an extensive analysis of the elements identified by different researchers. It is sufficient to mention four elements that seem to be at the core of 'cop culture'—(a) support for colleagues and the inappropriateness of close supervision; (b) what is termed 'the macho image', which includes heavy drinking, physical presence, and some attitudes that are sexist and racist; (c) the idea that rules are there to be used and bent; and (d) the sense of mission in police work.[70] The suggestion is that these and similar attitudes are wide-spread, not that they are universal. There may be differences from division to division, particularly between rural and urban areas. There may be individuals or

[67] In the *Crown Court Survey*, by Zander and Henderson, around 20% of barristers who received the brief only on the day of the hearing admitted that they had insufficient time to prepare (pp. 30–1). The vast majority stated that the short notice was sufficient.

[68] K. Hawkins, 'The Use of Legal Discretion: Perspectives from Law and Social Science' in K. Hawkins (ed), *The Uses of Discretion*, 1992, at p. 22.

[69] On the inspectorates, see B. Hutter, 'Varieties in Regulatory Enforcement Styles', (1989) 11 *Law and Policy* 153.

[70] For detailed discussion, see J. Skolnick, *Justice without Trial*, 1966; P. Manning, *Police Work*, 1977; S. Holdaway, *Inside the British Police*, 1983; D. J. Smith and J. Gray, *Police and People in London: the Police in Action*, PSI study, vol iv, 1983; and R. Reiner, *The Politics of the Police*, 2nd ed, 1992, ch.3.

groups, particularly women and some younger police officers, who accept few or no aspects of the culture. Senior officers may argue that changes are taking place, but the stronghold of the culture has always been in the lower ranks. The phenomenon of police culture has been observed so frequently that its existence as an entity cannot be put in doubt.

In an attempt to unravel the reasons which underlie the culture, we may begin by considering (a), support for colleagues and the inappropriateness of close supervision. In order to set aside the claim that this part of the culture has changed, it is worth recalling that two recent research studies for the Royal Commission on Criminal Justice found that the supervision of junior officers in the conduct of inquiries and in questioning was not the norm, and was often regarded as a breach of the trust that should be shown in every officer's skills.[71] This is linked to the idea of police solidarity and the duty to support a fellow officer, although it may have a darker side, as the Royal Commission recognizes in its reference to officers and civilian staff being 'deterred by the prevailing culture from complaining openly about malpractice'.[72] To some extent the isolated position of the police in society may breed a form of solidarity and defensiveness. To some extent the culture may reflect the differing perspectives of police officers 'at the sharp end' and of those officers who are managers, with the lower ranks covering for one another and trying to shield from senior officers various deviations from the rules.[73]

Perhaps the strongest evidence for the existence in the British police of (b), what is termed the 'macho image', which includes racist and sexist attitudes, came from the Policy Studies Institute, London, study of policing in London.[74] Other researchers refer to physical dangers of the job, to 'the alcoholic and sexual indulgences' of male police officers, and to the struggle of women police officers to gain acceptance.[75] But Reiner suggests that some allegations of police racism fail to take proper account of the nature of police work in a society that places ethnic minorities at a disadvantage in many respects.[76]

Central to the cop culture is (c), the idea that rules are there to be used and bent. There are two strands to this. The first emphasizes the use of the criminal law as a resource for legitimating or reinforcing police handling of a situation: the police officer has available a range of offences with which to support his or her authority, and may decide whether or not to invoke one of them as a reason for arrest and charge.[77] Of course this is hardly applicable to crimes such as murder, rape, and armed robbery, but it can be applied to the range of public

---

[71] J. Baldwin, *Supervision of Police Investigations in Serious Criminal Cases*, RCCJ Research Study No. 4, 1992; M. Maguire and C. Norris, *The Conduct and Supervision of Criminal Investigations*, RCCJ Research Study No. 5, 1992. [72] RCCJ, para. 2.65.
[73] See further Reiner, *op.cit.*, pp. 115–17. [74] Smith and Gray, *op.cit.*
[75] Reiner, *op.cit.*, pp. 124–5. [76] Reiner, *op.cit.*, p. 156 f.
[77] For a classic study that highlights this, see E. Bittner, 'The Police on Skid Row: a study in peacekeeping', (1967) *American Sociological Review* 32.

order offences, obstruction and assault on police officers, and a number of other charges. The primary objective of the police may be to keep the peace and to manage situations: in this they use and exert authority; anyone who resists that authority may be charged. The second strand concerns the various procedural rules about questioning, notably the Codes of Practice under the Police and Criminal Evidence Act. The reason why these rules are broken from time to time is that they are seen as unwise impediments to proper police work, standing in the way of vigorous questioning which will get at the truth, or (sometimes) will produce the results which senior police officers or the media seem to want. Indeed, it is thought to be a poor reflection on those who recommend and make the laws that they fail to understand the realities of police work. This led Smith and Gray to comment that deviations from proper procedures can be expected to continue 'as long as many police officers believe that the job cannot be done effectively within the rules'.[78]

These two strands coalesce to suggest that there is a police motivation that lies beyond and above the formal rules of the criminal justice system. It flourishes partly because of the discretion actually left to the police by the system, and partly because of their continued ability to circumvent what they regard as fetters unjustifiably imposed on them. This leads us to enquire about (d), the sense of mission in police work. It is an essentially conservative outlook, in social terms, which celebrates the position of the police as a 'thin blue line' standing between order and chaos. The mission is strengthened by seeing the police as being on the side of the right, serving society, and ranged against offenders and other miscreants who are in the wrong. Reiner describes the subtle interplay of three themes—'of mission, hedonistic love of action, and pessimistic cynicism'—that constitute the core of the police outlook.[79] Many officers join the police with a sense of mission, in terms of defending society and its institutions against attack and disorder, and then develop a kind of cynicism about social trends that seem to threaten existing ways of doing things. The Royal Commission appears to accept some such view:

> We recognize that police malpractice, where it occurs, may often be motivated by an over-zealous determination to secure the conviction of suspects believed to be guilty in the face of rules and procedures which seem to those charged with the investigation to be weighted in favour of the defence.[80]

To be sceptical about the moral quality of the police mission would be easy: it certainly contains its contradictions, in that it purports to emphasize established moral values but many officers rejoice in various sexual exploits, and in that it adopts a puritanical attitude towards drug-users but police alcoholism is

---

[78] Smith and Gray, *op.cit.*, p. 230; see also Reiner, *op.cit.*, pp. 81–5.
[79] Reiner, *op.cit.*, p. 114.   [80] RCCJ, para. 1.24.

a long standing problem.[81] Yet, these contradictions apart, there is a true sense in which the police are performing an essential and central social function. To this extent both the term 'police force' and its modern successor, 'police service', contain elements of realism. There is nothing unhealthy in having a sense of mission about that, any more than it is unhealthy for doctors, nurses, or even lawyers to have a sense of mission. Just as people are right to expect medical care when ill or injured, so citizens are entitled to expect official action when they fall victim to a crime or in the face of threats to good order. Often, this does amount to the protection of the weak against the predatory. But while the vital nature of this social function cannot be disputed, its definition can be. The police culture evidently defines it differently from Parliament, for example, since police officers often express contempt for 'legal restrictions'. There is no question that the maintenance of good order counts, but there is room for debate about what counts as the maintenance of good order.

JUSTIFYING 'UNETHICAL' BEHAVIOUR BY CHALLENGING THE ETHICS

We arrive, then, at the point of struggle for moral supremacy. The police would presumably claim a strong moral element in their mission. Is this really open to challenge? What ethics could call into question the vigorous pursuit of this apparently fundamental social function?

Let us begin by constructing a version of the mission. Some of the main elements have been described above, but there is a need for a rounded version that could fit the words and opinions of police officers. The key element is crime control: this is surely the point of the criminal justice system. It means that law observance should be maintained. In this the police are inevitably in the front line, having peace-keeping functions that (in terms of time spent) outstrip the processing of suspected offenders. A second element is that, where the interests of the defendant conflict with those of the victim or society, priority should be given to the latter. A third and connected element, following from the first two, is that the police should pursue this society-centred approach so far as is possible, exploiting any discretion left by the criminal justice system in order to further the conviction of the guilty. Taken together, these elements of crime control and the protection of society may be taken to establish a powerful case in favour of the police mission. If we are not to descend into anarchy, someone has to do it. Better that it be done in a committed way than without any sense of its social importance.

Assuming that there is some truth in this account, is it defensible? In my view almost every step suffers from confusion which, when examined, mixes

---

[81] Reiner, *op.cit.*, p. 124.

overstatement with understatement and neglects important features of social
life. It would be easy to claim that this is because I have formulated this
version of the police mission for my own purposes; but I would be happy for
my counter-arguments to be ranged against any other version of the police
mission that keeps faith with what considerable numbers of police officers say
and do. The counter-arguments are these. The first element refers to crime
control as if it were to be pursued without regard to any other values. Is it
plausible to advance such an uncomplicated notion? To take an extreme but
telling example, does it suggest that the police should be free to use repressive
measures wherever they regard them as appropriate, or that torture should be
available for use on those suspected of serious crimes? If the answers are
negative, then we need to adopt a more sophisticated and sensitive notion than
'crime control'. Many people might accept at first blush that crime control is
the ultimate aim of the criminal justice system, but on reflection they would
surely recognize that it ought not to be pursued without qualification. That
would lead to a police state.

The second element is that priority should be given to the victim or
society over the interests of the suspect/defendant. In the vernacular this
might be called 'toe-rag theory', since its essence is that the interests of the
innocent and good should be preferred over those of the suspect or defendant.
As one constable stated some years ago, 'Speaking from a policeman's point of
view it doesn't give a damn if we oppress law-breakers, because they're
oppressors in their own right.'[82] This seems to suggest that accused persons
should have no rights, or few rights, or at least rights that can be overridden
when that is necessary in the public interest (as interpreted by the police). This
is to turn the idea of rights on its head. The whole idea of rights is that they
respect the individual's autonomy, and ensure that the individual is protected
from certain kinds of inappropriate behaviour, and is furnished with certain
assistance, when he or she is in the hands of public officials. Rights have been
termed anti-utilitarian claims, in the sense that they represent claims that the
individual be not treated in certain ways even if that might enhance the general
good. However, the idea of priority for 'the interests of society' seems to
accord the individual suspect or defendant no particular rights, and to deny the
whole legitimacy of human rights such as those incorporated in the European
Convention.[83] Moreover, it does so at a stage before the suspect or defendant
has been convicted, thereby affirming a strong presumption of guilt arising

[82] Reiner, *op.cit.*, p. 111.

[83] This is not to overlook the importance of victims' rights, which may on occasion conflict with
those of suspects or defendants. However, this argument should not be taken as far as those who
readily convert 'the interests of society' to 'the interests of victims' would wish to take it. One
must first decide what the rights of victims should be: see the references in note 3, above. Once that
has been done, there will be few direct conflicts between victims' rights and those of suspects or
defendants.

from the investigating officer's belief. Is it really acceptable to place so much emphasis on the judgment of one or more police officers, especially when one element in the cop culture is a mutual support and respect for the skills of others which frowns on routine supervision?

These arguments also show the weakness of the third element, always seeking to promote the interests of society against those of the suspect. This is flawed for various reasons. Suspects are members of society. Even members of society who are unlikely to be suspected of crime might accept that those who are suspected should be accorded some rights. Few would agree that it should be for the police to decide which suspects should be accorded rights and which not. The notorious cases of miscarriage of justice leave us well aware that police officers' judgments of someone's guilt or innocence should not be determinative.

The conclusion is therefore irresistible that the 'police mission' described above cannot claim the moral high ground. It overstates the notion of crime control by assuming that this should be pursued either without qualifications or with only such qualifications as the police deem appropriate. It assumes that respect for the rights of suspects is bound to detract from crime control, and does so for insufficient reason. In this it understates the importance of respect for human rights even when accused of a crime. It also fails to recognize the findings of pyschologists such as Tyler, whose experiments suggest that procedural fairness is valued more highly by many citizens than the outcome of the procedure.[84]

These deficiencies in the version of the 'police mission' sketched above should not be allowed to overshadow the importance of convicting the guilty. Some statements of the importance of suspects' rights seem to neglect the social importance of convicting the guilty and dealing with crime. The fundamental reasons for having a criminal justice system are to reduce crime and to deal with offenders. Among the reasons for having a police force are to reduce crime and to apprehend and question suspected offenders. Statements of the rights of suspects and defendants cannot stand on their own, in isolation from the social functions of the system to which they apply. They leave the question of how to maximize the protection of suspects' rights, while ensuring the conviction of the guilty and the protection of victims and potential victims.

It is one small step from these ruminations to the conclusion that what is required is a balance between powers of crime control, and rights to protect suspects and defendants. But this is a step that should not be taken until there has been more discussion about the nature and significance of the rights. It would be far too casual to assume that, after recognizing the absolute right not to be subjected to torture, all other so-called rights can be traded off as part of some political compromise, wherever gains in crime control seem likely. The

---

[84] T. R. Tyler, *Why People Obey the Law*, 1990.

investigation of terrorist crimes or mass murders tends to bring these issues sharply into focus: the 'prevention of terrorism' legislation curtails or removes various rights accorded to persons suspected of other crimes, and yet some of the most notorious miscarriages of justice have been perpetrated against people suspected of terrorist crimes. While it would be wrong to overlook the importance to citizens of peaceful and crime-free living conditions, it is also right that persons suspected of crimes should be granted various facilities, and that the agents of law enforcement should behave towards them in particular ways—both of which the European Convention on Human Rights is designed to secure. The rights of victims, too, are not mere matters to be weighed in the balance, but are important in their own right. In the end, conflicts among rights and between rights and utility, have to be resolved at a political level. But the metaphor of balancing can seduce too easily: unless there is a clear recognition of all the relevant rights, of the justifications for recognizing them, and of their relative priority or 'weight', beware the concept of balance.

UNETHICAL STANDPOINTS?

We might now consider three standpoints that appear to ooze practicality and good sense, particularly among those who work in certain parts of the criminal justice system. The first, already mentioned in one context, is the argument that certain rules should be circumvented because the rule makers do not understand the practical problems. The second is that it is wrong to expect police, prosecutors, etc. to operate with 'their hands tied behind their back'. And the third is that when the CPS drops a case or when a court gives a lenient sentence, this is bad for morale in the system. All these standpoints are connected, but they deserve brief discussion individually.

Is it right to circumvent rules on the ground that the rule makers do not understand the day-to-day, on-the-ground problems of the criminal process? The claim is heard in various quarters. It is heard among some police officers in relation to the Police and Criminal Evidence Act and its Codes of Practice: these are restrictions imposed by people who expect 'results' and yet do not understand the difficulties the police have to encounter. There are three problems with a claim of this kind. Firstly, there is the constitutional argument: any person or organization that substitutes its own judgment from one reached through the appropriate democratic channels is behaving unconstitutionally. Secondly, there is the values argument: that this claim assumes that crime control, in a fairly absolute form, is the only worth-while value. It gives no weight to the protection of the rights of suspects. And third, there is the evidential argument: is it really true that 'the job' cannot be done if the restrictions are observed? In fact this is less likely to be a matter of evidence than a question of values again, since the claim that the job cannot be done suppresses the unarticulated clause, 'within the prevailing culture'. If a different culture prevailed, perhaps the job could be done. One can only plausibly assert that it cannot be done if one assumes no change in the culture. These three arguments expose the weaknesses of the claim that rules made by out-of-touch rule makers may be circumvented. They apply no less to the view said to obtain among some magistrates' clerks some years ago, that High Court rulings were there to be circumvented because 'the judges did not understand the practicalities, eg of dealing with truculent, often regular, customers, or a busy court schedule'.[85] This, again, seems to have been based on the assumption that either speed or the conviction of the guilty is important above all else.

The second claim is similar in some respects. It is that society expects the police to combat crime with their hands tied behind their backs, or that society expects prosecutors to obtain convictions with one hand tied behind their backs. The precise formulation varies, but the target is always the 'restrictions' imposed, usually by the legislature but sometimes by the higher judiciary. The claim could be countered by means of the three arguments deployed above—the constitutional point, the values argument, and the question of evidence. However, another argument is worth raising here: the assumption that respecting the rights of suspects significantly diminishes the number of convictions, and therefore the protection of the public and of victims. This is a complicated argument, requiring considerable space to develop and to rebut. Suffice it to say here that research suggests the number of extra convictions likely to result from, say, abrogating the right to remain silent during police questioning, without adverse inferences being permitted, is relatively small; and that must be set against the possibility of more convictions of the innocent if the rule were changed.[86] The existing law appears to have a greater impact on police perceptions than upon the outcome of cases.[87] This brings the discussion to the question of morale.

The third claim is that it is bad for police morals when the CPS decides to drop a prosecution commenced by the police. Parallel claims are sometimes heard when a court gives a low sentence on conviction, and there is also the suggestion that one reason why station sergeants tend not to refuse charges from officers who bring in arrestees is that it might affect morale. Now as an empirical proposition this claim may often be correct. Such events may reduce

---

[85] The words of a magistrates' clerk, quoted by A. Rutherford, *Criminal Justice and the Pursuit of Decency*, 1993, p. 62.

[86] RCCJ, para. 4.22, recommending (by a majority) no change in the law, for this reason. Notwithstanding this, the Government has pressed ahead with plans to restrict the right of silence, now enacted in the Criminal Justice and Public Order Act 1994.

[87] See R. Leng, *The Right to Silence in Police Interrogation*, RCCJ Research Study No. 10, 1993; M. McConville and J. Hodgson, *Custodial Legal Advice and the Right to Silence*, RCCJ Research Study No. 16, 1993.

police morale, as may new restrictions on their questioning of suspects, changes in their pay and conditions, and several other matters. The problem here is whether one should defer to the conservatism that underlies the morale of professions such as the police (or the Bar), a conservatism no doubt linked with a sturdy defence of the police mission discussed earlier. One reason for deferring to it would be that the mission of crime control is of supreme social importance and that it would be wrong to upset such a vital organisation as the police. However, an alternative approach would be to try to alter the culture that supports this version of the police mission, a culture that sees little reason for according rights to suspects. Two justifications for taking this course would be that it is ethically superior, and that the democratic institutions have decided that certain other values are worthy of respect.

CRIMINAL JUSTICE REFORM THROUGH ETHICS

Law enforcement agencies and the administration of criminal justice are governed by masses of legislative rules, and yet it is common ground that there are wide areas of discretion and that there must continue to be some areas of discretion. The next step, at least for those who favour the principle of legality as a general principle,[88] is to attempt to structure discretion by the use of guidance and guidelines. Other common features of reform proposals are better training of criminal justice personnel and better lines of accountability. Measures of this kind, espoused in various forms by such politically disparate groups as the Royal Commission on Criminal Justice, after their review of criminal justice processes, and by Michael McConville, Andrew Sanders and Roger Leng at the end of their sharply critical research report on police and prosecution services,[89] are now recognized to be far more promising than mere changes in legal rules. The reason for this is the strength of occupational cultures within such key agencies as the police, the prosecution service, the various regulatory inspectorates, defence solicitors, the criminal Bar, the Forensic Science Service, and so on. More has been said here about the occupational culture of the police, to some extent justifiably since they form the principle filter into the criminal justice system, but to some extent simply because there has been more research into the police. Since occupational cultures are so powerful, better understanding of their nature and their support systems requires further research into the professions.[90]

There is evidence that, whether coincidentally or in response to recent publicity about miscarriages of justice, there is now greater concern about

---

[88] For discussion, see P. H. Robinson, 'Legality and Discretion in the Distribution of Criminal Sanctions', (1988) 25 *Harvard Journal on Legislation* 393.

[89] M. McConville, A. Sanders and R. Leng, *The Case for the Prosecution*, 1991, ch.10.

[90] Cf M. McConville, J. Hodgson, L. Bridges, and A. Pavlovic, *Standing Accused*, 1994.

professional ethics in the criminal justice system. Even as moderate a body as the 1993 Royal Commission reported that it was 'struck by evidence of a disquieting lack of professional competence in many parts' of the criminal justice system.[91] The police service is at an advanced stage of preparing its code of ethics, and the CPS has recently published a *Statement of Purpose and Values*. The Bar and the Law Society, as is evident from chapters 3 and 4 herein, are aware of many of the issues. The significant step is to move away from the concentration on individual moral dilemmas and to confront the occupational cultures and traditional working practices of each profession, in so far as they may be inconsistent with a principled, ethical approach to criminal justice.

While issuing a few codes of ethics will not necessarily bring changes of outlook and practice, there can be little doubt that codes of ethics must play an important part in the dynamics of change. Although they tend to be addressed to individuals within each profession, they often form part of a package including 'mission statements' and 'declarations of purpose', thus recognizing that decision making takes place within an organizational setting. A draft of the Police Service's *Statement of Ethical Principles* includes two principles that are particularly relevant to our discussion. The first is the duty to 'uphold fundamental human rights, treating every person as an individual and display respect and compassion towards them'; the second is the duty to 'act only within the law, in the understanding that I have no authority to depart from due legal process . . . '. The first recognizes the idea of fundamental human rights, and the second confronts directly the cultural dispensation to bend rules 'in the interests of justice'. Apart from the obvious point that they would need to be harnessed to an effective system of accountability, it would be particularly important to promulgate the reasons behind the principles. At least the draft police code refers expressly to 'fundamental human rights', but an essential part of training must be to convey the reasons why these rights ought to be respected, whether by abstract instruction or by means of rôle-play exercises, debates, and so on. Otherwise, a statement of ethical principles would be a poor match for a well-entrenched occupational culture. The key questions must be addressed convincingly; why must I show respect towards someone who admits to a dreadful crime? If I feel that I can solve a difficult case by deviating from the rules, is it not in the interests of society that I should do so? Both the democratic argument and ethical principles should be elaborated in reply.

Part of the framework of the Police and Criminal Evidence Act 1984 was to recognize, as not all European countries have done, the right of a suspect in a police station to consult with a lawyer and to have a lawyer present during questioning. This right will only be of proper benefit to suspects if their legal

---

[91] RCCJ, para. 1.20.

advisers give them due protection from unfair police practices. The Royal Commission regards as 'disturbing' the findings of researchers that competent legal advice is not always given and that legal advisers sometimes remain passive while police officers break the rules by indulging in oppressive, threatening, or insulting practices.[92] Many practical improvements are necessary here, both in the organization of defence solicitors' practices and in the training of unadmitted staff. There are wider issues of policy concerning the legal aid system and the rôle of the defence solicitor.[93]

The literature of English criminal procedure is replete with statements about the proper rôle of the prosecutor. In the nineteenth century it was said that the motivation of a prosecutor should be that of a Minister of Justice,[94] and this was elaborated by Sir Herbert Stephen when he wrote that the object of the prosecutor should be 'not to get a conviction, without qualification, but to get a conviction only if justice requires it'.[95] Christmas Humphreys, writing as Senior Crown Counsel, stated that 'the Crown is interested in justice; the defence in obtaining an acquittal within the limits of lawful procedure'.[96] The rhetoric of this position recognizes that crime control should not be regarded as the sole or dominant aim of the prosecutor, and that the concept of justice also includes the recognition of certain rights of defendants and of victims.[97] The CPS's *Statement of Purpose and Values* contains a CPS commitment to 'treat all defendants fairly', and to treat victims with 'sensitivity and understanding'.[98] However, there is little elaboration of these principles, and unfortunately there is no attempt at justification and no practical examples are given. If a document of this kind is to have an effect on professional conduct within the Service, more emphasis must be given to justification, explanation, and training.

Much more could be said about ethical principles for the Forensic Science Service,[99] and about codes of ethics for the many other professional groups operating within the criminal justice system, such as the Inland Revenue, Customs and Excise, the Serious Fraud Office, and the regulatory agencies. Indeed, so diverse are the legislative frameworks and discretionary practices of these different agencies that one might call into question the justification for having separate statements of ethical principles. At a fundamental level one

---

[92] RCCJ, paras. 3.56 to 3.63.
[93] See M. McConville, J. Hodgson, L. Bridges and A. Pavlovic, *Standing Accused*, 1994.
[94] Crompton, J. in *Puddick* (1865) 1 F. & F. 497.
[95] H. Stephen, *The Conduct of an English Criminal Trial* (1926), p. 11.
[96] C. Humphreys, 'The Duties of Prosecuting Counsel', [1955] Crim LR 739, 741.
[97] Cf D. M. Nissman and E. Hagen, *The Prosecution Function*, 1982, p. 2: 'In pursuing his goal to seek justice, the prosecutor must punch through the tiresome criminal defender, whose goals are necessarily in conflict with the search for truth and justice.'
[98] Crown Prosecution Service, *Statement of Purpose and Values*, 1993, 8, 10; cf also their *Statement on the treatment of victims and witnesses by the Crown Prosecution Service*, 1993.
[99] RCCJ, paras. 9.34 to 9.36.

might ask whether it is justifiable to speak of an ethical approach to criminal justice in a system that institutionalises different approaches and different rights according to whether one's offence falls within the 'police' category or the 'regulatory' category, producing inequalities of treatment that are hard to defend.[100] There is a strong case for developing a statement of common ethical principles for those involved in the administration of criminal justice, to which further principles could be added for each particular agency or group.

CONCLUSIONS

The criminal justice system has moral dimensions other than the moral force of the law against those who do wrong. Among those other moral dimensions are that the rights of victims and witnesses should be respected, and that citizens who are suspected of, or charged with, offences must be dealt with in a way which respects their rights. Of course there is room for controversy about the particular rights of each kind that should be recognized, as the extensive philosphical literature shows, but the existence of the European Convention on Human Rights enables some progress to be made. It may properly be regarded as a basic specification of relevant ethical principles, although not an exhaustive one—it does not deal with victims, and says nothing about the ethical orientation of parties such as prosecutors, defence lawyers, or police officers. The European Convention may be seen as a higher law, standing above English legislation and case-law, although it is a form of positive law. It does not offer any clear theoretical basis for the rights it propounds, apart from a general reference in the Preamble to 'a common heritage of political traditions, ideals, freedom and the rule of law', but it can be regarded as an authoritative source of principles for legislators and judges. We then move to the political proposition that, once legislation has been enacted, it is not for any group of officials, however committed to a sense of mission that claims to be in the 'public interest', to go behind it. The legislation may respect some rights absolutely, and may embody some form of compromise between crime control and certain other rights. In terms of practical encounters between officials and citizens, the key point is that the officials should act in the spirit of the compromise, in a way that shows an understanding and an acceptance of those rights that they are required to respect. This should have its foundation in clear and practical codes of ethics that explain the justifications for respecting rights, and which are buttressed by effective training. In this way, any opposition between ethical conduct and occupational cultures may perhaps be minimized.

---

[100] Cf, eg A. Sanders, 'Class Bias in Prosecutions', (1985) 24 *Howard J.C.J.* 176, with the reference in J. Braithwaite, *Corporate Crime in the Pharmaceutical Industry*, 1984, ch.9, to the narrow concerns of 'liberal bleeding hearts'.

8

Legal Ethics: Its Nature and Place in the Curriculum

ALAN PATERSON

THE regulation of the professions is an area which has been attracting increasing international interest in the last decade. In the eyes of the dominant paradigm in the sociology of the professions—market control theory[1]—and indeed from the standpoint of many economists, professions are simply state backed cartels. On this view self-regulation has only served to restrict competition and to deceive the public.[2] As is well known, in the last decade the alleged excesses of self-regulation have come under increasing attack. A combination of an active consumer movement and interventionist government policies have seen a sustained assualt on restrictive practices in the professions during this period. To Abel, these steps towards deregulation spell the end of market control and the demise of professionalism.[3] There is, however, an alternative perspective. As I have argued elsewhere[4] professionalism can be perceived as a form of implicit contractualism in terms of which the profession in return for delivering competence, access, a service ethic, and public protection expects to receive reasonable rewards, status, constraints on competition, and autonomy. Viewed in this light the events of the last decade can be construed as no more than a renegotiation of the tacit contract placing a greater emphasis on the consumers' side of the equation,[5] while leaving the essential elements of professionalism intact. Such a readjustment of the balance between the lawyers' self-interest and the public interest may yet provide the appropriate balance between self-regulation and deregulation for which the commentators are striving.[6]

Given the centrality of ethical regulation to the legal professions under both the old paradigm and the new, it is surprising how little the nature or

[1] See M. Larson, *The Rise of Professionalism* (Berkeley: University of California Press, 1977) and R. Abel, *The Legal Profession in England and Wales* (London: Basil Blackwell, 1988).

[2] See R. Abel, 'Why does the ABA promulgate ethical rules?' 50 *Texas Law Review* 639.

[3] See R. Abel, 'The Decline of Professionalism?' (1986) 49 MLR 1.

[4] See A. Paterson, 'Professionalism and the Legal Services Market' in E. Skordaki and C. Willis (eds) *Lawyers and Social Change* (Oxford: Oxford University Press, forthcoming).

[5] A similar argument appears in R. Dingwall and P. Fenn, 'A Respectable Profession' 7 *International Review of Law and Economics* 51 who see professions as having entered an implicit bargain with the state, the terms of which are open to renegotiation—since privileges can be withdrawn by the state (p.62).   [6] See Dingwall and Fenn *op.cit.*

content of professional ethics has featured in the critical writings of modern scholars outside the United States. Perhaps because of this in the Anglo–American world alone legal and professional ethics appear to have a multiplicity of contents ranging from professional conduct to moral philosophy, and from professional practice to practice management. Certainly, when it comes to the curriculum there is much to be said for the conclusion of the Cotter Report[7] that all of these aspects should be taught, though at different times in the pre- and post-qualifying stages. For the purposes of this chapter, however, the primary focus will be on the core elements of professional responsibility, namely, the legal regulation and professional conduct of lawyers.

Even this is not narrow enough since there are wide-spread disagreements both as to the fundamentals of professional conduct and their origins. As we have seen Abel regards ethical rules or codes as self-serving protectionism rooted in opportunism. Certainly, Schneyer's study of the evolution of the American Bar Association Model Rules of Professional Conduct[8] demonstrates clearly that particular rules of professional conduct are often the battle-ground where interests of different factions within the profession (for instance the trial lawyers and corporate lawyers) conflict. Another school of thought[9] sees professional ethics as a collection of values derived from first principles. This school rejects the development of ethical codes and detailed rules since, like Abel, it considers that the rules contained therein never quite meet the facts of particular cases and are therefore of little guidance. Unfortunately, leaving it to the balance of conflicting principles which are intuitively divined but vary according to the circumstances, amounts to little more than a sophisticated form of relativism. This school, nevertheless, has much support amongst the student body and indeed the profession. Many of them consider that the study of professional ethics is a barren pursuit—since they feel that they already know what it is to be a moral person.[10] This confusion between ethics and professional ethics is exacerbated by the fact that most students, and not a few practitioners, believe that ethical dilemmas in legal practice are self-evident and resolvable by intuitive means. It was arguments such as these which prevented either branch of the profession in Scotland from promulgating codes of conduct until the last decade. How often the argument was repeated: 'we all know instinctively what it is to be ethical. If you spell it out all you do is show the cowboys of the profession how close to the wind they can sail.'

It is not just the sporting metaphors which are confused in that argument.

---

[7] B. Cotter, *Professional Responsibility Instruction in Canada* (Quebec: Conceptcom, 1992).

[8] T. Schneyer, 'Professionalism as Politics' in R. Nelson, D. Trubek and R. Solomon (eds) *Lawyers' Ideals and Lawyers' Practices* (Ithaca: Cornell University Press, 1992) p. 95.

[9] A recent exponent of this line of thinking is Alfred Phillips. See A. Phillips, *Professional Ethics for Scottish Solicitors* (Edinburgh: Butterworths, 1990).

[10] 'And what is good, Paedrus, and what is not good—need we ask anyone to tell us these things?' Robert Pirsig, *Zen and the Art of Motorcycle Maintenance* (William Morrow & Co.: New York, 1974).

It is, moreover, a curious argument for lawyers to advance since it could equally well be applied to the criminal law. The response of civil libertarians to the suggestion that we should not spell out the law, so that potential criminals can only discover *ex post facto* whether or not they have actually breached the law, can readily be imagined.[11] In reality the worlds of ethics and professional ethics only partly intersect. Not a few aspects of professional regulation, for example most of the rules on the attraction of business, owe their origins to questions of policy rather than morality. Certainly, highly moral students not infrequently fail examinations in professional ethics.[12] To counter such perceptions entails exposing the students to some of the many problems of professional ethics which arise and to which there is either no intuitively obvious right answer, or where the solution appears counter-intuitive. Such issues include: is it ethically permissible for lawyers to send fliers advertising their services directly to victims in a train crash with whom they have no prior connection? May lawyer/client confidentiality be breached in order to recover the lawyer's fee? Can the lawyer use the contents of a client's file to defeat a misconduct complaint lodged against him or her by the client? May a lawyer receive a legacy from a client under a will which the testator has handwritten at the direction of the lawyer? Not infrequently the answer to such questions differs depending on the jurisdiction in which it arises. The key point is that minds may differ on such issues and that the only safeguard for one's practicing certificate is knowledge of what the rules and principles actually require. Indeed the dangers of the intuitive approach include precisely the fact that it encourages lawyers to get into ethical dilemmas such as conflicts of interest without realising it. Once they have begun down the slippery slope the tendency is to get ever more embroiled as, in the conflict of interest example, their intuition rationalises the continued retention of both clients long after the objective bystander would have called a halt.

It can, on the other hand, be argued that the rules of professional conduct are akin to legal rules and principles (many of which are rooted in the law of agency)[13] which have evolved through the courts, the decisions of disciplinary bodies, and the practice rules of the profession. Unfortunately, in the United Kingdom these rules and principles are insufficiently developed.[14] This is in part due to the dominance until relatively recently of the intuitive school of thought, in part to the marked reluctance of solicitors to consider that the law

---

[11] cf the concerns caused by *D.P.P.* v. *Shaw* [1962] AC 220.

[12] Blinkered to the last, many regard such a failure as a much greater stain on their escutcheon than failing any other law examination.

[13] See eg The American Law Institute, *Restatement of the Law Governing Lawyers*, 1992.

[14] In the United States, by contrast, there is a very substantial jurisprudence across the individual states and by the American Bar Association itself in this field. There are many textbooks and journals in the area.

of agency applies to them,[15] in part to an unwillingness by the courts to wrest the responsibility for developing the principles from the professions and the disciplinary bodies,[16] and in part to a shortage of cases. Even in areas whose significance has long been established there are substantial lacuna. The paramount duty to the court owed by all lawyers is but one such area. We still do not know the full parameters of the boundary between 'actively' and 'passively' misleading the court which was initially sketched in *Meek* v. *Fleming* [1961] 2 QB 366 and *Tombling* v. *Universal Bulb Co. Ltd.* (1951) 2 TLR 289. In Scotland it is not even clear whether this distinction is recognized by the courts or whether counsel are under greater restraints than solicitors in this area. Nor is there clear cut guidance in either country as to how to deal with the perjuring client.

Again, in the increasingly important area of conflict of interest, tribunals and authorities in the United Kingdom have yet to grapple with such straight-forward issues as the obligations of the lawyer who is acting both for an insured and for the insurance company. Who is the real client when a conflict arises? Compared with the development of the topic in North America the case-law on conflict of interest in the United Kingdom is only in its infancy, although there have been a few useful decisions in recent years.[17] Nevertheless it surely cannot be long before our courts begin to grapple with the problems caused by successive conflicts[18] and the additional difficulties caused by the exponential growth in size of our major city firms and the proliferation of their international branch offices. In Scotland, the dearth of case-law is especially marked since the neglect of the subject area has been reinforced by the usual scarcity problems which exist in small jurisdictions. For example, while it has long been established that contracts between lawyers and their clients must be 'fair and reasonable',[19] it has never been established whether the same test is

---

[15] The case of *Brown* v. *Inland Revenue* [1965] AC 244 is a particularly clear illustration of this tendency. In all the common law world the only jurisdiction which interprets the law of agency, such that the interest on client accounts belongs to the lawyer, is the United Kingdom. At least in England and Wales the view has been taken that commissions not declared to the client belong to the client as the principal in the transaction. In Scotland the majority of the Council of the Law Society takes the view that where an agent is employed to do work which is not, in the ordinary course of business, done gratuitously, eg, to effect insurance, and the principal pays nothing for his services, he, the agent, may retain any commission received from a third party. (Under this view of the law the principal is presumed to assent to the agent receiving a commission, however much the commission exceeds the fee which could reasonably be charged for performing the service.)

[16] cf *E* v. *T* 1949 SLT 411: 'I shall not attempt to define professional misconduct. But if the statutory tribunal, composed as it always is of professional men of the highest repute and competence, stigmatise a course of conduct as misconduct, it seems to me that only strong grounds would justify this Court in condoning as innocent that which the Committee have condemned as guilty' per Lord President Cooper.

[17] eg *Re a firm of solicitors* [1992] 1 All ER 353.

[18] See now *Re a firm of solicitors* [1995] 3 All ER 482.

[19] see eg *Aitken* v. *Campbell's Trustees* 1909 SC 1217.

applicable in the case of gifts. Again, it is far from clear whether information as to a future crime with the potential for injury or even death, or information as to the true author of a serious crime for which another is being tried, would be exempted from the legal professional privilege in Scotland. Other areas where guidance is lacking include the ethics of negotiation,[20] the allocation of decision making authority between lawyer and client, and when, if ever, delay is a legitimate strategy in litigation.

While the dearth of academic and critical writing in the field can be regretted and the shortage of case-law remarked on, it is even more disappointing that the reasoning deployed by the courts and the disciplinary tribunals in recent decades has rarely provided useful guidance on matters of principle.[21] This is particularly applicable to Scotland, but in truth the approach taken to intentionality and misconduct is unsatisfactory on both sides of the border. In two recent cases the Inner House of the Court of Session (the Scots equivalent of the Court of Appeal)[22] stressed that in assessing whether a course of action amounts to professional misconduct it is not just a question of whether a practice rule or a common law standard has been breached, but also the degree of culpability of the solicitor's actions in all the circumstances. It was established in *Council of the Law Society* v. *J* 1991 SLT 662 that 'the circumstances' could never include the fact that the solicitor was ignorant of a new practice rule which had only recently come into force. Somewhat surprisingly, however, the Court also ruled that the fact the solicitor's breach of the practice rule involved no prejudice to the client might be relevant to establishing misconduct, and not just a point which went to mitigation of sentence. Similarly, both the courts and the tribunal in Scotland appear to have suggested that being an inexperienced assistant or trainee goes to culpability. These rulings seem hard to reconcile with well-established decisions on both sides of the border to the effect that ill health or substance addiction only go to mitigation and not to culpability. To make matters worse the Court of Appeal has recently ruled that since the aim of the Disciplinary Tribunal is the protection of the public and the profession, some considerations which would ordinarily weigh in mitigation of punishment in a criminal case have little application in a misconduct case. Thus they concluded that it was not an argument against suspending a solicitor from practice that the solicitor might be unable to re-establish his practice when the period of suspension was over.[23]

---

[20] eg, can one mislead the other side in a negotiation about matters such as the sum which your client would be prepared to accept in settlement?

[21] It seems likely that the three problems are interconnected. We are unlikely to witness a change in the judgment styles in this field until appellate courts or academic writers begin to demand greater intellectual rigour from the first instance decision makers.

[22] *Sharp* v. *The Council of the Law Society of Scotland* 1984 SLT 313 and *MacColl* v. *Council of the Law Society of Scotland* 1987 SLT 525.

[23] See *Bolton* v. *Law Society* [1994] 2 All ER 486.

If this decision is curious, the latest offering from the Privy Council in this field, *Clark Boyce* v. *Mouat [1993] 4 All E.R. 268*, is disappointing. The case offered an opportunity to provide a wide ranging exposition on conflict of interest, its forms, rationale, and solutions. The single judgment, however, enunciates the largely unexplored doctrine that solicitors can continue to act in situations of conflict, provided their clients give their informed consent. This doctrine is accepted in the United States,[24] but in a far more rigorous and narrowly confined form than that put forward by the Privy Council. Moreover, the American cases have set limits to the doctrine, indicating the situations where the seriousness of the conflict is such that no amount of informed consent can permit the lawyer to continue to act. While this was hinted at in the Privy Council, almost no guidance was provided as to where the limits of informed consent should be drawn. At best this case must count as an opportunity missed to provide much needed guidance to the profession. At worst it is an open invitation to streetwise solicitors to run the risk of conflicts of interest in the hope that their clients' informed consent can be 'obtained' at a later stage if serious problems arise. However, the utility of such a strategy remains unproven since, to further complicate matters, it is unclear whether the case, which was fought on the basis of breach of contract and of fiduciary duty, will also be regarded as determinative of the ethical issues, or whether the Solicitors Complaints Bureau or the Discipline Tribunal will reject or curtail the informed consent doctrine.

WHAT SHOULD BE TAUGHT IN PROFESSIONAL ETHICS?

Given the debates as to the nature and content of the subject, the paucity of United Kingdom materials in the area, and the reluctance of the courts and tribunals to lay down clear guidelines in the field, it is perhaps hardly surprising that its place in the curriculum should also be problematic. Quite apart from the critique of the intuitive school who, as we have seen, believe that it is pointless to study professional ethics at all, there is the closely related viewpoint that it is of precious little use when it is taught. These critics point to the fact that in most of the major corporate scandals in recent years, on both sides of the Atlantic, the lawyers have been singularly ineffective in persuading their clients that honesty is the best policy. Similarly, researchers who have interviewed in-house lawyers have reported relatively few accounts of instances when the lawyers found themselves restraining their clients from unethical or illegal conduct.[25]

A quick and partial answer to this is that almost certainly none of the

---

[24] See eg C. Wolfram, *Modern Legal Ethics* (West Publishing Co., 1986) pp. 337–49
[25] See eg Eve Spangler, *Lawyers for Hire* (New Haven: Yale University Press, 1986).

lawyers in question had had any serious training in professional ethics. Such training is a relatively recent phenomenon, even in the United States, where it only became wide-spread after 1974 in the aftermath of Watergate, when the American Bar Association required it to be taught in all accredited law schools. It can also be objected that the critics are being unfair since nobody criticises teachers of tort when lawyers forget limitation periods. It is wholly unrealistic to think that professional ethics classes will prevent professional misconduct. What they can do is sensitize new entrants to potential problems and place them on their guard; it can also provide then with suggestions as to what to do, and who to consult, when they are faced with an ethical conundrum.

Indeed, contrary to the views of the students and critics, it can be argued that it is growing ever more important to study and teach professional ethics. This is because of the effect of de-regulation and market forces on both sides of the Atlantic. As competition within the profession and between the profession and other professions has increased, so the tension for firms between operating as a business and as a professional unit has grown. Indeed, Marc Galanter and Thomas Palay have argued[26] that the tension is inherent in the very form of organisation adopted by law firms—particularly the larger ones. These firms have been growing dramatically in size on both sides of the Atlantic in the last decade and now account for very significant proportions of the practising profession.[27] This tension has profound implications for legal educators who in future will have to provide better training to would-be lawyers, both in the business sphere (for example management training, time management, computerization) and in the professional sphere (by greater skills training, for instance drafting, interviewing, and negotiation). To a certain degree these objectives are being met by the new Legal Practice Course, the Professional Skills course, and Continuing Legal Education courses such as Best Practice. However, there is an even stronger case for proper training in professional ethics and the rôle of the lawyer to assist the lawyers of the future in managing the tension between economic considerations and professional practice. It remains to be seen whether the Legal Practice Course and the professional skills course will be sufficient to achieve this.[28]

Part of the problem of what to teach stems from the pluralistic or multi-layered aspects of professional responsibility. It encapsulates not merely the rules of professional conduct, but also unprofessional conduct, inadequate professional services, written practice standards, the law of negligence, and

---

[26] 'The Transformation of the Big Law Firm' in R. Nelson *et al.* (eds) *op.cit.*

[27] Curiously this is even more true for England and Wales than in the United States. The top 15 firms in London employ nearly 10% of all solicitors in private practice in England and Wales.

[28] Certainly they have been helped by the existence of the sixth edition of the very useful *Guide to the Professional Conduct of Solicitors* (London: The Law Society, 1993).

the law of agency, not to mention aspects of the law of evidence, professional practice, and professional etiquette. To teach these in isolation from each other is to provide only a partial picture to students. They need to be encouraged to see that there is an array of norms and sanctions surrounding them, that interconnect in their implications and sometimes even in their consequences.

WHEN SHOULD THE COURSE BE TAUGHT?

The Cotter report argues persuasively[29] the case for aspects of professional responsibility to be taught in all stages of legal education from pre-law or first year law courses to honours, and from the practical course to continuing professional development. While accepting that such a proposal sounds suspiciously like empire building, it may none the less reflect the reality that there are differing strands to the subject which are hard to combine into a single class. The strands range from ethical debates such as 'defending the guilty', 'the hired-gun model and the corporate polluter', and 'the limits to confidentiality' to a scrutiny of the principles of the law of agency; from a contextualist account of the ætiology of professional rules[30] to understanding ethical dilemmas as part of clinical legal education.

At present few jurisdictions if any can actually boast a satisfactory curriculum at all these levels of instruction. In the United Kingdom there is some introductory material in legal system courses but very little elsewhere in the undergraduate curriculum. At present Strathclyde is the only Law School in Scotland where aspects of professional ethics appear in Honours courses from the perspective of the sociology of the professions, but this course has few counterparts in England and Wales. Jerome Frank, the famous American fact sceptic, considered that there was no point in providing ethical training except in a clinical context.[31] However, this is impractical in the United Kingdom where few Universities provide clinical training. Moreover, there is evidence from the United States that, in practice, instructors in clinical programmes find that they have insufficient time to provide ethical training when in the middle of a case.

WHERE SHOULD PROFESSIONAL ETHICS BE TAUGHT?

Should professional ethics be taught as a course on its own or as a pervasive or integrated element in all practical courses? In the Legal Practice Course

---

[29] *op.cit.* ch.3. A similar argument seems to have been accepted at the Second Consultative Conference of the Lord Chancellor's Advisory Committee on Legal Education and Conduct in its review of legal education in July 1994. (Conference Proceedings, Discussion Group 2 pp. 2–3).

[30] See eg Schneyer *op.cit.*

[31] J. Frank, 'Why Not a Clinical Lawyer-School?' 81 *U. Penn Rev* 907 (1933) p. 922.

professional conduct is described as a pervasive course, but in practice it is taught both as a free standing module and pervasively—an approach which is also followed at the Continuing Legal Education stage. This is surely the right solution. If it is accepted that Professional Ethics is not rooted in intuitive notions of good behaviour, but rather founded on fiduciary obligations which pervade the law of agency, then the case for a free standing course showing the interdependent and interrelated nature of the subject is a strong one. A pervasive approach on its own would find it difficult to achieve this. Thus the study of conflict of interest as part of a practical conveyancing course would almost certainly fail to explore the wider aspects of conflict of interest, not to mention its interdependence with the doctrine of confidentiality. Similarly, to study fees and the taking of commissions in a context that is completely divorced from the examination of client property and contracts with clients, or, indeed, conflict of interest, is to miss the important principles and interconnections which run throughout each of these areas. Moreover, the pervasive approach runs the risk that if time constraints become a problem in the course then the ethical inserts may be amongst the easiest to drop or curtail. This may reinforce the final objection to the pervasive approach, namely, that while in one light it points to the importance of the subject that it appears in every other subject, to the student the lack of a free standing course in its own right in the area may appear an indication that it is peripheral to their practical training.

HOW SHOULD PROFESSIONAL ETHICS BE TAUGHT?

This question raises two issues. The first is a variant on the question of what should be taught, for it relates to the approach or perspective which should be adopted in teaching professional ethics. The second issue relates to technique—which methods of instruction should be adopted? As we shall see the issues are interrelated. As to the framework to be adopted, the lack of experience in teaching the subject in the United Kingdom has prevented significant debate on the topic. In the United States, with nearly twenty years of teaching professional ethics, it is not surprising that the pedagogical debates between those who focus largely on the codes of professional ethics in their classes, and those who feel that ethical training must go further by examining the fundamentals of the lawyer's rôle in society, have been keenly fought.[32] In many respects these dialogues have mirrored those between black letter,

---

[32] See eg E. Chemerinsky, 'Pedagogy Without Purpose' 1985 *American Bar Foundation Research Journal* 189; T. Schneyer, 'Professional Responsibility Casebooks and the New Positivism: A Reply to Professor Chemerinsky' 1985 *ABFRJ* 943; and E. Chemerinsky, 'Training the Ethical Lawyer: A Rejoinder to Schneyer' 1985 *ABFRJ* 959. Chemerinsky describes the debate as 'a battle for the soul of the legal profession of the future'.

contextualist, and critical legal scholars. Typically, ethics courses in the United States have tended to be rather traditional with a strong emphasis on the rules—an approach which is popular and understood by the students, whose first concern is to learn enough to pass the bar examination in the subject. However, over the years the critiques of the adversarial system and the rôle of the zealous advocate have been mounting,[33] and with it the emergence of ethics courses that look at the conflicting duties of lawyers, examine critically the rôle of the lawyer in society, and point to the deficiencies of the ethical codes as vehicles for resolving the moral dilemmas which arise in legal practice.

If there is no consensus on the approach to be taken, there is little more on appropriate educational formats. Thus there is no single method of instruction that has gained universal approval. If the focus is on the evolution of professional codes or rules of practice in a contextualist framework, then the seminar format is best. Through the use of written materials highlighting competing drafts and the submissions of different factions within the profession,[34] it is possible to show the political and contingent nature of aspects of professional responsibility. The seminar or small group format is also best for ethical debates such as the morality of representing a corporate polluter, defending the guilty or perjuring client, or establishing the limits of confidentiality when confronted with other values, for instance freedom, life, or the avoidance of physical harm.[35]

If the aim is to provide an overview of the central core of the subject and its interconnections as part of vocational training, then the lecture and tutorial approach of the United Kingdom and Canada,[36] or the large class socratic approach of the United States, may be the answer. However, it is probably the case that, amongst teachers of ethics courses which emphasize the legal regulation and professional conduct of lawyers, there is a growing consensus in favour of problem oriented courses with simulation, video and rôle plays, and a rejection of the lecture as preferred format.

As Cotter argues[37] present approaches to instruction in professional responsibility have, with some exceptions, been somewhat conventional and unimaginative. It is quite clear that formal lectures are not the best format for ethical learning. Vocational training is frequently adult education, an environment where active learning is perhaps even more desirable than it is amongst undergraduates. Even in the case of school leavers the view is increasingly

---

[33] See eg W. Simon, 'Ethical discretion in Lawyering' 101 *Harv Law Rev* 1083 (1988), R. Wasserstrom, 'Rôles and Morality' in D. Luban ed, *The Good Lawyer* (Totowa, New Jersey: 1984) and R. Gordon and W. Simon, 'The Redemption of Professionalism' in Nelson *et al* (eds) *op.cit.*

[34] See eg Schneyer, *op.cit.* on the making of the ABA Model Rules.

[35] eg should a lawyer in receipt of confidential information as to a future crime of violence, a kidnapping, or an admission of guilt in relation to a crime for which an innocent party is facing the death penalty, be permitted to disclose that knowledge without fear of professional discipline?

[36] See the Cotter Report *op.cit.* ch.2.   [37] para 3.18 *et seq.*

being taken that learning in a University context should be becoming more interactive in its nature.[38] However, the sheer range of case-books available in the United States in this field[39] is a sharp testimony to the dissension which continues to prevail over the most effective format or ordering to adopt in this field. Even the question whether it is best taught by a full-time member of Faculty or a part-time lecturer from practice is unresolved. A partial solution to both of these questions may come from involving the students themselves in the teaching (and therefore the learning) process. A format in which the students provide some aspects of the formal presentation in class, including the scripting of rôle plays, may provide a form of participatory learning if the pitfalls can be avoided.[40] They, after all, may well be better at communicating with their peers than the lecturer. If the latter can set the parameters for the script, the themes for debates, and the principled basis for exposition, the execution can be left to selected members of the class in each week.[41]

The rôle play script which follows comes from a class in professional responsibility of Strathclyde University in 1993 on the topic of Duties to the Court. It demonstrates some of the strengths and weaknesses of the participatory approach. It shows clearly the advantages of humour and using student authors who are on the same wavelength as the rest of the class. It also draws on in-jokes and visual cues with which the class had become familiar (bar room scenes are popular with student authors). However, it also epitomizes some weaknesses. The script is too clever and, since it involves a play within a play, is difficult to grasp when presented to an unsuspecting audience. It also is weaker at doctrinal exposition and therefore suffers in its educational content. Nor does it engage the rest of the class in ethical debate. Nevertheless, the approach has sufficient promise to justify further exploration of its pedagogical merit, as the search for the optimum format of teaching and learning professional responsibility continues.

---

[38] See the MacFarlane Report on *Teaching and Learning in an Expanding Higher Education System*, 1993, and the Entwhistle review of *The Impact of Teaching on Learning Outcomes in Higher Education* (Sheffield: CVCP, 1992). See also the *Consultation Paper: Review of Legal Education* (LCACLEC, 1994), pp. 24–5 and M. Partington, 'Maintaining Quality in Legal Education' Keynote Address, Second Consultative Conference of the Lord Chancellor's Advisory Committee on Legal Education and Conduct on Legal Education, (Conference Proceedings, 1994) p. 7.

[39] There are probably more case-books in this area than in any other area of substantive law in the United States.

[40] These are many. Student forms of communication are difficult to censure and rapidly become competitive with each succeeding group endeavouring to outdo its predecessor in terms of humour, vulgarity, bad taste, etc. Once established such patterns are hard to break, moreover they lead the participants to concentrate more on the impact of the rôle play than the educational content of the problem in question.

[41] Under this approach each group within the class is responsible for the teaching of the class on at least one occasion. This will involve the lecturer in a pre-class meeting with each group to discuss the format and content of the class.

[FOUR CHARACTERS IN SEARCH OF A RÔLE PLAY]

ANNOUNCER: 20th Century Theatre Productions proudly present 'Four Characters in Search of a rôle Play.'

CRIMINAL: I have been charged with appearing in a criminally bad rôle play exercise.

SOLICITOR: That's interesting because at this very moment I'm appearing in one myself. Tell me more about the background to this charge and how you intend to plead.

CRIMINAL: I'll be pleading not guilty. The background is that I was witnessed entering this lecture room at or around 11 o'clock this morning. As it is well known that there is no point in going to this lecture unless you have to, and that you only have to if you are taking part in the rôle play, suspicions were aroused and the matter was reported to the procurator fiscal who is taking a hard line in these matters.

SOLICITOR: I can see how incriminating these circumstances would be. What exactly is your defence?

CRIMINAL: My defence is that I did not intend to appear in a **bad** rôle play but intended to appear in a good one. I am entirely prepared to admit to having been involved in a rôle play and that it was very bad—it even had a bar room scene in which two solicitors have an informal discussion over a drink—but as there was no intention *videlicet* there was no crime.

SOLICITOR: That sounds to me a sound basis in law. You realize that this is a very serious charge and that if you are found guilty you will probably pass the Diploma in Legal Practice and be sentenced to a very long career as a solicitor in private practice.

CRIMINAL: I'm aware of that. I really do need your help on this one.

SOLICITOR: I'll see what I can do.

ANNOUNCER: The following week.

SOLICITOR: I have been examining the statutory basis on which you are charged. I am sorry to have to tell you that appearing in a criminally bad rôle play is an offence with strict liability. This, the statute says, is for reasons both moral and æsthetic. I wonder what your response is to that.

CRIMINAL: In that case I must say that we will just have to find another line to take. I will commit myself to denying that I was ever at the lecture.

SOLICITOR: But there must have been dozens of potential witnesses.

CRIMINAL: True. But none of them could possibly be described as credible. I mean—just look at them. There's probably none of them awake, never mind paying attention. No, this seems like a sure fire line of defence to me. If the Crown can pull dirty tricks such as founding crimes on strict liability, then the ordinary citizen has to be entitled to defend himself by any means he can.

SOLICITOR: Your outburst throws me into a professional dilemma in which my duty towards my client conflicts with my duty to the court. This will have to be resolved in one way or another before we can properly proceed.

CRIMINAL: [*Putting his jacket on and taking two cans of beer from a plastic bag.*]

Perhaps what you need is the benefit of a bar room scene in which two solicitors have an informal discussion over a drink.

[*The criminal is transformed into the 2nd solicitor*]

2ND SOLICITOR: Did anything interesting happen to you at work today?

SOLICITOR: Funnily enough something interesting did happen today. You'll remember I was telling you about the client of mine accused of appearing in a criminally bad rôle play and who wanted me to collude in preparing a fictional defence. Well, today the client from Case no 26, page 180 of the National Course Materials, came into my office and asked me to do exactly the same thing.

2ND SOLICITOR: I see. These two cases can therefore be considered together and resolved on the same basis.

SOLICITOR: Exactly. What we need now is a scene by which we can set out clearly the issues involved and show what their resolution might be.

2ND SOLICITOR: But let's not do it here. Since this strict liability business came into being you know that if there's one setting in which you can't resolve a rôle play any more it's the one we're in right now

[*Pause. Both solicitors look perplexed and pensive.*]

By the way, you could really do with a hair cut you know?

SOLICITOR: [Jabs the air with his finger on discovering a way forward.]

In that case I'd better go to the hairdressers.

[*One seat is removed and the other is placed centre stage.*]

BARBER: Good morning, sir, what can I do for you?

SOLICITOR: I'd like an imaginary hair cut, please.

BARBER: So what do you do then?

SOLICITOR: I'm a solicitor, specializing in rôle plays at Strathclyde University.

BARBER: You know, I've always wanted to ask a solicitor how can you defend someone whom you know is guilty?

SOLICITOR: Well, that's not a problem. But you know I've always wanted to ask a pretend barber, is a solicitor entitled to withdraw from acting for his client?

BARBER: Have you got an example on your mind?

SOLICITOR: Well, I was acting for a bloke charged under the Criminal Rôle Play Offences (S) Act who originally said he was innocent but now tells me he deliberately and maliciously acted in an appalling rôle play but still wishes me to defend him and tender a plea of not guilty. Can I terminate the relationship?

BARBER: Well sir, the principle is as found on page 164 of the Professional Ethics Materials. You must have good cause and give reasonable notice of intention to terminate.

SOLICITOR: Would you, in your capacity of pretend barber, say that lying constitutes a serious break-down in confidence between solicitor and client?

BARBER: Yes, you do not have to withdraw but you are entitled to. Of course, this only applies when your withdrawal will not prejudice your client's interest, for example in the run-up to a trial, but not during the conduct of it, or indeed when there would not be sufficient opportunity for another agent to adequately prepare your client's defence. And of course you must withdraw where continuing would cause you to breach the rules of conduct.

SOLICITOR: And, am I entitled to charge my client when I have terminated the relationship, and would I have a lien over the precognitions already taken?

BARBER: As a pretend barber, I can tell you. A solicitor always has a right of lien over his client's papers except when the exercise of it would obstruct the course of justice. This applies even when you have received a mandate to deliver a former client's papers to his new solicitor. As to payment, were your client paying privately you would be entitled to payment for work done up to the moment of withdrawal, but you would encounter difficulty from the Legal Aid Board for any work done in a trial you don't complete yourself. How's that for you, sir?

SOLICITOR: That's fine, thanks.

ED: Something for the week-end, sir?

9

Large Law Firms and Professional Responsibility

MARC GALANTER AND THOMAS PALAY

THE DOUBLE IMAGE OF THE LARGE FIRM

THE large business law firm, built around the promotion to partnership tournament, was invented a century ago.[1] It is, in a Darwinian sense, a success story. In spite of intermittent contractions, large firms are flourishing. There are more of them, they are bigger than ever, they command a bigger share of an expanding market for legal services. The large law firm is also a success in a deeper sense, as a social form for organizing the delivery of comprehensive, continuous high-quality legal services. Like the hospital in the practice of medicine, the large firm has become the standard format for delivering complex high-quality services. Many features of its style—specialization, team-work, continuous monitoring on behalf of clients, representation in many forums—have been emulated in other vehicles for delivering legal services. The specialized boutique firm, the public interest firm, the corporate law department—all model themselves on the style of practice developed in the large firm. From its original American embodiment, the large firm device has been adapted by lawyers in Canada,[2] Australia,[3] and Britain[4] and is spreading rapidly in many other countries.[5]

In its American setting, the large law firm has had an ambivalent relationship to legal ethics and professional responsibility. On the one hand the large law firm has been esteemed not only for its technical performance but as a

---

[1] On the emergence and spread of the tournament device that undergirds the large law firm, see M. S. Galanter and T. M. Palay, *Tournament of Lawyers: The Transformation of the Big Law Firm* (University of Chicago Press; Chicago, 1991).

[2] R. J. Daniels, 'Growing Pains: The Why and How of Law Firm Expansion', *University of Toronto Law Journal*, 43 (1993), 147–206.

[3] O. Mendelsohn and M. Lippman, 'The Emergence of the Corporate Law Firm in Australia', *University of New South Wales Law Journal*, 3 (1979), 78098.

[4] R. G. Lee, 'From Profession to Business: The Rise and Rise of the City Law Firm', *Journal of Law and Society*, 19 (1992), 31–48; J. Flood, 'Megalaw in the U.K.: Professionalism or Corporatism? A Preliminary Report', *Indiana Law Journal*, 64 (1989), 569–92.

[5] Y. Dezalay, 'The *Big Bang* and the Law: The Internationalization and Restructuring of the Legal Field', *Theory, Culture & Society*, 7 (1990), 279–93; Y. Dezalay, 'Territorial Battles and Tribal Disputes', *Modern Law Review*, 54 (1991), 792–809. See generally A. Tyrrell and Z. Yaqub, *The Legal Professions in the New Europe* (Blackwell; Oxford, 1993).

setting for the most elevated professionalism. A generation ago, Jerome Carlin studied the New York bar and found that large firm lawyers not only had the largest incomes, served the most affluent clients, and were the best trained and most technically skilled lawyers, but that they experienced

maximum pressure to conform to distinctively professional standards, as well as the more ordinary ethical norms; at the same time they are insulated from pressures to violate [those professional standards].[6]

In technical skill, collegiality, and probity, the large firm seemed to provide a venue for the most exemplary professionalism. In his foreword to Carlin's book,[7] Geoffrey Hazard noted that ironically the traditional badges of the profession—an independent general practice rendering personal service to all sorts of people—were no longer the marks by which the truly 'professional lawyer' was identified.

But there is an other hand. Coupled with this high regard is a long tradition of reproach of the large firm for abandoning the professional calling and becoming a mere business. Before the turn of the century there was already a sense that the profession had compromised its integrity and, by too close embrace of business, its identity. In 1895 the *American Lawyer* complained that:

[T]he typical law office . . . is located in the maelstrom of business life . . . in its appointments and methods of work it resembles a great business concern . . . the most successful and eminent of the bar are the trained advisors of business men . . .
[The bar] has allowed itself to lose, in large measure, the lofty independence, the genuine learning, the fine sense of professional dignity and honor . . .
[F]or the past thirty years it has become increasingly contaminated with the spirit of commerce which looks primarily to the financial value and recompense of every undertaking.[8]

After the turn of the century, John Dos Passos complained:

From 'Attorneys and Counselors at Law' they became agents, solicitors, practical promoters, and commercial operators . . . Entering the offices of some of the law firms in a metropolitan city, one imagines that he is in a commercial counting-room or banking department.[9]

---

[6] J. Carlin, *Lawyer's Ethics—A Study of the New York City Bar* (Russell Sage Foundation; New York, 1966), 168–9.   [7] *Ibid.* at xxiii.
[8] American Lawyer, 'The Commercialization of the Profession', *The American Lawyer*, editorial, (Mar. 1895), 84–5. (This is not the intense monthly that has since 1979 chronicled (and cheered on) rapid change in the world of large law firms, but a long extinct legal newspaper of the same name, published in New York from 1893 to 1908.) 'Bar' is used here not in the English sense, but in the American sense of the entire body of legal professionals.
[9] J. Dos Passos, *The American Lawyer: As He Was—As He Is—As He Can Be* (The Banks Law Publishing Co.; New York, 1907), 46.

It was not only a distinctive ambience that was lost, but the connection with the pursuit of justice:

It may . . . safely be said that the prevailing popular idea of the lawyer, too often justified by facts is, that his profession consists in thwarting the law instead of enforcing it . . . The public no longer calls them 'great' but 'successful' lawyers . . . It is the common belief, inside and outside of the profession, that the most brilliant and learned of the lawyers are employed to defeat or strangle justice.[10]

The frenetic pace and intense specialization of the large firm repelled many established lawyers.[11] But others were more sanguine about the changes. In a 1904 address to the New York State Bar Association, a lawyer observed unapologetically:

The law business is not what it used to be. This expression 'law business' itself marks a certain change. This business side of the profession has assumed paramount importance and the profits of the business are our most practical concern.[12]

By the 1930s, the scale and stability of the large law firms was recognized in the pejorative phrase 'law factory'.[13] Describing the bar in 1933, Karl Llewellyn observed that corporate practice had become 'itself a business . . . [with] a large staff, a highly organized office, a high overhead, intense specialization'. These firms attracted the 'ablest of legal technicians' and fostered a 'lopsided' business perspective that ignored the wider public functions of the bar.[14] Specifically, critics deplored the distributive implications of the development of the large firm. A. A. Berle ascribed to it the abandonment of the notion that the lawyer 'was an officer of the court and therefore an integral part of the scheme of justice' and its replacement by a notion of the lawyer as 'paid servant of his client . . . [T]he complete commercialization of the American bar has stripped it of any social functions it might have performed for individuals without wealth'.[15]

This grim assessment was shared by Chief Justice Harlan Fiske Stone, who described '[t]he successful lawyer of our day . . . [as] the proprietor or general manager of a new type of factory, whose legal product is increasingly the result of mass production methods'.[16] Stone deplored the commercialization and deprofessionalization of the large firm lawyer:

---

[10] *Ibid.* at 130–1.

[11] W. Hobson, *The American Legal Professional and the Organizational Society* 1890–1930, (Garland Publishing; New York, 1986).

[12] E. P. White, 'Changed Conditions in the Practice of Law', *The American Lawyer*, 12(2) (Feb. 1904), 52.

[13] This term is used by Karl Llewellyn in a 1931 book review, *Colombia Law Review*, 31 (1931), 1218. In a 1932 New Yorker profile of Paul Cravath, the author notes that '[t]he blasphemous youngsters just out of law school refer to [the Cravath firm] . . . as 'the factory' and it does have, indeed, the efficiency and production of a first-rate industrial plant.' M. Mackaye, 'Profiles: Public Man', *New Yorker*, 7(46) (1932), 23.

[14] K. Llewellyn, 'The Bar Specializes-With What Results?', *Annals*, 167 (1933), 179.

[15] A. A. Berle, 'Modern Legal Profession', *Encyclopedia of the Social Science*, 5 (1933), 343.

[16] Stone, 'The Public Influence of the Bar', 48 (1934), *Harvard Law Review*, 6.

More and more the amount of his income is the measure of success. More and more he must look for his rewards to the material satisfactions derived from profits as from a successfully conducted business, rather than to the intangible and indubitably more durable satisfactions which are to be found in a professional service more consciously directed toward the advancement of the public interest . . . [I]t has made the learned profession of an earlier day the obsequious servant of business and tainted it with the morals and manners of the marketplace in its most anti-social manifestations.[17]

Thus the large firm was felt to be profoundly at odds with professional traditions of autonomy and public service.

In its stable 'Golden Age' around 1960, inhabitants and observers regarded the large firm world as sadly declined from an earlier day when lawyers were statesmen and served as the conscience of business.[18] Echoing laments that have recurred since the last century, partners complained to sociologist Erwin Smigel that law was turning into a business.[19] No longer, another observer reflected, did young associates regard themselves as servants of the law and holders of a public trust: 'they are too busy fitting themselves for existence in the 1950's, when efficiency, accuracy, and intelligence are the only values to be sought'.[20]

As large firms have grown and multiplied, despondency about the decline of law practice from its virtuous and collegial past has intensified. Within the legal profession itself, many share the sense that law has freshly descended from a noble profession infused with civic virtue to commercialism.[21] In the most erudite and theoretically sophisticated account of decline, the Dean of the Yale Law School counsels idealistic young lawyers to stay clear of large firms, whose 'harshly economizing spirit' and 'increasingly commercial culture' is inimical to the commitment to public service that is the hallmark of professional identity.[22]

---

[17] Stone, 'The Public Influence of the Bar', 48 (1934), *Harvard Law Review*, 6–7.

[18] On the 'Golden Age' see Galanter and Palay, *supra* note 1 at ch.3.

[19] E. Smigel, *The Wall Street Lawyer: Professional Organization Man?* (Indiana University Press; Bloomington, 1969), 303–5.

[20] M. Mayer, 'The Wall Street Lawyers: Part II: Keepers of the Business Conscience', *Harper's Magazine*, 212 (1269) (1956), 56.

[21] The latest entry is S. M. Linowitz with M. Mayer, *The Betrayed Profession: Lawyering at the End of the Twentieth Century* (Charles Scribner's Sons; New York, 1994). The most scholarly is A. T. Kronman, *The Lost Lawyer: Failing Ideals of the Legal Profession* (Harvard University Press; Cambridge, 1993). The most dyspeptic is P. M. Brown, *Rascals: The Selling of the Legal Profession* (Benchmark Press; New York, 1989). The literature is vast. See, eg, A. M. Adams, 'The Legal Profession: A Critical Evaluation', *Dickinson Law Review*, 93 (1989), 652. ('[T]he . . .most pervasive manifestation of the change in the legal climate is the decline of professionalism and its replacement with commercialism.'); N. Bowie, 'The Law: From a Profession to a Business', *Vanderbilt Law Review*, 41 (1988), 741; L. Caplan, 'The Lawyers' Race to the Bottom', *N.Y. Times*, (6 Aug. 1993), A-29. The bar's 'official' account of the danger of commercialization is the ABA Commission on Professionalism, *In the Spirit of Public Service* (1986) (known as the Stanley Report, for Chair Justin Stanley).

[22] Kronman, *supra* note 21, at 378–9.

Distress about lost virtues has been a recurrent companion of élite law practice since the formation of the large firm a hundred years ago.[23] The 'earlier day' when virtue prevailed lies just over the receding horizon of personal experience. Lawyers' sense of decline reflects the gap between practice and professional ideology: in the flesh, working life is experienced as more mundane, routine, business-like, commercial, money driven, client dominated, and conflict laden than it is supposed to be. It is easy to believe that the way it is supposed to be is the way that it used to be.[24]

THE TROUBLE WITH LAWYERS

So we find a curious double image in which large firm lawyers embody the professional ideal of technical proficiency and service to clients, at the same time that the firm is seen as betraying other aspects of professionalism. Complaints within about the loss of collegiality and the abandonment of public-spiritedness are matched by misgivings without about the effects of large firm lawyering. For even as large firms solve the problem of providing quality legal services to large entities, they raise problems of access to justice. By efficiently assembling great concentrations of talent and resources, and placing them at the service of the powerful economic actors (and occasional rich individuals) who can afford their fees, large firms accentuate the disparity in ability to use the legal system.[25]

In a complex, highly technical system that requires individualized service by highly trained and expensive specialists, there is a major problem of providing legal service to the poor and disadvantaged—and to individual persons generally. In Britain the chief means of addressing this disparity is provision of legal aid; in the United States the emphasis is ready access through the contingency fee. But even if individuals obtain competent lawyering to address those predicaments the remedy of which generates a fund of cash, they are unlikely to obtain the co-ordinated strategic use of the legal system that is afforded the corporate clients of large law firms.

In short, one of the persistent and important critiques of the large American law firm is that it does too much for the rich and too little for the poor. This is part of a wider critique that faults the legal profession for abandoning its obligation to promote justice. This 'public justice' critique, most prominent in the 1960s and 1970s, was manifest in Ralph Nader and the

---

[23] Galanter and Palay, *supra* note 1, at 11, 36; R. Gordon, 'The Independence of Lawyers', *Boston University Law Review*, 68 (1988), 43.

[24] Lawyers are not the only legal actors beguiled by a nostalgic reconstruction of the past. See M. S. Galanter, 'The Life and Times of the Big Six: Or, The Federal Courts Since the Good Old Days', *Wisconsin Law Review*, 1988 (1988), 921 (describing the misperception by Supreme Court Justice of change in Federal Court dockets).

[25] M. S. Galanter, 'Why the "Haves" Come Out Ahead . . .', *Law & Society Review*, 9 (1974), 95.

consumer movement, the access to justice movement, the establishment of the federally-funded Legal Services Program, and the development of public interest law. Its high-water marks were a 1978 speech by President Jimmy Carter, reproaching the legal profession for its betrayal of justice in favour of seeking advantage for its paying clients, and the report of the Amercian Bar Association's Kutak commission seeking to revise the rules of professional conduct by accentuating the public duties of lawyers and limiting their license for adversarial combat.[26]

During the 1980s this 'public justice' critique was eclipsed by a very different attack on the legal profession.[27] Lawyers were seen as the promoters and beneficiaries of excessive legalization and runaway litigation. They were depicted as parasites whose predations unravel civil society and undermine the economy. This predator view reached a crescendo in the final years of the Bush administration, with Vice-president Dan Quayle leading the charge with the assertion that America had seventy per cent of the world's lawyers and that they were undermining the country's economic competitiveness. Attacks on predatory lawyers and crazy lawsuits emerged as a major theme in the losing Republican presidential campaign of 1992.[28]

The anti-lawyer campaign resonated with élite groups: business people, doctors, politicians, and media pundits concurred on the unwholesome effects of lawyers. The flavour of this is manifest in a widely repeated story:

A doctor, a lawyer, and an architect were arguing about who had the smartest dog. They decided to settle the issue by getting all the dogs together and seeing whose could perform the most impressive feat.

'Okay, T-Square', ordered the architect, and T-Square trotted over to a table and in four minutes constructed a complete scale model of Chartres Cathedral out of toothpicks. The architect slipped T-Square a cookie, and everyone agreed that it was a pretty impressive performance.

'Hit it, Sawbones,' commanded the doctor. Sawbones lost no time in performing an emergency Cæsarian on a cow. Three minutes later the proud mother of a healthy little heifer was all sewn up and doing fine. Not bad, conceded the onlookers, and Sawbones got a cookie from the doctor.

---

[26] The background and reception of the Carter speech and the Kutak report are recounted in M. S. Galanter, 'Predators and Parasites: Lawyer Bashing and Civil Justice', *Georgia Law Review*, 28 (1994), 638–43. The Kutak proposals aroused fierce opposition from various sectors of the bar and were vitiated at a series of ABA meetings in 1982 and 1983.

[27] The 'public justice' critique retains some vitality. Indeed one of the public's chief complaints is that lawyers have abandoned the pursuit of justice. Hart Survey, *infra* note 33, at Table 10.

[28] M. S. Galanter, 'News from Nowhere: The Debased Debate on Civil Justice', *Denver University Law Review*, 71 (1993), 77–113.

'Your turn, Loophole' said the lawyer. Over went Loophole, smashed the cathedral, mangled the calf, screwed the other two dogs, took their cookies, and went out to lunch.[29]

Mirroring their masters, the other dogs are constructive, creative, helping; the lawyer's dog is destructive and predatory—it not only contributes nothing, but destroys the contributions of the others, appropriates their deserved rewards, and violates them 'personally'. This captures some of the intense resentment of lawyers by élite groups. The media reflected (and fostered) wide-spread popular disdain for lawyers. One symptom of this is a tidal wave of jokes about lawyers, exemplified by the story recounted above, riddles like 'What do you call 60,000 lawyers at the bottom of the sea?' (Answer: a good start!), and a book of cartoons entitled *Dead Lawyers and Other Pleasant Thoughts.*[30]

Anti-lawyer humour itself became a political issue in the Spring of 1993 when the president of the California Bar Association blamed lawyer bashing for encouraging attacks on lawyers like the mass murder in a San Francisco law office by a disgruntled client.[31] Although few rallied to his proposal to treat attacks as 'hate speech', the profession is desperately concerned to mend its reputation.[32] Two recent public opinion surveys portray the contours of public disapproval.[33] The National Law Journal poll documents a decline in public regard for lawyers since 1986, while at the same time the portion of the population using lawyers' services increased sharply. People are generally satisfied with their own lawyers. Indeed, although many respondents said they were charged too high a fee, most said they were more satisfied than dissatisfied with their lawyer's performance.[34]

But when viewed in the aggregate, lawyers are held in low regard. Almost three-quarters of the population thinks that the United States has too many lawyers.[35] Only forty per cent of the public hold a favourable attitude toward lawyers—less than half the percentage that think well of teachers or pharmacists. Only stockbrokers and politicians are rated lower.[36] The respondents

---

[29] This story can be found in many collections of lawyer jokes. This version is adapted from B. Knott, *Truly Tasteless Lawyer Jokes* (St Martin's Paperbacks; New York, 1990), 4–5. To 'eat [someone's] cookies' is to vanquish that person. J. E. Lighter, *Random House Dictionary of American Slang*, (Vol 1; Random House; New York, 1994), 695.

[30] Wiley, *Dead Lawyers and Other Pleasant Thoughts* (Random House; New York, 1993).

[31] J. Hiscock, 'Lawyer Dying for a Laugh', *Daily Telegraph*, (7 July 1993), 12.

[32] D. O'Briant, 'Open Season on Lawyers', *Atlanta Journal and Constitution*, (9 July 1993), ('The American Bar Association recently decided to allocate a half-million dollars for a public relations blitz to polish the tarnished image of lawyers.').

[33] The ABA commissioned a comprehensive survey of public attitudes towards the standing of attorneys. Results were published in G. A. Hengster, '*Vox Populi*: The Public Perception of Lawyers: ABA Poll', *American Bar Association Journal*, (Sept. 1993), 60. The survey, conducted by telephone with 1,202 adult participants, was carried on by Peter D. Hart Research Associates, Inc., Jan. 1993 (Hereafter Hart Survey). The National Law Journal poll surveyed 815 people in mid-July. Results were published in R. Samborn, 'Anti-Lawyer Attitude Up', *National Law Journal*, (9 Aug. 1993), 1.   [34] Samborn, *supra* note 33, at 20.   [35] *Ibid.* at 1.

[36] Hart Survey, *supra* note 33, at Table 1.

thought lawyers were smart and good problem solvers, but greedy, successful money-makers, lacking in both honesty and compassion.[37] But in view of the historic affinity of lawyers with the powerful and wealthy, this profile of public attributes is quite surprising. For it is the top people who are most negative about lawyers: those with higher incomes, and more education, and more direct experience with the legal system.

Americans who are more critical than average tend to be more establishment, upscale, and male. The higher the family income and socioeconomic status, the more critical the adults are.

Pluralities of college graduates feel unfavorably toward lawyers, while pluralities of non-college graduates feel favorably.

By and large those who see lawyers in a more favourable light than average tend to be downscale, women, minorities and the young.[38]

Quite a reversal from an earlier day when lawyers were seen as part of the establishment and supporters of the status quo!

PROFESSIONAL RESPONSIBILITY AND THE *PRO BONO* OBLIGATION

It is in this context that we turn to the most recent developments in professional responsibility and their relation to large law firms. Large firms rarely engage in the characteristic sins of the smaller practices—the abuse of clients by peculation, neglect, or incompetence. Although there is some client grumbling about excessive staffing and high fees, the typical misdeeds of large firms are not lack of zeal, disloyalty, or under-performance. Instead, subservience to the valued client may tempt them to 'over-perform', leading to a compromise of obligations to other parties and to the larger legal system.[39] In the aftermath of the collapse of many savings and loan associations, regulators have pursued large law firms for being uncritically co-operative with the schemes of their financial clients. From 1989 to 1993, regulators brought over ninety cases against law firms.[40] In a 1992 proceeding that shook the upper reaches of the profession, Kaye Scholer, a Wall Street firm, paid a forty-one million dollar settlement rather than face seizure of its assets that would have threatened its

---

[37] Hart Survey, *supra* note 33, at Table 7.

[38] *Ibid.* at 4–5. (The order of the sentences in the above quotation have been changed from the original format.)

[39] D. Wilkins, 'Who Should Regulate Lawyers?', *Harvard Law Review*, 105 (1991), 819–20 usefully explicates the distinction between 'agency' problems, (eg, inattention, negligence, defalcation) and 'externality' problems (ie, lawyers and clients acting together to harm others— frivolous pleadings, misrepresentations of clients' financial positions, and other misdeeds that harm others or the legal system rather than the client).

[40] H. Weinstein, 'Attorney Liability in the Savings and Loan Crisis', *University of Illinois Law Review*, 1993 (1993), 53.

very existence. The following year Jones Day Reavis & Pogue, the second largest United States firm, paid a record fifty-one million dollars to settle government claims that it helped conceal fraud by convicted financier Charles Keating.[41] In each of the above instances, the case was resolved by a consent decree that set out stiff new rules for the respective firm's banking practice. Large law firms are on notice that major difficulties may ensue if they are insufficiently critical and detached from their corporate clients.

The assault here comes from government regulators who can move aggressively in the prevailing atmosphere of scorn for lawyers. At the same time there is pressure from **within** the profession to address the problems of access and disparity by embracing the notion of mandatory *pro bono* service. In February 1993 the American Bar Association's House of Delegates modified its model ethical rule commending *pro bono*, to provide that every lawyer 'should aspire' to devote fifty hours a year to *pro bono publico* service, of which a 'substantial majority' should go to the poor and to organizations that help the poor.[42] Since the enforceable ethical rules are enacted by the courts and bar in each state, this provision is not enforcable as such, but it provides a powerful push for bar groups to consider how to implement *pro bono* requirements. Four state bars had enacted such 'hours' obligations before the ABA pronouncement and a fifth enacted one by mid-1994. Like the ABA rule, all provided 'should' rather than 'shall': they were ethical obligations but not enforceable through the disciplinary process. A few local bars, in which membership is voluntary, have imposed *pro bono* requirements as a condition of membership.[43]

The idea of mandatory *pro bono*, which has been around for the last twenty years or so, appeals to those who share the public justice critique of the profession. Joining these supporters are many who are alarmed by external attacks on the legal profession. Mandatory *pro bono* commends itself for its equalizing thrust and its display of professional *noblesse*.

The supporters of mandatory *pro bono publico* service seem to be reading public opinion accurately. Almost three-quarters of the respondents to the aforementioned 1993 National Law Journal poll thought lawyers should be required to spend some of their time on community service—a sharp increase since the 1986 poll.[44] Other survey data suggests that this is a passive low intensity preference: when asked to volunteer a change that would improve the legal system only five per cent proposed equalizing access to justice or

[41] S. Terry, 'Paying the Price and Bearing the Burden', *Washington Post*, (26 Apr. 1993), F7.

[42] American Bar Association, ABA Model Rules, Rule 6.1. The rejection of earlier attempts to mandate a specific amount of *pro bono* service is detailed in E. F. Lardent, 'Mandatory *Pro Bono* in Civil Cases: The Wrong Answer to the Right Question', *Maryland Law Review*, 49 (1990), 92–9.

[43] Telephone interview with B. V. Groudine, Assistant Committee Counsel, American Bar Association Standing Committee on Lawyers' Public Service Responsibility, (26 Aug. 1994).

[44] Samborn, *supra* note 33, at 22. 73% of the respondents favoured a mandatory requirement, up from 55% in the 1986 poll.

expanding *pro bono* services.[45] Still, hearing about lawyers providing free legal service to the needy ranked highest among items improving respondents' opinion of the profession.[46]

Of course this notion of an obligation to devote a portion of one's time to public service applies to **all** lawyers, not just to lawyers in large firms. But there is a substantial connection between large firms and support for *pro bono*. Large firms have had the most visible *pro bono* programmes—and large firm lawyers have been the most enthusiastic and outspoken supporters of the concept.[47] The amount of *pro bono* activity by law firms is uneven among firms of all sizes, but media accounts suggest that generally there is more *pro bono* among the largest firms and the amount is increasing.

To test this impression, we matched the *American Lawyer's* annual surveys of *pro bono* activity (available since 1990) with the *American Lawyer* reports on firm size, revenues, and estimated profits and with our own data set on firm growth rates.[48] In general we found that *pro bono* activity was positively related to the size and economic performance of the firm. We used four measures of *pro bono* activity (total hours of *pro bono* activity for the firm, the number of lawyers providing twenty or more hours of *pro bono* service during the year, hours per lawyer engaged in *pro bono* work, and the percentage of lawyers at the firm who reported twenty or more hours of *pro bono* activity). *Pro bono* activity, as measured by each of these four measures, increased between 1990 and 1993. In the fifty-nine firms for which complete data were available for both 1990 and 1993, total hours of *pro bono* work increased forty-five per cent. This resulted from more lawyers contributing more hours each: the number of attorneys reporting twenty or more hours of *pro bono* activity increased by over sixty per cent while the average hours per attorney increased by almost one-third. The percentage of attorneys at these firms who contributed twenty or more hours increased by thirty-four per cent (but still totalled less than forty per cent of lawyers at these firms). Overall, *pro bono* activity grew faster than the size, revenue, or profits of these firms. In general the level of *pro bono* activity was positively related to firm performance.

Thus the data suggest that the larger the firm and the greater its gross

---

[45] Hart Survey, *supra* note 33, at 28.

[46] In the ABA survey 43% said such information improved their opinion of lawyers 'a lot' and another 27% reported 'some' improvement. At the other end of the scale, only 17% and 39% reported similar effects from learning that '[l]awyers help defend the average person from unjust actions by big business or the IRS [Internal Revenue Service].' *Ibid.* at 31.

[47] One of the most trenchant critics of mandatory *pro bono*, noting that its strongest support comes from the upper strata of the legal profession, argues that large firms will be the real beneficiaries of such programmes. J. R. Macy, 'Mandatory *Pro Bono*: Comfort for the Poor or Welfare for the Rich', *Cornell Law Review*, 77 (1992), 1119–21.

[48] The detailed results are presented in M. S. Galanter and T. M. Palay, 'The Public Service Implications of Firm Size and Structure', in Robert Katzmann, ed, *The Law Firm and the Public Good* (Brookings Institution Governance Institute; Washington, 1995).

revenues the more willing it is to encourage or permit *pro bono* activity. Why should this be? Some would argue that large firms, or at least some of them, have been the site of a long tradition of public service, even though that tradition is presently in some disarray. Conceding that 'public service' is a category far broader than '*pro bono*' as currently understood, it is evident that *pro bono* work by large firms has been neither typical nor continuous.

The present *pro bono* surge is not the large firms' first encounter with expectations of organized *pro bono* work. In the late 1960s there was a great contraction in the supply of talented associates. The Vietnam War draft diverted law graduates to other occupations in which they could obtain deferments. Simultaneously, when 1960s activism induced disdain for corporate practice among students seeking work in poverty law and public interest law, the percentage of élite law graduates entering private practice fell precipitously.[49] Confronted by criticism that their work was unfulfilling and inimical to the public interest, many firms acceded to demands that recruits be able to spend time on '*pro bono publico*' activities.[50] In 1970 the *Wall Street Journal* reported that 'now it's common for [the big corporate law firms] to permit their attorneys to spend substantial portions of their time in noncommercial work'.[51] But just a few years later, this commitment had largely dissipated,[52] only to be rekindled in the 1980s, when 'voluntary *pro bono* programs enjoyed an unparalleled level of support, funding and growth'.[53]

We submit that there are structural reasons why large firms find regular organized *pro bono* service more congenial than do their smaller counterparts. On the whole, large firms with hundreds of lawyers can adapt readily to the *pro bono* obligation by appointing partners (or retaining outside specialists) to manage it, and assigning staff to deal with the logistical problems of finding and screening suitable cases. A large volume of *pro bono* work projects a favourable image of public service at the same time that it provides both an asset for recruitment of young lawyers and regular opportunities for development of professional skills such as trial advocacy. Smaller firms, unable to enjoy similar economies of scale in organizing their *pro bono* work, find it considerably more disruptive and burdensome.

The large firm setting is home to the most intense efforts to institutionalize *pro bono* obligations. In May 1993 the American Bar Association launched its 'Law Firm *Pro Bono* Challenge' calling on the five hundred largest law firms in the country—that is, roughly all firms with more than

[49] Galanter and Palay, *supra* note 1, at 56, n.122.

[50] J. Berman and E. Cahn, 'Bargaining for Justice: The Law Student's Challenge to Law Firms', *Harvard Civil Rights-Civil Liberties Law Review*, 5 (1970), 16–31.

[51] C. Falk, 'Many Lawyers Take Up Political, Social Causes on their Firms' Time', *Wall Street Journal*, (20 May 1970), 1.

[52] S. Tisher, L. Bernabei, and M. Green, 'The Sad State of *Pro Bono* Activity', *Trial*, 13(10) (1977), 43–6. [53] Lardent, *supra* note 42, at 90.

seventy lawyers—to contribute an amount of time equal to three to five per cent of the firm's total billable hours each year. This effort was resoundingly endorsed by Attorney General Janet Reno. By late May some 155 law firms had signed on.[54] Some of the largest firms declined to participate on the ground that the programme's definition of *pro bono* work was too restrictive and objected to the requirement that a law firm commit a percentage of its total hours rather than a fixed number.[55] Unlike the American Bar Association Model Rules, which declares the obligation of individual attorneys, the Challenge includes an undertaking to modify firm arrangements by eliminating barriers to *pro bono* work and nurturing 'a firm culture in which *pro bono* service is a routine and valued part of each individual's professional life'.[56] A year after the Challenge was issued, the total number of signatory firms was 164, only slightly higher than the initial sign up.[57] Subsequently, news about the programme has been sparse.

If *pro bono* were to become mandatory for all lawyers, it would very likely include arrangements for making *pro bono* obligations transferable. That is, there would be a market in which lawyers could arrange to pay others to discharge their obligation, or be paid to do *pro bono* work for others.[58] Existing legal services offices would be strengthened and a whole new category of *pro bono* providers might appear. But it seems likely that most large firms would operate their own *pro bono* programmes, with long term effects that no one can predict.[59]

So, to summarize, we have a curious situation in which lawyers are under attack by élites, but are seen as flawed yet useful champions by the poor and less advantaged. Major regulatory initiatives promise to make large firms hold themselves more independent of their major business clients—at the very time that these clients are trying to reduce their dependence on outside law firms and gain more control over costs. And, finally, the large law firms, embracing *pro bono* representation of the poor, are the leading edge of the profession's initiative in redefining itself as a vehicle of public justice.

We do not argue that such service is a necessary and inevitable feature of the large business law firm—a claim which its history surely falsifies. But neither is it incompatible—at least from the point of view of the lawyers in those firms. It remains to be seen how their clients will react and how they will respond to client pressures.

[54] W. J. Dean, 'The ABA's Challenge to Law Firms', *New York Law Journal*, (24 May 1993), 3.
[55] D. Knox, 'Was *Pro Bono* Challenge Too Challenging?', *American Lawyer*, (June 1993), 26.
[56] Dean, *supra* note 54.
[57] W. J. Dean, 'Highlights of the 1994 Conference', *New York Law Journal*, (6 May 1994), 3.
[58] D.Luban, *Lawyers and Justice: An Ethical Study* (Princeton University Press; Princeton, 1988) 277–89; M. S. Galanter and T. M. Palay, 'Let Firms Buy and Sell Credit for *Pro Bono*', *National Law Journal*, (6 Sept. 1993), 17–18; M. Coombs, 'Your Money of Your Life: A Modest Proposal for Mandatory *Pro Bono* Services', *Boston University Public Interest Law Journal*, 3 (1993), 215–38; Linowitz, *supra* note 21, at 161–2.   [59] Katzmann, *supra* note 48.

PRO BONO ABROAD?

As the American style large firm spreads around the globe, it is an open question whether the *pro bono* gene will manifest itself elsewhere. Our interviews of lawyers in large London solicitors firms from 1990 until 1994 elicited little sense of distress about the increasingly commercial character of law practice. Interviewees unselfconsciously spoke of 'the law business'. For the most part they were quite sanguine about recent changes and free of expressions of nostalgia about lost professional virtue. There was no sense that the profession was under attack. And there was hardly a glimmer of interest in expansive *pro bono* activity, although inquiry revealed that several of the firms we visited had substantial *pro bono* programmes. Such interest, where it exists, remains low key, valued more as a recruiting device than a bulwark protecting professional identity from attack. Perhaps we failed to ask the right questions, but we detected no counterpart in the London large firm world to the American sense that large firms might have a special obligation to remedy serious deficiencies in access to justice. In May 1994, a Law Society working party firmly rejected any mandatory contribution of legal services or compulsory financial support.[60]

Perhaps this should not surprise us, for legal aid for the poor was firmly institutionalized in Britain as a state responsibility prior to the emergence of large firms. And lawyers there have not been subjected to withering attack by élite groups and broader public opinion. But these contrasts, in turn, are located in a world in which many forces are driving the legal systems of the industrialized nations in a common direction.[61] The development in England of the large law firm is in itself a striking instance of such convergence. So before we take the present divergence on *pro bono* as permanent, it is useful to recall that in their 'Golden Age' in the 1950s and early 1960s no one would have predicted that the thrust for strong *pro bono* commitment in the United States would come from the large firms.

Of course we don't know how the present spurt of interest in incorporating *pro bono* into the large firm will play out. Lawyers are adaptive and the large law firm has proved a resilient form. Is it resilient enough? The question is nicely put in one of the few lawyer jokes that depicts the world of the large firm:

A senior partner at a major New York law firm . . . was asked by the Manhattan Chamber of Commerce to address its membership.

---

[60] Law Society, *Solicitors Serving Society: A Report of the Pro Bono Working Party* (The Law Society; London, 1994).

[61] M. S. Galanter, 'Law Abounding: Legalisation Around the North Atlantic', *Modern Law Review*, 55 (1992), 1–24.

Accepting months in advance, he forgets about the engagement until, cleaning off his desk late one Friday evening, he notices the date scheduled in his calendar for the following Monday. With a big week-end at the beach house on tap, there's no time to write a speech.

Instead, he calls in a bright young associate.

PARTNER: Smith, I have to address the Chamber on Monday night and because of a client commitment all week-end, I can't do it myself. You'll have to write it for me. Have it on my desk by noon Monday.

ASSOCIATE: But sir, my girlfriend and I have reservations at -

PARTNER: On my desk at noon. No ifs, ands, or buts.

Comes Monday at 12, the speech is delivered, freshly typed and bound in a neat plastic folder. The partner, on his way to a client meeting that will last until the evening, stuffs the speech in his brief-case without reading it. Later that night, standing before the audience of 500 business executives (many clients and potential clients), he delivers the speech, which turns out to be a literary pearl filled with humorous anecdotes, wonderful insights, and bright observations on the law, business, and modern society. Near the end, it reaches a crescendo that has the audience on the edge of its seats.

'Before I leave you tonight,' the partner reads, 'I want to share with you my ultimate vision for using the law not only to resolve disputes, but to create a new chapter in the history of mankind. A chapter of unparalleled peace and prosperity world-wide. To accomplish this, I will suggest that—he turns the page, curious himself to read this remarkable plan, only to find, in capital letters, IMPROVISE, YOU SON OF A BITCH.[62]

---

[62] M. Stevens, *Power of Attorney: The Rise of the Giant Law Firms* (McGraw Hill; New York, 1987), 179–80.

10

Doctoring Legal Ethics: Studies in Irony

DEREK MORGAN

'A Watergate Mini Quiz: Which of the following Watergate thugs were lawyers?
a Richard Nixon
b. John Mitchell
c. Spiro Agnew
d. G. Gordon Liddy
e. John Dean
f. Charles Colson
g. Robert Mardian
h. Herbert Kalmbachi
i. John Erlichman
j. Donald Segretti
Answer: a, b, c, d, e, f, g, h, i, j' [1]

THE AGE OF SCEPTICISM

That lawyers have long excited conflicting emotions may be gauged by comparing the opinion of Cicero with that of Shakespeare, two commentators from different eras and cultures chosen at random. For Shakespeare the starting point for the good life was obvious. "Lawyers, my part in their downfall" was encapsulated in Dick the Butcher's wisdom; 'The first thing we do, let's kill all the lawyers.'[2] Cicero was of a more sanguine temperament; he portrayed the attorney as a servant of the public whose house is 'without doubt the oracular seat of the whole community.'[3]

Such caricatures and sentiments are remarkable of most professions. What I think emerges as interesting from the Watergate narrative, apparently told at the expense of the whole American legal profession which Brallier captures, is something of a different order.

First, and I suspect most important, is that for lawyers and other members

[1] Jess M. Brallier, *Lawyers and Other Reptiles*, (Chicago, Contemporary Books, 1992) at 74
[2] Shakespeare, *King Henry the Sixth–Part Two*, Act 4 Scene II, l7 3
[3] Cicero, *De Oratore*, I.45, in *The Correspondence of M. Tillius Cicero*, (Dublin, Hodges Figges, 1915, ed. Robert Yelverton Tyrell and Louis Claude Purser)

of present societies under a certain age, the nature and force of the point which it seeks to make will be less significant than for other, older citizens who lived through the unfolding drama and debacle of Watergate. It will mean something different to lawyers and citizens of the Euro-American culture[4] than it will mean to lawyers and citizens from Central and Eastern European, Asian, Indian and Pacific Rim or other states. These peoples do not share the same cultural assumptions, let alone the same cultural history against which the Watergate break-in is framed and famed.

Thirdly, unless read against a certain background, a certain cultural understanding, (of the nature of the American presidency and standards to be applied and accepted in public life generally in the 1950s, 1960s and 1970s—to speak only of the middle twentieth century), the saga of Watergate, involving so many lawyers, would have less significance for a more modern audience. The Presidency in the United States has been subject to a number of Special Prosecutors since the time of Watergate. American Presidencies, prior to the 1970s, particularly that of John F. Kennedy, have been subject to a vast re-colouring, the common and popular phrase might be deconstruction and reconstruction, in the past 15 years.

I want to suggest what might be called the Age of Scepticism, an age in which enquiry into formerly sanctified and sanitised public institutions and aspects of public life is now no longer unthinkable in the way in which it was previously, has led to a different, perhaps a new and more urgent puzzlement about the nature and meaning of ethics in many aspects of public and private life. This is crudely illustrated by the existence in the United Kingdom of a now semi-standing body, under the Chairmanship of Lord Nolan, to investigate and make recommendations on standards of conduct in public life, and what political commentator Andrew Marr has identified as a waning appetite for political debate which is becoming 'tinged by distaste.'[5] It bears witness to the force of the argument created and popularised by a generation of feminist writers that the personal is political and the political is personal. General concern with ethics has, it seems, become a defining stigmata of the closing decades of the century.[6]

---

[4] I use this term in the way that I have learnt it from anthropologist Marilyn Strathern, *New Certainties for Old? The Case of Enabling Technology*, (Lancaster, Centre for the Study of Cultural Values, University of Lancaster), 1994, at 6 (and see her important *After Nature: English Kinship in the Late Twentieth Century*, (Cambridge, CUP, 1992), where 'the awkwardness of the hybrid term conveys its application as both wider and narrower than anything one might wish to attribute to the citizens of Northern Europe and North America.'

[5] Andrew Marr, *Ruling Britannia*, (London, Michael Joseph, 1995) at 34

[6] I use ethics here initially in the classical sense understood within moral philosophy, as the theory of the good life involving the study of value, both the empirical question of what people value but also the normative question of what it is right or appropriate to value. Whether particular professional ethics give rise to obligations imposed upon members of that professional above and beyond general (ordinary) morality is a difficult, and much argued point which, in this essay, I do not address.

Even more obvious than the uncertainties of world economics and world politics was the social and moral crisis, reflecting the post-1950 upheavals in human life, which also found widespread if confused expression in these Crisis Decades. It was the crisis of the beliefs and assumptions on which modern society had been founded since the Moderns won their famous battle against the Ancients in the early eighteenth century—of the rationalist and humanist assumptions, shared by liberal capitalism and communism . . .[7]

FASHIONABLE AREAS OF INTELLECTUAL INQUIRY

In this essay, in which I am charged to consider whether the study of legal ethics has anything to learn from other sites of professional ethics, particularly medical ethics, I want to offer some reflections on what Hobsbawm identifies as 'the crisis of beliefs and assumptions.' I will suggest that while the balance of symmetries and asymmetries in the provision of medical and legal services make me *cautious* (no more, certainly not yet sceptical) about suggesting that, at the level of *specific situational* concerns, much can be read from one branch of the applied ethics discipline to another, I will suggest that there are sufficient symmetries to make the nature and form of ethical argument in health care available as template from which to begin to forge a distinctive account of legal ethics. In particular, I will suggest that a study of medical ethics has the possibility to contribute to the emergent study of legal ethics in three particular ways. First, in illuminating what the nature of ethical controversy consists in; secondly, how it may emerge as a dynamic and not a static mode of analysis, and thirdly, how debates within philosophy and ethics are transforming the nature of the arguments, the possibility of the subject and the construction of the basis of ethics itself. In particular, I want to reflect on some of the macro-ethical considerations affecting medical ethics (Cranston identifies such concerns as being as much political as ethical[8]) which in my view may be of value in consideration of legal ethics.

In parallel with the changes suggested by Galanter[9] as characteristic of North Atlantic legal life and the place of law in society there has been, through the globalisation of life, a re-introduction of a concern with the plurality of legal, ethical, social and moral systems which occupy the peoples of the world. Indeed, one of the most significant changes to arrive in the office of the modern lawyer in the past decade is the transnationalisation of legal services (the other, I believe, is the strong and unrelenting forces of competition and the

---

[7] Eric Hobsbawm, *Age of Extremes: The Short History of the Twentieth Century 1914-1991*, (London, Michael Joseph, 1994) at 11

[8] Ross Cranston, , 'Legal Ethics and Professional Responsibility above, p. 6.

[9] Marc Galanter, 'Law Abounding: Legalisation Around the North Atlantic' (1992) 55 *Modern Law Review* 1-24. I draw extensively upon this essay below.

consumerism which accompanies it[10]). Yet, unlike medicine, where there are
some agreed core elements to ethical codes which are almost universal, this
plurality of law knows relatively little of agreed international codes of ethics.
Medicine has become familiar with such developments, beginning in the
modern age with the judgment of the Nuremberg Military Tribunals, whose
ten principles according to which medical research should be carried out
following prosecution of Nazi officers for War Crimes committed during the
second world war form the basis first of what became known as the Nuremberg
Code.[11] This has been followed by other documents of ethical aspiration of
which the World Medical Association's Declaration of Helsinki 1964[12], the
Declaration of Geneva,[13] and the Declaration of Tokyo,[14] are the best known
examples. For law, concerns with ethics have been thrown up in part by this
internationalisation of business and practice which has brought its practitioners
into working and social contact with lawyers and business people from
different and diverse cultural and ethical backgrounds with different expectations about etiquette and ethics in doing business together.[15] This has produced
more debate of where the end points are; it has perhaps fostered the search for
some ethical core. As John Flood has percipiently suggested

The recurring theme in the literature of globalization and change . . . is that change is
dependent on correctly interpreting and adapting to diverse cultures. In using this term I
refer to the cultures of nations and periods and the specific cultures of social and
economic groups. As might be expected, a term like 'culture' is a highly contested
one. The push of globalization has been checked by the mediation of culture, which is
forcing mutations in organizational forms and modes of doing business that, for the
most part, professions were unprepared for.[16]

The hegemony of Western modes of thought, which have much dominated
Western political, social and moral philosophy for the last two hundred years
or so, have been as Hobsbawm intimates, under an assail of the kind which is a

[10] The essays collected in Yves Dezalay and David Sugarman, *Professional Competition and
Professional Power: Lawyers, Accountants and the Social Construction of Markets*, (London,
Routledge, 1995) provide an excellent point of reflection on this question.
[11] For an accessible source for the judgments see Ian Kennedy and Andrew Grubb, *Medical
Law: Text with Materials*, (London, Butterworths, 2ed., 1994) at 1011–24
[12] Recommendations guiding medical doctors in biomedical research involving human subjects,
(as amended 1975), extracted in Kennedy and Grubb, *op. cit.*, at 1024–26
[13] As amended at Sydney, 1968, Solemn Pledge on admission to the Medical Profession, set out
in J. K. Mason and R. A. McCall Smith, *Law and Medical Ethics*, (London, Butterworths, 4 ed.,
1994), Appendix B
[14] Statement on the Torture and other Cruel, Inhuman or Degrading Treatment or Punishment,
set out in Mason and McCall Smith, *op. cit.*, Appendix D
[15] I regard this as a slightly different example, perhaps a variant on what Marc Galanter has
called 'More Modalities, More Voices.' See his Chorley Lecture at the London School of
Economics, published as 'Law Abounding: Legalisation Around the North Atlantic' (1992) 55
Modern Law Review 1 at 11.
[16] John Flood, 'The Cultures of Globalization: Professional Restructuring for the International
market' in Yves Dezalay and David Sugarman, *op. cit.*, 139 at 140

new phenomenon. This produces tensions as much as it produces questions apparently demanding new or certainly radically different answers or approaches of a kind which the West has not really seen since the times of the Crusades in the twelfth century.

Let me make it clear at the outset, again, that I am *not* concerned with canvassing select topics in which ethical concerns appear to have some commonality between the study of medicine and the study of law. Obvious candidates for such a project would have been confidentiality, conflicts of interest and the respective responsibility of the professional to the individual and to the wider public good or interest. One example of my meaning here, of the kind of analysis which I could have offered but have not done, will suffice. Take the question, 'should a doctor ever lie?' (and substitute for it, for that is what this form of comparative ethics suggests, 'should a lawyer ever lie?')

Now this question is, of course, one of a quite different order, one which I venture will be readily identified by lawyers, from the question, 'should a doctor always be candid?' There is, from many points of view, not only the ethical, a vast difference in the two following responses to the question; 'did my father die peacefully last night?' One answer, the truthful one, is yes he did; he died peacefully at 4 am. Another, a candid one, replies, yes he died peacefully at 4 am; of course he was by then quite heavily sedated following several hours of delirium, and had been given pain control measures to ease the consequences of his fall from bed at 12.30, where he lay in his own despoilment for over two hours until a nurse discovered him at 3 am.

There are some who hold that any form of lying, or deception, is always a wickedness, and can never be condoned. There are few who would be so absolute, and many, I think, who would readily appreciate the distinction between the two answers given above or who, after reflection, would condone the answer given truthfully in the first case. Of course, to say that this is all highly context dependent begs another series of questions. To describe the doctor in the above example as 'economical with the truth' is to commend her in some way for the discretion which she showed in the discharge of her answers to the inquirer. In other contexts, such economy would be rightly condemned, when, for example, what is being made clear by the questioner is a demand not only for the truth, but indeed the whole painful truth. Part of the judgment of the ethical approach to the answer will reside in whether the whole truth is, so to speak, volunteered, or extracted piece by piece from a reluctant interlocutee.

There is of course, an irony, noted by Jenny Levin, that in the past two decades or so academic lawyers have eagerly entered the fray in thinking and writing about medical ethics but have failed to show the same alacrity towards the legal profession.[17] Thus, there are few comprehensive considerations of

---

[17] 'An Ethical Profession?' (Swansea, University of Wales Swansea) Inaugural Lecture at the University of Wales Swansea, 24 October 1994, at 13. There is an interesting point here which concerns whether *academic* lawyers are of the same *profession* as those who practice law, which I cannot pursue here.

ethical rules in the context of legal practice in the United Kingdom, if we
conceive of the study of legal ethics as constituted by analysis of comprehensive texts and finely honed codes of ethical conduct promulgated by the legal
profession, supplemented by an 'extensive body of case law, literature, of
scholarship, analysis and commentary on these ethical rules, similar to that
which exists in relation to other legal rules and doctrines.'[18] Even in this sense,
Codes of Ethics are, as Levin has observed, a very recent phenomenon in the
UK, as in other western European countries.[19] On examination, she has
suggested that the Code of Conduct of the Bar,[20] and of the Law Society[21]
for example, deal only with the traditional concerns of the profession—'the
regulation of entry, with other restrictive practices designed to eliminate
competition and preserve or enhance status. Much of this is dealt with in
considerable detail—for example the solicitors rules on advertising, the
obtaining of practising certificates, preventing fee sharing; barristers rules
relating to wigs, eating dinners, not eating dinners in the company of solicitors, and so on.'[22] But, as Ross Cranston has here recalled in his editorial
essay, concerns with ethics in the legal profession can go much wider than this.
And it does not follow from the fact that one can describe an activity as self-
interested that it is no more than an economic ideology.[23] There is, of course,
another irony to observe; that legal ethics has to a large extent proceeded
without asking whether and if so what it has to learn from moral philosophy as
applied in medicine and health care, or other specific professional locations.

Medical Ethics, Environmental Ethics, Business Ethics, Engineering
Ethics, Research Ethics; all have become fashionable areas of intellectual
enquiry and professional concern in a way which would perhaps have been
if not unthinkable then at least highly unusual a generation ago. One of the
interesting features which I want to reflect upon in this essay is the *apparently*
late arrival of Legal Ethics as a proper subject of concern at the moral
quadrille. This, of course, raises the need to be clear about what we understand ethics to mean (in the sense of medical ethics or legal ethics), at what
levels we are suggesting their impact, and what force or authority we are
implying to the ethics so identified. At once it will become clear that we are
dealing with essentially contested notions in each stage. It will be necessary,
then, briefly to survey the field of contemporary ethics and the levels at which

---

[18] Levin, *op. cit.*, at 8. This form of scholarship has a much more secure lineage in the United
States and is beginning to emerge with strength in other common law jurisdictions; see, for
example, Stephen Parker, and Charles Sampford, *Legal Ethics and Legal Practice*, (Oxford, 1995).
[19] Levin, *op. cit.*, at 8
[20] *Code of Conduct of the Bar of England and Wales*, (London, The General Council of the Bar,
1990 ed.)
[21] *The Guide to the Professional Conduct of Solicitors*, (London, Law Society, 6th ed. 1993)
[22] Levin, *op. cit.*, at 15
[23] A point nicely made in Daryl Koehn's considered book, *The Ground of Professional Ethics*,
(London, Routledge, 1994) at 3

they might operate. That forms the burden of the next section of this essay. Thereafter, I want to make some observations on the usefulness or otherwise on trying to read across from one field of applied ethics, that of medicine, to another, that of law. Here, I identify some parallels and asymmetries which need to be taken into account in making this assessment. Again, I want to make clear that my thesis is concerned not with canvassing specific issues but rather with looking at the shape and nature of the ethical template. I shall do that by considering one example of what I shall call a macro-ethical consideration, and one example of a methodological kind in medical ethics. I shall attempt to show how the stencils drawn from these templates can accommodate an analysis of legal practice and legal ethics.

WHAT SORTS OF ETHICAL ARGUMENTS ARE THERE?[24]

Bernard Dickens has conveniently identified four types of approach to ethics which serve as a useful base from which to examine the practice of medicine; what may be called a natural law or duty based ethics, utilitarian or consequentialist base ethics (I would have reversed that order as utilitarianism is but one form of a consequentialist argument), principle based ethics and feminist ethics (what I would have identified as feminist approaches to ethics).[25] To those I would have added two others; postmodern ethics, of the kind discussed by Bruce Jennings[26] and 'the new pragmatism' as Susan Wolf has called it.[27] At the risk of doing violence to all, let me briefly review the salient referents of each approach. Those that will be particularly familiar I have treated in the most cursory manner.

a) Natural law or duty based ethics claim derivation from natural reason, and seek to distinguish virtue from vice as a matter of the inherent quality of the act. Unethical actions violate universal reasoning based on moral duties, or, in religious versions of Natural Law, they violate divine intentions for how human beings should live. Divine intentions are known by revelation to chosen or learned officers of the faith. When an act is inherently vicious or bad, none of its consequences can be considered virtuous or good, and complicity in the commission is as culpable as committing the wrong itself. Principles of natural law or duty are declared as a matter of authority and since all people are

---

[24] Accessible introductions and bibliographical references are available in Peter Singer, (ed.), *A Companion to Ethics*, (Oxford, Basil Blackwell, 1991), Roger Scruton, *Modern Philosophy*, (London, Sinclair-Stevenson, 1994) ch.20 and at 559-64, and Elizabeth Frazer, Jennifer Hornsby and Sabina Lovibond, *Ethics: A Feminist Reader*, (Oxford, Basil Blackwell, 1992)

[25] After Bernard Dickens, 'Law, Ethics and Justice in Human Reproduction' paper presented at the UNESCO International Symposium on Ethics in Medicine and Reproductive Biology Paris, 6-8 July 1994.

[26] Bruce Jennings; 'Possibilities of Consensus: Towards Democratic Moral Discourse' (1991) 16 *The Journal of Medicine and Philosophy* 447-63

[27] (1994) 20(4) *American Journal of Law and Medicine* 395-415

governed by the same duties, all are bound to common obedience. By these principles, ethical relativity is denounced, and some acts, such as lying, are invariably considered wrong.

b) Consequentialist or Utilitarian Ethics judge acts according to whether or not they are useful in promoting human well-being or happiness. Right acts maximize desirable outcomes and wrongful acts cause or contribute to undesirable results. Distinctions between desirable and undesirable outcomes are based on the values of participants in a community of interest, who will in practice compose a political or jurisdictional entity. There is no requirement that utilitarian ethical principles be universal or enduring, since what is desirable or useful in one place or time may not be in another. Interests and the desirability of outcomes change over time, depending on pragmatic considerations. Utilitarian ethics are relative to circumstances.

c) Principle based ethics identify a small number of principles that ethical conduct should consider and prioritise. The principles themselves do not conform to any order of priority, so that the exercise of ethical decision-making requires the decision-maker to determine which prevails when their observance would produce conflicting results. A decision is ethical not simply because of its content but because of the process of due consideration of the principles that have produced it.[28] The commonly (but not universally) accepted principles are:

- respect for persons, which includes i) autonomy of capable persons and ii) protection of persons incapable of autonomy;
- beneficence, meaning the duty to do good and to maximize good, which some consider to include but others distinguish from
- non-maleficience, meaning the duty to do no harm or to minimize harm and the risk of harm; and
- justice, the ethical principle to which the law primarily devotes itself, which requires equal treatment of equal cases, equitable distribution of benefits and, for instance, due remedies of injustices.

d) Feminist approaches to ethics are not a series of monoliths , but cover a wide spectrum of approaches and preferences. There a number of unifying themes, although fissures in the unity, like all approaches to ethical questions, open and close from time to time. 'Perhaps the greatest philosophical achievement of feminism over the last twenty years (though this achievement rests, of course, on earlier work) has been to demonstrate in practice—in the practice of moral and political philosophy—that the long absence of women's generic interests from the agenda of these subjects could not be innocently explained.'[29] The overarching theme of feminist approaches to ethics is the

---

[28] The classic text in Medical Ethics has become Tom Beauchamp and James Childress' *Principles of Biomedical Ethics*, (Oxford, OUP, 4th ed., 1994). See also the voluminous Raanan Gillon and Ann Lloyd (eds), *Principles of Health Care Ethics*, (Chichester, Wiley, 1993).

[29] Frazer, Hornsby and Lovibond, *op. cit.*, at 4

reaction against and response to these exclusions from traditional centres of ethical authority (in which Plato and Aristotle are particular exemplars[30]). They are unified by assertion of the legitimacy of women's experiences of injustice and perceptions of right conduct to reshape social attitudes and laws. Particularly, but simplistically, they may be characterised by the conviction that women live according to an ethic of care for and connectedness with others rather than a male-gendered autonomous independence (to counter which BT is currently employing Bob Hoskins, for example), and an incentive to empower women to be in control of key decisions of their lives. Not all women are feminists and, not all who recognise the importance of feminist approaches to ethics are women.

e) an influential version of post modern ethics argues that moral decision making in medicine (as in other professional and public organizational settings) is becoming increasingly institutionalized and subject to formalized procedures and constraints. Bruce Jennings has suggested that across a broad range in the landscape of contemporary medicine

. . . ethical choice and agency are now embedded as never before in a network of explicit rules and formal procedures and processes for making decisions. These rules stipulate (within certain limits) what types of decision may be made, how they may be made, by whom, and with the assistance of what resources.[31]

Such rules are increasingly becoming institutionalized. This, for Jennings, means that they are embedded in the organisational form of statutes, court opinions, administrative mandates, and institutional protocols. This 'embeddment' has important relationships with the kinds of ethical concerns and the way in which they are expressed, it shifts the primary focus of ethical theory towards an understanding of morality 'as a socially embedded practice'. The 'classical' approaches (exemplified in the different theoretical practices of Plato and Kant) invest far more moral authority in the practice and the results of philosophical reflection than they are able to sustain and seem to require a neutral and insulated space for such reflection, cut off from the space of public discourse and deliberation.[32]

The shift thus identified is part of a rethinking of the very nature of ethical theory itself: its relationship to the human subjectivity and the cultural context that produces it, the kind of knowledge it can be expected to provide and the

---

[30] For considerations of these exclusions see Genevieve Lloyd, *The Man of Reason: ' Male' and ' Female' in Western Philosophy*, (London, Metheun, 2nd ed.,1992), and specifically in relation to the family, Derek Morgan and Gillian Douglas, 'The Constitution of the Family: Three Waves for Plato' in Derek Morgan and Gillian Douglas, (eds.), *Constituting Families: A Study in Governance*, (Stuttgart, Franz Steiner, 1994) at 7–21. A good introduction to feminisms in health is Helen Bequaert Holmes and Laura Purdy (eds), *Feminist Perspectives in Medical Ethics*, Bloomington, Ind. Indiana University Press. 1992)

[31] Bruce Jennings; 'Possibilities of Consensus: Towards Democratic Moral Discourse' (1991) 16 *The Journal of Medicine and Philosophy* 447–63   [32] *Ibid*, 450

force and authority of its claims and its relationship to practice are part of the reconstruction underway. This kind of 'post-modern' philosophical reorientation of moral philosophy so fundamentally affects our grasp of the relationship between theory and practice that, Jennings proposes, it cannot but have a profound effect on applied ethics. It exposes the extent to which classical ethical theories ' . . . rest on assumptions about the transcendent character of reason and a "philosophy of the subject" . . . that are no longer tenable.'[33] In other words, it is being claimed that ethical conclusions are produced and constructed rather than found from contemplation. The older questions are being displaced by a newer—post-modern—approach which aims to examine and explore the way in which crucial questions ' . . . have to do with the way in which the meanings and legitimacy of moral notions are established, reinterpreted or transformed over time.'[34] Again, these transformations have important consequences for the ways in which we conceptualise and even describe the setting of a legal framework and the establishment of ethical standards for regulating scientific and technical societies.

In relation to each type of these ethical approaches, there are more or less well suited levels of analysis. Thus, we might typically identify micro, macro, and meso level approaches. Microethics, characterised by person-to-person ethics and exemplified by ethics influenced by traditional religious doctrines, have concerned themselves with individual conscience and relations between individuals. Macroethics concern relations among groups, and between a group and an individual within or outside the group, while meso ethics, located between these other levels of analysis, is concerned with bureaucratic, administrative and management decision making tasks, particularly with allocations of resource. Examples from each of these levels of analysis could, and in a fully articulated analysis would need to be given, in order to substantiate any thesis which seriously purported to argue that there were cross-over possibilities in the study of one department of applied ethics to another, in the simple way that I am proposing might be achieved here. I do not propose to make that fully articulated move, but, later, to give one example of the uses of the macro level analysis which for the present will have to stand for the fuller thesis.

f) the rise of a 'New Pragmatism' as Susan Wolf has proposed it might be called, shares something in common with both feminist approaches to ethics and concerns with morality 'as a socially embedded practice'. She has suggested that the old paradigms in bioethics, especially that of principled based approaches, are under attack from a number of quarters; a plethora of alternative approaches is emerging and a new empiricism is challenging the content of previously accepted principles. Burgeoning feminist and race-sensitive work has rendered suspect any bioethical approach geared to the generic 'patient', and methodological reassessments suggest the need to return

---

[33] *Ibid*, 448   [34] *Ibid*, 448

to cases rather than principles, to narratives rather than norms. This shift is being mirrored or shadowed in new paradigms in health law.[35] The goal of this new, emergent, pragmatic paradigm is to change the nature of ethical colloquy about access (in this case) to health care. Bioethics and law have until recently been characterised by 'conversations among the experts, governed by top down theory and the elegance of abstract pronouncements, largely inattentive to differences of race, ethnicity, gender and insurance status.'[36] Wolf suggests the marking out and pursuit of a new path,

. . . one more winding and complex. This is a path shaped by the twists and turns of empiricist investigation, with detailed attention to context. It will be wide enough to accommodate multiple proposals and critiques as to method, full with attention to feminist, race-attentive, and other contributions. It will be teeming with people, the patients and research subjects whose fates are most at stake in clinical settings.[37]

The importance for this analysis in relation to medical ethics or bioethics is that not only does it echo the suggestions for a re-characterisation of ethical concerns which Jennings has predicted, it has extraordinary parallels with the arguments of the European social philosopher, Ulrich Beck. This in turn reflects back on the work of the American legal scholar, Marc Galanter. A tangential passage to explore this connection will afford a suggestive perspective on paths for ethical enquiry.

SECRET FAREWELLS TO EPOCHES: TWO VIEWS OF THE CATHEDRAL

Ulrich Beck is concerned to describe the process of 'reflexive modernization' within medicine. This 'institutionalized . . . noiseless social and cultural revolution' has secured for medicine as a professional power a fundamental advantage against political and public attempts at consultation and intervention. His thesis suggests the dangers of uncontrolled or unregulated uses and developments of science and technology. He has argued that while the latest research results constantly open up possible new applications, because this happens at such a rapid, exponential rate, the process of implementation is practically uncontrolled. Accordingly, while medicine supposedly serves health, it has in fact 'created entirely new situations, has changed the relationship of humankind to itself, to disease, illness and death, indeed, it has changed the world.'[38]

---

[35] Wolf, (1994) 20(4) *American Journal of Law and Medicine* 395–45 for a comprehensive review   [36] Wolf, *op. cit.*, at 415   [37] *Ibid.*

[38] Ulrich Beck, *Risk Society: Towards a New Modernity*,(London, Sage, trans. Mark Ritter 1992; originally published as *Riskogellschaft. Auf dem Weg in eine andere Moderne*, (Frankfurt, 1986), 204). This work is further explicated in his exchanges with Anthony Giddens and Scott Lash in Beck, Giddens and Lash, *Reflexive Modernisation: Politics, Tradition and Aesthetics in the Modern Social Order*, (Oxford, Polity Press, 1994). There are excellent discussions of this work

In its fields of practice, clinical diagnosis and therapy, it not only controls the innovative power of science, but it is at the same time its own parliament and its own government in matters of 'medical progress.' When it has to decide on 'malpractice', even the 'third force' of jurisprudence has to take recourse to medically produced and controlled norms and circumstances, which according to the social construction of rationality can ultimately be decided only by medical people and by no one else.[39]

The principles of 'reflexive modernisation' developed and deployed by Beck in the 'sub-politics of medicine'—what he calls but 'an extreme case study' of more general questions in and facing scientific and technical societies— involve the divergence of diagnosis and therapy in the current development of medicine which results in a dramatic *increase* of so-called chronic illness, '... illnesses that can be diagnosed thanks to the more acute medical and technical sensory system, without the presence or even prospect of any effective measures to treat them.'[40] His thesis here is that progress necessarily implies unplanned excess, the harmful effects of which are unintentional.[41]

The importance of this observation is this; *if the costs of progress are unintentional, they may well be equally unforeseeable*, while nonetheless statistically quantifiable as risks. Social costs become difficult to guard against or anticipate or even calculate. As the process of what Beck calls the 'noiseless social and cultural revolution' within medicine ('the institutionalised revolution'[42]) is amplified, the role of law, it seems to me, is metamorphosed: whether it keeps pace with the demands of those changes is another question, an empirical or evaluative one to be set alongside a series of conceptual ones. In relation to medicine, the interesting question for the lawyer is; what is the most appropriate or sensitive regulatory response? I want to suggest, however, that for the current thesis, the importance of Beck's analysis is that it may be possible to trace the same kind of metamorphosis, *mutatis mutandi*, in law. While there is apparently less silence, more visibility in the nature of the changes which take place and in their institutional nature, in fact the nature of what Galanter calls 'Law Abounding'— is more subtle in its effects and more complex in its forms. It produces ' ... an uncomfortable sense that the world has been legalised—that our world of primal experience has been penetrated, permeated, colonised and somehow diminished by a

---

in the independently acclaimed work of Zygmunt Bauman, especially his *Postmodern Ethics*, (Oxford, Basil Blackwell, 1993) and *Life in Fragments; Essays in Postmodern Morality*, (Oxford, Basil Blackwell, 1995). Bauman owes and acknowledges a clear intellectual debt to one of the early sceptics whose writings on medical ethics are of a seminal quality, Hans Jonas; see particularly his *Philosophical Essays: From Ancient Creed to Technological Man*, (Englewood Cliffs, NJ, Prentice Hall, 1974) and *The Imperative of Responsibility: In Search of an Ethics for the Technological Age*, (Chicago, University of Chicago Press, 1984). There are parallels here with the work of Marc Galanter in law to which I want to return.

[39] *Ibid* 210   [40] *Ibid*, 204   [41] *Ibid*., especially 209   [42] *Ibid*., 206 and 209–10

derivative and unprofitable layer of the legal.'[43] But in what sense has this happened noiselessly as a social and cultural revolution? Certainly, there has been 'an enlargement of the legal world' which has brought with it unforeseen and unforeseeable consequences. At 1990 there were more lawyers in the United States than in the rest of the world combined. America had four times the number of lawyers per capita as Britain, five times per capita as Germany, ten times per capita as France and twenty times the number per capita as Japan.[44] In short, however, the amount of law has increased exponentially,[45] and it has become more pervasive.[46] Perhaps of equal or greater significance, however, is the rôle different forms of *regulation* used throughout the legal system to control, regulate or facilitate a wide and diverse range of economic and social functions.[47]

Since the 1970s, however, there has also been a remarkable change in the way in which Euro-American societies *make* law which in part parallels the description which Jennings offers of the institutionalisation of rules in medicine. Not only this, but the effective forms of accountability in the making of these laws are under severe strain. Examples from the British parliamentary system in the past ten years could be multiplied several-fold and reproduced internationally, but two will suffice. First the Community Charge, introduced under the provisions of the Local Government Finance Act 1988 and the Local Government and Housing Act 1989.[48] On this, the leading commentators observe that

As with most controversial government Bills, the standing committee was a futile marathon. Between mid-January and mid-March 1988, the committee held 35 sessions, sitting for a total of 120 hours . . . The committee's proceedings went almost unnoticed by the press. A colossal amount of committee time was spent on the first few clauses . . . after which the government resorted to a guillotine so that most of the later clauses went through with virtually no debate . . . it was scrutiny by slogan and soundbite.[49]

---

[43] Marc Galanter, 'Law Abounding: Legalisation Around the North Atlantic' (1992) 55 *Modern Law Review* 1–24 at 1

[44] J D Davidson and W Rees-Mogg, *The Great Reckoning*, (New York, Simon & Schuster, 1993) at 120   [45] Galanter, *op. cit.*, at 6 and text accompanying notes 41–57

[46] Galanter, *op. cit.*, at 13-14 and text accompanying notes 96–106. There is an amusing and instructive account of the way in which Bill Twining tests and demonstrates this point to his students in Twining, *Blackstone's Tower*, (London, Sweet & Maxwell, 1994).

[47] For a recent, comprehensive analysis see Anthony I Ogus, *Regulation: Legal Form and Economic Theory*, (Oxford, Clarendon Press, 1994) passim. For an earlier review of the 'statutorification' of the legal system see Guido Calabresi, *A Common Law for the Age of Statutes*, (Cambridge, Mass., Harvard University Press, 1982) and the references cited therein.

[48] For commentary on the legislation see John McEldowney, *Public Law*, (London, Sweet & Maxwell, 1994) at 354–59

[49] David Butler, Andrew Adonis and Tony Travers, *Failure in British Government*, (Oxford, OUP, 1994) at 116

The limitations of the Community Charge legislation, like the later Child Support Act 1991, were pointed out by the Committees before the legislation was passed. They were taken seriously 'only after there had been riots in the streets and threats of violence against public servants.'[50] And the problems which the *making* of laws reveal carry dangers not just for the parliamentary process itself, but for those whose professional duty is to work with those laws for and on behalf of others. Difficulties are expressed by both barristers and solicitors. James Goudie QC, has observed that 'legislation is becoming increasingly inaccessible . . . and . . . impossible to understand. Unintelligible legislation is the negation of the rule of law and of parliamentary democracy.'[51] An officer of the Law Society bluntly suggested that lawyers were constantly ' . . . trying to find out what [statute law] is in force, when it came into force . . . and when they have found out, what the hell it means.'[52] The identification of this gap between the intended, unintended, foreseen and unforeseeable consequences of legal change, and some of its potential consequences was first proposed by John Griffiths' important essay 'Is Law Important?'[53]

Marc Galanter has identified some of the common elements that surround and infuse what he has called the North Atlantic legal cultures. Within their richer, more informed, more diverse societies;

- there are more laws, more lawyers, more claims, more strategic players of the law game, such that societies spend more, absolutely, on laws and lawyers;
- legal institutions including courts and firms increasingly operate in rational, business-like manners and lawyers, judges and administrators are more entrepreneurial and innovative in designing and re-designing institutions and procedures to respond to the demand to be more cost-effective;
- the law is plural, decentralised, issuing from more sources, and more rules are being applied by more actors to more varied situations which mean that legal outcomes are more contingent and changing;
- outcomes are increasingly negotiated rather than decreed, such that law is less autonomous, less self-contained and more open to methods and data from other disciplines;
- because law is contingent, flexible and technically sophisticated, it is increasingly costly. Thus most people are priced out of the market for direct use of law. Law operates increasingly through indirect symbolic controls rather than through imposing physical coercion.[54]

An analysis of *medical* progress as itself institutionalized discloses that there

---

[50] Andrew Marr, *op. cit.*, at 69
[51] *Making the Law*, (London, Hansard Society, 1993) at 8   [52] *Ibid.*
[53] (1979) 54 *New York University Law Rev.* 359
[54] Marc Galanter, 'Law Abounding: Legalisation Around the North Atlantic' (1992) 55 *Modern Law Review* 1–24 at 24

has been 'a revolution of the lay public's social living conditions without its consent.'[55] Indeed, in an arresting phrase, Beck describes this process as a 'secret farewell to an epoch of human history' in which the principles of technological feasibility and arrangement encroach on the subjects in such a way that the very foundations of a model of 'progress' which implicates a subject who is supposed ultimately to benefit from the process, are cancelled. In a strikingly similar vein Galanter has suggested that

In this new world of more law, more pervasive law, and more information about law, law itself is being transformed. . . . As the law expands and penetrates the world, it changes in the process. Its institutions flourish but lose their autonomous, self-contained quality. On every front we can observe the boundaries of the legal world becoming blurred and indefinite: . . . law firms become more like businesses; courts become more like other governmental bodies and their judgments increasingly resemble legal scholarship, . . . the traffic is not uni-directional—other institutions and discourses absorb legal ideas and simulate legal forms.[56]

Recalling the basic principles of democratically based societies in which central issues of public policy affecting the future of society are the subject of public debate to shape the political resolve, Beck fears that the developments of modern technology have set in motion processes which undermine the 'idea of democracy from inside.' Technology and medicine are becoming the instruments of uncontrolled 'sub-politics', where, in the sub-politics of medicine, there is no parliament and no executive in which the consequences of a decision might be examined before it is taken. There is even no social forum for decisions. ' . . . [T]he highly bureaucratized developed Western democracies check every act for its conformity with legal requirements, terms of reference and democratic legitimation; at the same time it is possible to escape all the bureaucratic and democratic controls and to take closed decisions despite the hail of general criticism and scepticism in a world which escapes parliamentary control and in which the very bases of existing life and previous patterns of social control can be completely neutralised.'[57] The parallels with changes in the legal order which I have attempted to suggest indicate that the sketch which Beck has provided of the medical form of the cathedral might be perceptible in the shadow which it throws onto the legal.

SYMMETRIES AND ASYMMETRIES

I want now to turn to consider the conditions in which I believe it is possible to achieve that read over between law and medicine, or more specifically, between medical ethics and legal ethics. My argument here is that while there

---

[55] Beck, *op cit.*, 206   [56] Galanter *op. cit.*, at 17–18   [57] *Ibid.*, 208

are of course some important asymmetries between medical and nursing practice and the practice of law (of which an appreciation is necessary properly to identify the transplantability between medical and legal ethics) and the histocompatability is not, as it were, a complete match, there is sufficient to believe that some grafting would succeed.

One important asymmetry (I do not necessarily want to equate this with difference) is that in legal practice, importantly, the concern is *generally* with the client's property or affairs. Affairs here can properly be understood to include incidentals to the person him or her self—such as involvement with the criminal justice system or the family jurisdiction of the court. In medical practice, typically, one deals not with the person's property and affairs, not even with that persons' body, but with *them*; when the doctor cuts in the operation he or she cuts not my body, he or she cuts me. But as far as ethical concerns are the subject of inquiry, one important consideration presently focuses attention in both lawyering and doctoring; that the practice is or should be concerned with the nature of the relationship between the professional and others.[58] Importantly, is the lawyer, any more or less than the doctor, personally responsible, morally or legally for the conduct of a case or the performance of a procedure or an operation? Are responsibilities owed to third parties other than the client or the patient?

Another important divergence is that in general terms, the issues in medicine are to a much greater degree determined than they are in legal practice. The reason for this lies, I think, in the nature of the concerns which are central to the practitioners in the two disciplines. Confidentiality will serve as a workable example. The doctor is primarily concerned to protect patient confidences in order to protect the patient's interests and the continued integrity of the doctor-patient relationship. The lawyer, in contrast, has a stronger (though not an exclusive) business interest in protecting client confidences in order to protect his or her own business, as well as to discharge any duties he or she may owe to the client.

Despite this limited catalogue of divergence, there are important points of contact between models (or ideal types) for the two professions which may make the possibility either of a comparative ethical analysis worthwhile or the suggestion of mutual areas of learning to be contemplated seriously. First, both professions are openly acknowledged to owe responsibilities beyond the bounds of the professional-client relationship, whether in the case of lawyers to the court, to their partners (even at the sake of personal or institutional cost), or whether in the case of doctors, to other professionals or to the public interest.

Secondly, both professions have been subject to enormous changes wrought at the hands of the state, determined to bring principles of market

[58] Jenny Levin, *op. cit.* at 17

organisation, if not market forces, closer to the operation of everyday life in professional practice. Both have been subject to changes heralded by the information revolution, which have raised similar questions of a legal as well as of an ethical kind; confidentiality, privacy, and the primacy of the client's interests, appear to be remarkably similar. But I am drawn to be sceptical about how far *these* similarities are anything more than superficial. Both professions have also been subject to enormous changes, which I have partly discussed above, in the nature and the extent of the good (health care or law) which could be made available (or foist upon) members of the public. One implication of this similarity I want to trace in the following section.

Both professions, whether at the level of rhetoric or practice (this is the source of sometimes loud and occasionally fruitful debate) are similarly defined by a distinctive commitment to benefit the client, a commitment that in each case appears to be limited to benefits which the client has assented to. This is a more complex argument from symmetry, for discussions in medical ethics and law in the past decade have been much preoccupied with the extent to which a doctor may proceed in the best interests of the patient when the patient does not him or her self identify their best interest in the same way, or indeed, according to the same set of values. Insofar as medical practice *itself* throws up real dilemmas for the ethical practice of law this is a clear area of overlap.

But there two further and important symmetries, which are identified by Daryl Koehn, which make the case for suggesting that the study of legal ethics can be enriched by a study of the forms, nature and content of ethical arguments in medicine and health care, more pressing and secure. As she demonstrates, professions such as the medical profession and the legal profession (she discusses others in the course of her thesis) *may*[59] 'represent the only mechanism we have for collectively providing ourselves with the goods of health [and] legal justice . . .'.[60] This has two consequences; first, their practitioners are bound by the trust which we, as citizens, place in them. It is this, for example, which make the particular study of, say, confidentiality or whether professionals are ethically bound to keep to the promises which they have made to those whom they are treating or serving, worthy of and susceptible to comparative analysis.

Secondly, because these are the *chosen* responses which we as a community have made to the problems of delivering help to the ill, the injured, the sick, or advice and assistance to the accused, the troubled, the concerned or the dispossessed, because we have ' . . . collectively preferred an arrangement in which the professions are to some sense and to some degree independent of state control,'[61] we need to press for a clarification of *whose* ethics we are

---

[59] I show how this assumption could be challenged in the next section.
[60] *The Ground of Professional Ethics*, (London, Routledge, 1994) at 5–6   [61] *Ibid.*, at 6

addressing before we collapse the distinction between professional and ordinary morality. Although this is a difficult point, and is not without controversy or objection,[62] it is so nicely illustrated in the field of medical ethics that it is worth recalling the observation here of Franz Inkelfinger, the former editor of the New England Journal of Medicine as he dies of cancer;

> I do not want to be in the position of the shopper at the Casbah who negotiates and haggles with the physician about what is best. I want to believe that my physician is acting under a higher moral principle than a used car dealer. I'll go further than that. A physician who merely spreads an array of vendibles in front of his patient and then says "Go ahead, you choose, it's your life" is guilty of shirking his duty, if not malpractice.[63]

There is, I feel, much that the study of legal ethics could learn simply from that observation.

Finally, although this is infrequently acknowledged, and there are existent and emergent tensions generated by it, both legal and medical professionals work in areas in which market provision plays an important, although as yet asymmetrical part. The doctor, unlike the lawyer, as an allocator of state goods based upon a merit-good system, has responsibility to the state for the way in which he or she discharges professional practice. The lawyer does not, or at least not to any thing like the same extent, act in this way.[64] This reflects a *crude* dichotomy between the practice of law and the practice of medicine, at least in the United Kingdom. It lies at the heart of any debate which asks to what extent, if at all, the development of legal ethics can draw upon or learn from medical ethics. At least at their respective cores, and at least for the time being, the practice of law is a private, business oriented profession; the public practise of medicine is seen as imposing duties upon its practitioners of a very particular kind. This does not imply that solicitors act first and foremost as business people and only, if at all, as an afterthought to the ethical consequences or dimensions to their practice. Nor would it suggest that if they were properly to be regarded as businesses, that they would thereby be entitled, let alone enjoined, to act as they please. Those conclusions would depend on very different moves, and I return to make some observations on them, below. But as Cranston has suggested,

---

[62] Koehn returns to consider the most significant objection to her point, and offers her response in *loc. cit.*, Ch. 8, 'The professional and the public good.'

[63] F G Ingelfinger, 'Arrogance' (1980) 304 *New England Journal of Medicine* 1507–11

[64] The arguments in this section draw also from a reading of R G Lee, [q]What Good is Health Care?' which forms part of the argument in R G Lee and Frances H Miller, *Health Care Allocation and the Law: Who Gets What and Why?* (Aldershot, Dartmouth, in preparation) and from conversations with Bob Lee. I am grateful for permission to cite this argument, although Bob Lee would not necessarily agree with the use to which I have put it or the conclusions which I draw from it.

any association with the profession dispels the suggestion that the profession's ethical codes are self-interest writ large. There is a genuine concern with high ethical standards, not least so as to maintain the profession's public standard.[65]

Lawyers' firms do turn away business because of, say, a conflict of interest even when it will cause them financial harm, or where it could benefit one partner but jeopardise the standing of the firm. There are obvious exceptions to this, as the development of what be called 'Chinese Wall Syndrome' in City of London solicitor's offices implies. But, it might be suggested that extant ethical rules exist to control the longer term business interests of solicitors against possible short-term incentives. For lawyers, then, ethical rules may presently be seen as long-term cost-benefit rents to prevent short-term profit taking, and almost every individual example of a traditionally conceived legal ethical rule can be explained according to this analysis. While this does not necessarily hold for rules of medical ethics, such that these symmetries and asymmetries in the provision of medical and legal services make me *cautious* about suggesting comparisons at the level of *specific situational* concerns, I want to reiterate that there are sufficient symmetries to make the nature and form of ethical argument in health care valuable in the study of legal ethics.

IDENTIFYING MISSING QUESTIONS IN LEGAL ETHICS.

In this section I want to draw on one example from the field of macro-ethical questions in health care and one from a methodological or conceptual debate which I hope will show that the study of legal ethics enjoins the inquiry of deep philosophical questions, as much as into the micro and meso concerns with which the subject has, in its more developed forms, come to be associated. The first is an example of a debate which is more philosophical in character. I have chosen it in order to illustrate the kind of what I am minded to call the 'missing question' in legal ethics. I do not mean by this that it is not a question which has not been asked. What I mean is that unless it is sometimes reiterated or restated, there is a temptation to assume that we are *all agreed on the purposes of ethical study*, that we will, in other words, without an occasional reminder, miss the point of ethical argument in law. It is the sort of question, if you like, which raises questions about the business of ethics and the ethics of business.

The relevant exchange is between English philosopher Bernard Williams and the American writer Robert Nozick. For health care I want to suggest we substitute legal need or legal services in order to explicate the point I want to illustrate. The ground of their debate is a macro-ethical one; one which as I

---

[65] Cranston, 'Legal Ethics and Professional Responsibility' above, p. 1.

have said, Ross Cranston identifies as much as a political question as an ethical one.

The immediate focus over which Nozick joins with Williams concerns the proper grounds of allocation of the scarce good that it seems to be universally acknowledged that health care has become. One possible approach is that health care should be given to those who in some way, judged against some sort of criterion, deserve it; that a just system of health care allocation should be backward looking, asking what has the individual done in the past to safeguard, preserve or damage their own health such that the state should reward (or discipline) them in its response. In this sense, state policy would be delivered through its gatekeepers, the medical, nursing and other social welfare professions. An alternative model would be a needs based model, a forward looking model, in which treatments might still be denied, or prioritised, according to need.

Other possible grounds of distribution exist, but I want to take just two examples of the directly competing notions of what might be entailed in the state's responsibility and obligations for health care and compare the libertarian position offered by Williams with that of the conservative Nozick. Williams argues that

Leaving aside preventive medicine, the proper ground of distribution of medical care is ill health: this is a necessary truth. Now in very many societies, while ill health may work as a necessary condition of receiving treatment, it does not work as a sufficient condition, since such treatment costs money, and not all who are ill have the money; hence the possession of sufficient money becomes in fact an additional necessary condition of actually receiving treatment.[66]

Nozick urges that 'it cannot be assumed that equality must be built into any theory of justice.'.[67] He says of the passage quoted from Williams that he seems to be arguing that if among the different descriptions applying to an activity, there is one that contains an 'internal goal' of the activity, then 'the only proper grounds for the performance of the activity, or its allocation if it is scarce, are connected with the effective achievement of the internal goal.' Thus, according to Nozick's reading of Williams, 'the only proper criterion for the distribution of medical care is medical need.' To this Nozick objects.

Does it follow, he asks, that the internal goal of an activity should take precedence over, for example, a person's particular purpose in performing the activity? If someone becomes a barber (or might we add, a lawyer?) because he or she likes talking to a variety of different people, is it unjust of them to allocate services to those to whom they most like to talk? Or, if they work as a barber in order to pay tuition at school, may they not cut the hair of only those

---

[66] Williams, 'The Idea of Equality' in Peter Laslett and W G Runciman, (eds), *Philosophy, Politics and Society* 2 series, Oxford, Basil Blackwell, 1962, at 110-31

[67] *Anarchy, State and Utopia*, (Oxford, Basil Blackwell, 1974), at 233

who tip well? Nozick ponders why the doctor's skills and activities should be allocated differently, via the 'internal goal' of medical care. When the layers of Williams' argument are peeled away, he writes,

what we arrive at is the claim that society (that is, each of us acting together in some organised fashion) should make provision for the important needs of all its members. . . . Despite appearances, Williams presents no argument for it. Like others, Williams looks only to questions of allocation. He ignores the question of where things or actions to be allocated and distributed come from. Consequently, he does not consider whether they come already tied to people who have entitlements over them (surely the case for service activities, which are people's actions), people who therefore may decide for themselves to whom they will give the thing and on what grounds.[68]

Nozick's argument has, in turn, been criticised. Len Doyal and Ian Gough reject it as incorporating a Lockean view of ownership, an essentially individualistic view in which I and only I am entitled to decide what to do with the fruits of my labour. For them this is flawed in its descriptive nature of production. Production, they write, is ' . . . a social process in which many mix their labour [and] any rights associated with ownership can no longer be focused exclusively on the individual.'[69] How would this analysis speak to the business, if that remains an acceptable descriptive term, of lawyering?

A further important, recent criticism has come from within the conservative tradition to which Nozick appeals. John Gray has objected that the night watchman state of the kind advocated by Nozick is incompatible with what he calls 'limited government', of which conservative government is the embodiment.

A limited government has tasks that go well beyond keeping the peace— . . . It has also a responsibility to tend fragile and precious traditions, to protect and shelter the vulnerable and defenceless, to enhance and enlarge opportunities for the disadvantaged, to promote the conservation and renewal of the natural and human environment and to assist in the renewal of civil society and the reproduction of the common culture without which pluralism and diversity become enmity and division.[70]

The implications of this argument for health care are important, far reaching and challenging. I am interested in those. But I am also interested to know whether, for example, the protection and shelter of the vulnerable includes payment for their retention of lawyers to argue on their behalf. What fragile and precious traditions are included, and which not, in Gray's elegy of limited government? And not only which traditions, but whose; in a plural, multi-

---

[68] Ibid. at 234–35. I learned of this debate and began to understand its subtleties from lectures given by John Day, of the University of Leicester. His own interpretation of it, and his response, are now recorded in his essay, 'Justice and Utility in Health Care' in Lincoln Allison, (ed.), *The Utilitarian Response: The Contemporary Viability of Utilitarian Political Philosophy*, (London, Sage, 1993) at 30   [69] *A Theory of Human Need*, (London, Macmillan, 1991) at 137–8
[70] John Gray, *Beyond the New Right*, (London, Routledge, 1993), at 50

cultural, mixed ethnic society, do some traditions outrank others, or do all fall to be considered according to some general criteria of tradition? As Marilyn Strathern has reminded us, there is much of importance attached to the naming of 'tradition.'[71]

Gray expounds these normative or evaluative criticisms in the concluding chapter of his book. Arguing, with critics such as Ivan Illich that it must be accepted that there are limits to health care, Gray's first concern is with the over medicalisation of life and death. Secondly, and this is related, he complains that modern medical care and treatment cannot be shown to have provided benefits proportionate to the claims made for it or indeed proportionate to the costs lavished on it. As Thomas McKeown has shown, improvements in health care have arisen much more from developments in sanitation, environment and personal life style than they have from individual 'medical' breakthroughs.[72] Third, much of what has been incorporated within modern medical care lies, in truth, outside the medical domain 'and can be performed safely and intelligently by trained lay people.'[73] Much of what is *routinely* provided by lawyers masquerades under the euphemism of legal services and would be amenable to the same analysis.

I offer this example of work in medical ethics, however, as being primarily an illustration of the need to examine the range of assumptions which a fully worked essay of legal ethics would address. For instance, we might start by examining whether the practice of lawyering was or should be undertaken by professionals at all, rather than, say small, medium and large sized businesses, and whether, if that were so, a business is the sort of enterprise to whom ethical analysis may properly be applied.

Now, one possible objection to the use of this example would be to suggest, at the outset, that lawyering skills are not a scarce good and that this renders any sense of an analogy with medical care redundant. A moment's reflection begins to dispel this fault-finding exercise, for it begs the question of access to law. Whether this is framed or appears in the form of legal aid cuts, (which raise a meso-ethical human rights question[74]) or in Galanter's identification of the world of 'New Legalism,' some people fall from the lawyering net;

The increase in the number and variety of legal actors, in the number of decision-makers, in the amount of authorative material, in the span of legal theory, in the amount of available information, in expenditures for legal services and the consequent intensity

---

[71] Marilyn Strathern, *op. cit.*, at 4

[72] McKeown, *The Role of Medicine*, (Oxford, Basil Blackwell, 1979) passim

[73] Gray, *op. cit.*, at 168

[74] It has been suggested that Government plans announced in a Green Paper in May 1995 could lead to breaches of both the European Convention on Human Rights and the United Nations International Covenant on Civil and Political Rights; opinion of Michael Beloff QC and Murray Hunt prepared on behalf of Liberty, referred to in *The Independent*, 1 September 1995, at 6

of lawyer work—all of these multiply the opportunities for unforeseen juxtaposition and the incentives for innovative enterprise to undermine established theories, rules and practices. . . . With the multiplication of authorative learning, the incorporation of ever more external material, the circulation of ever more detailed information at ever greater velocity, law becomes more contingent. . . . But as this vast, endlessly receptive law is pressed into service to address a host of substantive problems, it becomes less knowable and less predictable.[75]

Although a lot of lawyering and judicial work remains of a mundane, repetitive nature, as the law becomes more voluminous, more complex and more uncertain, the costs of using it increase.[76] To say that legal services are not a scarce good simply overlooks the fact of life that many people are priced out of the market for direct use of law in most matters. This has the paradoxical effect, according to Galanter, of changing the legal game in a whole variety of ways. An important one for my present argument is that as law becomes more contingent and more expensive, it becomes 'more accessible and more participative in the sense that there are more effective "strategic" legal actors.'[77] As more people can play the legal game the game changes. One possibility is, of course, that the nature of doing the business of lawyering can change as well. Certainly, there is a change in the role of courts, or at least our perception of their role. Legal actors 'improvise resolutions to disputes involving particular combinations of facts, parties, evidence, public sentiment and available knowledge.'[78]

While these resolutions are authoritative, their contingency is widely recognised; 'they are not inalterable fiat, building blocks in the temple of ages, but contingent and temporary.'[79] As with Jennings' suggestion that 'post-modern' philosophical reorientation of moral philosophy fundamentally affects our grasp of the relationship between theory and practice, so Galanter's claim is that legal conclusions are produced and constructed rather than found from contemplation. Not only are we being asked to understand morality 'as a socially embedded practice' where the crucial questions ' . . . have to do with the way in which the meanings and legitimacy of moral notions are established, reinterpreted or transformed over time,'[80] the same demands are being made in respect of law.[81]

In this way, the questions, 'what sort of thing is a law firm?,' 'what sort of being is a lawyer?' which initially look as though they may generate only a descriptive reply, (such that there is no implied evaluation against which their conduct or actions can be judged), can be framed as seriously incomplete. Any complete enumeration of the properties of a law firm must make some

[75] Marc Galanter, 'Law Abounding: Legalisation Around the North Atlantic' (1992) 55 *Modern Law Review* 1–24 at 19   [76] *Ibid*, at 20   [77] *Ibid*, at 20–1
[78] Perhaps the most remarkable example of this can be found in the High Court of Australia decision in *Queensland* v *Mabo* (1992) 142 CLR 1   [79] Galanter, *op. cit.*, 21
[80] *Ibid*, 448   [81] Did the realists know and predict this all the time?

reference to some conception of those types of action that are appropriate to it or which it is under some kind of obligation to perform; simply to describe a law firm without making some reference to its *function* as well as its *form* would be seriously incomplete. If this is so then it seems impossible to speak of a law firm (or any other social construct) in purely descriptive terms, as if from within some kind of moral vacuum. If this is the case (and only if this is the case) then it will make sense to apply moral discourse, indeed moral judgments, to the activities and behaviour of a law firm; it will be possible, indeed desirable, to say 'this is a good law firm' or 'that is a bad law firm' and mean by that that its activities can properly be the subject of moral endorsement or approbation.

There are those who argue that moral language can not properly be applied to businesses.[82] Yet, while most agree that private businesses bear some social responsibilities,[83] accepting this general point hardly settles the more complex question of what the content and scope of these responsibilities are.

An important element in reaching this conclusion consists in approaching the question 'what sorts of action are appropriate to a law firm?' In other words this question is itself logically prior to the supposedly descriptive one; 'what sort of a thing is a law firm?' This appears counter-intuitive; putting the consideration of the sort of things that X should do before the question of what sort of thing X is. In the case of physical objects it would look decidedly odd to prioritise the questions in this way. To ask whether this is a good glove would depend, at least in part, on whether the object of which this was being asked was a 'a continuous surface infolded on itself . . . [with] five outpouchings'[84] or a scarf. But this condition does not necessarily hold for a social construct, such as a law firm or other business; it is as though we are hostage to the notion that institutions, such as a law firm must have and indeed have only one purpose. But we can change institutions and use them for whatever purpose we choose; 'the meanings and legitimacy of moral notions are established, reinterpreted or transformed over time.'[85]

Some of the most interesting questions of legal, as with other professionally situated ethics, arise from the way(s) in which what the subject might consist in are conceptualised, and the sorts of questions which we allow should

---

[82] see, eg, M Velasquez, 'Why Corporations are not Morally Responsible for Anything they Do' in Beauchamp and Bowie, *op. cit.*, at 69–76; and M Keeley, 'Corporations as Non-Persons' (1981) 15 *Journal of Value Enquiry* 119–55. For a recent British examination of the question of responsibility and blame as applied through the criminal law and its values system see Celia Wells, *Corporations and Criminal Responsibility*, (Oxford, Clarendon, 1993) ch.5

[83] Tom Beauchamp, Norman Bowie, 'Corporate Social Responsibility' in Tom Beauchamp, Norman Bowie, eds., *Ethical Theory and Business*, (Englewood Cliffs, NJ, Prentice Hall, 2nd ed., 1983) at 52–7

[84] As recorded in Oliver Sack's classic essay on the effects of visual agnosia, *The Man Who Mistook His Wife for a Hat*, (London, Picador, 1986) at 13   [85] Ibid, 448

be asked. That is one of the foremost lessons which can be brought as a template from the study of ethics as applied to medical practice. Let me give one illustration from recent debates in medical ethics to illustrate this point. The aim of medical ethics, according to John Harris[86] is to produce answers to the moral questions raised by medical practice. Further than that, he avers that it is the task of medical ethics to give the answers that it is rational to give. But, as Anne Maclean has objected, it is possible to give different judgments on the question what should the rational actor do, all of which can be supported by moral reasons, or with reference to moral notions, standards, values or principles.[87] Thus Harris:

Just as the proper business of medicine is not merely to understand the nature and causes of illness, but to try to prevent or cure it, so the proper business of medical ethics is not merely to understand the nature of the moral problems raised by medical practice but to try to resolve them.[88]

Maclean's challenge to this is put in the following, fundamental way:

philosophy as such delivers no such verdict upon moral issues; there is no unique set of moral principles which philosophy as such underwrites and no question, therefore, of using that set to uncover the answers which philosophy gives to moral questions. When bioethicists deliver a verdict upon the moral issues raised by medical practice, it is their own verdict they deliver and not the verdict of philosophy itself. . . . [this] is not to deny that there can be rational answers to moral questions; it is to deny that for any moral question, there is a uniquely rational answer to it which can be uncovered by philosophical enquiry.[89]

The contingent nature of the inquiries available to us, the dependence on vision and perspective, which Maclean alludes to here, have an important impact on the enterprise of philosophising itself. While going far beyond the concerns with which Maclean is occupied, it is possible to suggest a link between the arguments which she is concerned to clarify and the recent shift away from epistemological questions about the relationship between a rational, knowing subject and a rationally knowable, objective morality as the primary focus of ethical theory towards an approach which aims to understand morality 'as a socially embedded practice'.

CONCLUSION

Medical ethics may help to sensitize the emergent field (in the UK at least) of legal ethics to the nuances and limitations of arguments in ethics and of the

---

[86] John Harris, *The Value of Life*, (London, Routledge, 1985)

[87] Anne Maclean, *The Elimination of Morality; Reflections on Utilitarianism and Bioethics*, (London, Routledge, 1993) ch. 1   [88] Harris, *op. cit.*, at 4   [89] Maclean, *op. cit.*, at 5

philosophies from which they derive or are drawn. They may also assist in explaining that ethical movement is an important part of doing or studying ethics; it would be partial to describe ethics or ethical modes of analysis as static, unchanging or of low viscosity. Of course, there are some within (medical) ethics who are critical of those movements. The debate between Harris and McLean which I have rehearsed is one example of that. Contrast the nature of that debate with the views offered by Bruce Jennings, who challenges the whole way in which the debates between the utilitarian Harris and the deontologist McLean proceed. Jennings offers a completely different interpretation of the nature of ethical debate. This is parallelled by Susan Wolf's identification of different paradigms in Health Law and Ethics. Ulrich Beck and Marc Galanter have suggested that there are unplanned and unforeseeable consequences attached to the nature and pace of change which we have become accustomed, if we are perspicacious, to witness. The movements in the relationship between law and medicine, and between medicine and law and society is nowhere better captured than in a metaphor for change adapted from Antoine de Saint-Exupéry; ' . . . we lack a perspective for judgement of transformations that go so deep. . . . To grasp the meaning of the world of today we use a language created to express the world of yesterday.'[90] Perhaps the real irony of legal ethics is that lawyers should have been doing so much in philosophy and ethics while not realising that the shifting currents of philosophy and ethics could offer so much potential to the radical transformations of law.

I said in the introduction to this essay that I wanted to offer some reflections on why it is that legal ethics has been a late arrival in the department of moral philosophy. Following the exploration which I have taken, I am now in a position to offer some cursory observations. A fuller examination must await another time. There are, I want to suggest, four reasons, of greater or lesser magnitude which may account for this. First, English law lacks a defining cultural moment which has prompted a wholesale re-evaluation of a whole domain of practice, such as (in medicine) the Nuremberg Tribunals and (in the United States) Watergate. Obviously, the latter touched not only lawyers, although it concerned many who were formerly or actively licensed; but it touched a nerve so deep in American society that few of its major institutions escaped review and revision. Secondly, the English legal profession has traditionally been preoccupied with etiquette in the belief that this *was* ethics, or that it was a satisfactory substitute for it. Literally, the language and manners of yesterday have been used as though it could be used to express the manner and meaning of the world today.

Thirdly, the need to explicate and examine legal ethics has come about largely as a result of what Eric Hobsbawm has called the social and moral crisis of foundational beliefs and assumptions in societies themselves. What I

---

[90] Antoine de St Exupéry, *Wind, Sand and Stars*, London, Pan, (1939, 1975 ed.) 39–40

have earlier called the Age of Scepticism has dulled the edge of critical observation and comment on the activities of those, such as lawyers, who have not been subject to especial ethical examination until recently. The transformation of the nature of lawyering has only recently become seen as a fundamental renegotiation of the nature of the enterprise. It is only recently that its practitioners have come to realise that they are faced with a *choice* of continuing to be seen and describe themselves as a learned profession under-written by Codes of Practice or as businesses, underscored by the ethical imperatives and inclines of business communities.

Fourthly, the opening of inquiry by those previously excluded from it, such as women and minorities, has shaken the nature and purposes of the protective assumptions within which the profession has previously worked. The identification and emergence of these hidden voices means that there is a real and forceful constituency to address in the task of producing and constructing meanings and legitimacy as societies work out how to embed their newly framed practices. The 'new pragmatism' suggests a variety of narratives within medical ethics and law, environmental ethics and law, to take two examples, such that it becomes clear that law itself stands in the light of these narratives, and that the practice of law, and law itself, may have been responsible for or implicated in producing or sustaining these challenged forms. Law itself, legal practice, thus emerges as a candidate for a change of form; a precursor to this is an examination of the ethics of lawyering in order to assess the need for and possibilities of change. In other words, legal ethics emerge as a response to ethical and philosophical challenges in other areas of moral enquiry.

Throughout, I have been concerned here to suggest an *additional* way of understanding legal ethics which may itself come to contribute to the general study of applied ethics as a department of moral philosophy. Legal ethics, so conceived, is I believe an important mode of study. It seeks to combine the preoccupation of early twentieth century moral philosophy with meta-ethical study *about* ethics with later developments in modern moral philosophy which have been more concerned with *taking part in ethics*.[91] Additionally, it draws in contemporary critics who identify the possibility, indeed the inevitability of a shift away from epistemological questions about the relationship between a rational, knowing subject and a rationally knowable, objective morality as the primary focus of ethical theory. Instead, this conception of ethics is drawn towards an approach which aims to understand morality 'as a socially embedded practice' having to do with the way in which the 'meanings and legitimacy of moral notions are established, reinterpreted or transformed over time.'[92]

---

[91] In the senses in which those activities are examined in Peter Singer, *Applied Ethics: Introduction,* (Oxford, OUP, 2ed. 1993) at 2

[92] See, for example, Bruce Jennings, 'Possibilities of Consensus: Towards Democratic Moral Discourse' (1991) 16 *The Journal of Medicine and Philosophy* 447-63, at 448

Index

duty to give full and frank disclosure,
137–8
duty to Legal Aid Fund, 135–6
legal professional privilege, 138–40
privilege from without prejudice
negotiations, 142–3
privilege in conciliation, 140–2
professional responsibility, and, 131–43
Police
'cop culture', 162–3, 164
'mission', 165–7

Regulatory regime, 2–6
Bar Code of Practice, 3–5
courts, and, 2–3
general law, 2
Law Society Code of Practice, 3–5
moral relativism, and, 5
political issues, 6
public pressure, and, 3–4
Responsibilities of legal profession, 27–30
access to justice, and, 28–9
discrimination, and 27–8
law reform, 28
law teachers, 29–30
Rules
ethics, and, 146–8

Secrecy, 7–10
disclosure on grounds of public interest, and,
7–8
implied term, 7
lawyer/client privilege, and, 8–10
professional codes, 7
Solicitors, 99–113
analysis of Practice Rules, 106–7
contact with witnesses, 85–6
current rules, codes and principles, 100–8
deregulation in 1980s, 106
distinguishing mere regulation from core
ethics, 105–8
independence, 106
non-statutory Principles and Codes, 103–5
objectives and principles of future change,
112–13
pressures external to profession, 111
pressures internal to profession, 110
professional ethics statistics 1993, 109
professional rules, codes and principles
affecting, 99-113
statistics, 100
statutory rules and codes, 101–2
Solicitors Complaints Bureau, 3–4